OXFORD **IB PREPARED**

# PSYCHOLOGY

## IB DIPLOMA PROGRAMME

Alexey Popov

OXFORD
UNIVERSITY PRESS

# OXFORD
## UNIVERSITY PRESS

Great Clarendon Street, Oxford, OX2 6DP, United Kingdom

Oxford University Press is a department of the University of Oxford.
It furthers the University's objective of excellence in research,
scholarship, and education by publishing worldwide. Oxford is a
registered trade mark of Oxford University Press in
the UK and in certain other countries

British Library Cataloguing in Publication Data
Data available

978-0-19-843416-0

10 9 8 7 6 5 4 3 2 1

Paper used in the production of this book is a natural, recyclable
product made from wood grown in sustainable forests.
The manufacturing process conforms to the environmental regulations
of the country of origin.

Printed in China

**Acknowledgements**

**Photo credits:**

**Cover:** Lisa Alisa/Alamy Stock Photo.

**Photos: p31:** ZEPHYR/Science Photo Library; **p37:** Vasiliy Koval/
Shutterstock; **p56:** Dean Drobot/Shutterstock; **p73:** Orbon Alija/
iStockphoto; **p75:** Recep-bg/iStockphoto; **p92:** H.S. Photos/Alamy Stock
Photo; **p96:** Big_and_serious/iStockphoto; **p112:** Monkey Business
Images/Shutterstock; **p114:** pixelfusion3d/iStockphoto; **p115:** The
nature of love. Harlow, Harry F. American Psychologist, Vol 13(12), Dec
1958, 673-685/Public Domain; **p116:** FatCamera/iStockphoto; **p131:**
Ivan Smuk/Shutterstock; **p133:** Carolyn Jenkins/Alamy Stock Photo;
**p142:** Mavo/Shutterstock; **p150:** RichardBakerStreetPhotography/
Alamy Stock Photo; **p152:** SolStock/iStockphoto.

Artwork by Thomson and Q2A Media Services Pvt. Ltd.

Every effort has been made to contact copyright holders of material
reproduced in this book. Any comissions will be rectified in
subsequent printings if notice is given to the publisher.

# Contents

Answers to the practice exam paper questions in this book can be found on your free support website. Access the support website here:

www.oxfordsecondary.com/ib-prepared-support

# INTRODUCTION

This book provides coverage of the IB Diploma syllabus in Psychology with a focus on assessment. It should not be used to study IB Psychology in isolation from other resources, but it will provide effective support for exam preparation when used in combination with other books.

To enhance your knowledge and skills and to maximize your exam performance, this book scrutinizes the structure of your exams, assessment criteria, possible questions and other elements that are important for focused revision.

## Book structure

In **Part 1** we provide **general guidance** that is not specific to particular content.

We give an overview of the structure of the exam papers: which paper covers which part of the course, how many marks each paper is worth, how many questions there are and from which elements of the syllabus these will be taken.

We also explain how topic headings and command terms are used to formulate questions. Specific exam questions in IB Psychology cannot be predicted; the examiners want to test your skills rather than your ability to memorize answers and reproduce them. However, there are certain boundaries beyond which questions cannot be asked, and it is important to be aware of these boundaries to stay focused on the course requirements. To an extent you can predict the **range** of possible questions.

We unpack the assessment criteria in all the rubrics that are used for different assessment components. An explanation is provided for crucial details that often become a source of ambiguity, confusion or varying interpretations. Similarly, we unpack command terms and analyze essential differences between them, with a discussion of what needs to be focused on when the same question is preceded by different command terms. This is helpful because fully meeting the requirements of the command term is necessary to gain marks in any IB Psychology essay.

In the general guidance we also discuss how essay responses can be structured to maximize demonstration of knowledge and understanding, and to enhance the critical thinking component of the essay. We propose a distinction between two generic approaches to structuring an essay: a "study-based approach" and an "argument-based approach". This is embedded in a discussion of what it means to "demonstrate evidence of critical thinking" and "use research to support arguments" in a Psychology essay.

Finally, we provide an overview of some common mistakes that are recurring in student papers based on our analysis of examination results from previous years.

**Parts 2–8** focus on **content-specific guidance**. There are seven units that are externally assessed through extended response essays: Biological approach to behaviour, Cognitive approach to behaviour, Sociocultural approach to behaviour, Abnormal

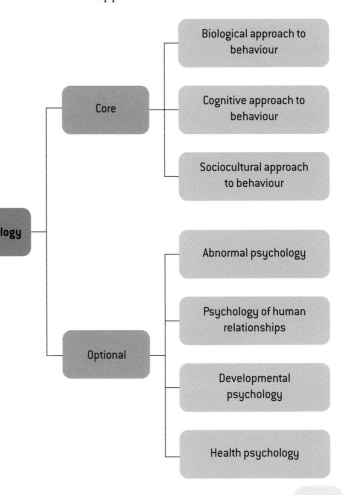

psychology, Psychology of human relationships, Developmental psychology and Health psychology. Each of these units is broken down into topics, and each topic is broken down into "content headings".

For each content heading, the questions that are typically asked by students (and teachers) are as follows.

- How might exam questions be asked for this content heading?

- What are the arguments that students can build their response around?

- What research studies can be used to support the answer?

- What are the common mistakes made by students in their responses to these questions?

We address all of these questions briefly for every content heading by including two compulsory sections and two optional sections. The compulsory sections are the key conceptual understandings relevant to the content heading (these appear as regular text) and key research studies (these appear in a special box). The optional sections only appear where relevant. These include additional information on how exam questions will be formulated (this appears in a box on top of the page) and common errors (these appear in a specially designed box).

After each of the seven units we have included sample student responses with examiner comments and marks. Sample responses are selected with diversity in mind: they come from a range of abilities, a range of topics and content headings and a range of potential types of exam questions. There are sample responses to generic questions on research methods and ethics, HL extensions and various other "tricky" questions. The focus is on including more responses that score high marks and providing average and weak responses only for the purposes of comparison. The reasoning behind this is that students benefit

more from being exposed to a larger number of high-quality responses, but they also need a baseline to compare these responses with.

The first three units (Biological approach to behaviour, Cognitive approach to behaviour and Sociocultural approach to behaviour) contain two short-answer sample responses and two extended responses each. The options (Abnormal psychology, Psychology of human relationships, Developmental psychology and Health psychology) contain two extended responses each.

**Part 9** of the book includes a section specifically devoted to paper 3. Each of the static paper 3 questions is unpacked and discussed. A sample stimulus is included along with two sample answers and examiner marks and comments.

In **Part 10** of the book we focus on the internal assessment (IA). Again, this directly addresses the difficulties that are commonly encountered by teachers and students while carrying out the task. We look at the assessment criteria one by one and interpret each of them. Assessment criteria are "operationalized", in the sense that we discuss what specific elements should be present in the IA and what requirements they should meet to be marked highly on this or that descriptor. One of the common causes of concern and misunderstanding in the current IB Psychology syllabus is how the IA investigation should be related to the background theory/model. To help with this, we provide a "study menu" with examples of research articles that could be taken as a basis for the IA investigation, and a clear indication of what counts as the theory/model in this research article, and where it can be found.

In **Part 11** of the book there is a full exam-style paper, the markscheme for which can be found online at **www.oxfordsecondary.com/ib-prepared-support**.

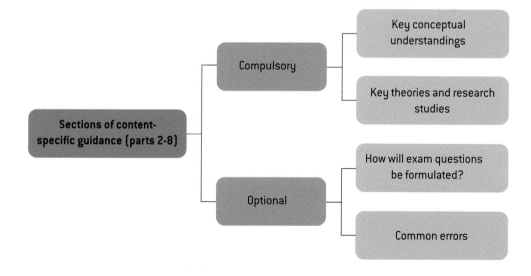

# 1 GENERAL GUIDANCE

## 1.1 THE STRUCTURE OF EXAM PAPERS

The IB Psychology syllabus is the main reference document that you need to have available while reading this book. It is provided in the IB subject guide and your teacher can share it with you.

The examination in IB Psychology for HL (higher level) students will consist of four parts: paper 1, paper 2, paper 3 and the internal assessment.

The differences between HL and SL (standard level) exams are as follows.

✔ SL paper 1 follows a slightly different structure (there are no HL extensions).

✔ SL students study only one option for paper 2, whereas HL students study two options.

✔ SL students do not take paper 3.

✔ There is no difference between HL and SL in the internal assessment.

**Paper 1** tests your knowledge of the core content of the syllabus: Biological approach to behaviour, Cognitive approach to behaviour and Sociocultural approach to behaviour.

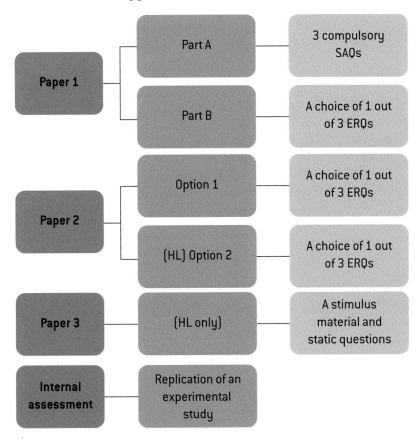

▲ Figure 1.1.1 Assessment components in IB Psychology

The paper follows this structure.

- Section A (1 hour): three compulsory short-answer questions (SAQs), one from each approach to behaviour (Biological, Cognitive, Sociocultural).

- Section B (1 hour): you choose one out of three extended response questions (ERQs), one from each approach to behaviour (Biological, Cognitive, Sociocultural). For HL students, one, two or all three of these ERQs will come from the HL extensions (The role of animal research in understanding human behaviour, Cognitive processing in the digital world, The influence of globalization on individual behaviour).

**Paper 2** tests your knowledge of the options. The IB Psychology syllabus offers four options for study: Abnormal psychology, Psychology of human relationships, Developmental psychology and Health psychology. HL students study two of these options and SL students study only one. Hence the duration of the paper is 1 hour for SL students and 2 hours for HL students.

For each option, paper 2 will give three ERQs, and you choose one out of the three to answer.

It is useful to know that each option is broken down into three broad topics. (For example, Abnormal psychology is broken down into Factors influencing diagnosis, Etiology of abnormal psychology and Treatment of disorders.) One essay title will come from each of these three broad topics.

**Paper 3** tests your skills related to approaches to research and ethics. It will have stimulus material that describes a research study in approximately 500 words. The study can be quantitative, qualitative or a combination of both. You will be asked a set of questions that tap into your ability to apply knowledge of research methodology and ethics to the stimulus material. The duration of this paper is 1 hour. The questions are known in advance. Only HL students take paper 3.

The **internal assessment** in Psychology is the same for HL and SL students. As the name suggests, this component is assessed internally, which means that you get marked by your teacher. (A random sample of student work in your school gets selected and sent to the IB for moderation; if the moderation results in a change of marks for the sample, marks for the rest of the students are adjusted accordingly.) Internal assessment in Psychology requires you to carry out a replication of a published experimental research study and report on the results. It is the final report that is evaluated.

The total mark that you get in the subject is a weighted sum of all the marks you get for individual components. The weights differ for HL and SL students; they are summarized in Table 1.1.1.

| Assessment component | Weighting HL | Weighting SL |
|---|---|---|
| External assessment (5 hours) | 80% | 75% |
| Paper 1 (2 hours) | 40% | 50% |
| Paper 2 (2 hours) | 20% | 25% |
| Paper 3 (1 hour) | 20% | |
| Internal assessment: experimental study | 20% | 25% |

▲ Table 1.1.1 Weighting of assessment components

# 1.2 HOW EXAM QUESTIONS WILL BE FORMULATED

In preparation for your exams it is important to know what to expect. The syllabus is built in a way that encourages holistic understanding of topics rather than rote memorization. For this reason, you are not given any clear list of pre-defined questions for the exam, and the exact way the exam questions will be formulated is, to an extent, unpredictable. Based on the question you get, it is your job (and your skill) to choose relevant material and present arguments in a way that is focused entirely on the requirements of the question.

This is not to say, however, that there are no rules in formulating exam questions. Although a certain amount of unpredictability does exist, some things you can know in advance. This section is a summary of such things.

## Paper 1: SAQs and ERQs

You get short-answer questions (SAQs) in section A of paper 1. As the name suggests, these questions require a more concise answer. Since you get three compulsory SAQs, you will have approximately 20 minutes to answer each of them.

SAQs are marked out of 9 marks each and assessed using a rubric.

The extended response question (ERQ) in section B of paper 1 is worth 22 marks and marked against a set of five criteria. You have 1 hour to write an ERQ response.

*For the assessment rubrics and their analysis, see pages 8–14.*

To know what to expect from exam questions, you need to know that SAQs and ERQs have different sets of command terms associated with them. These command terms are summarized in Table 1.2.1.

If you look at the syllabus, you will see that each unit is represented as a table (see the Appendix). For an example, Table 1.2.2 gives the syllabus for the unit Biological approach to behaviour.

| SAQ command terms | ERQ command terms |
|---|---|
| Describe | Discuss |
| Outline | Evaluate |
| Explain | To what extent |
| | Contrast |

▲ Table 1.2.1 Command terms used in the SAQs and ERQs

| Topic | Content |
|---|---|
| The relationship between the brain and behaviour | Techniques used to study the brain in relation to behaviour |
| | Localization of function |
| | Neuroplasticity |
| | Neurotransmitters and their effects on behaviour |
| Hormones and pheromones and their effects on behaviour | Hormones and their effects on behaviour |
| | Pheromones and their effects on behaviour |
| The relationship between genetics and behaviour | Genes and their effects on behaviour |
| | Genetic similarity |
| | Evolutionary explanation for behaviour |
| HL extension: The role of animal research in understanding human behaviour | For all three topics in this unit, and with reference to research studies, HL students should study:<br>• the value of animal models in research to provide insight into human behaviour<br>• ethical considerations in animal research. |

▲ Table 1.2.2 The syllabus table for Biological approach to behaviour*

(* *This is a simplified table; the actual syllabus table in the IB Psychology Subject Guide contains additional information.*)

There are two columns in Table 1.2.2: "Topic" and "Content". Throughout the book we will sometimes refer to these as "column 1" and "column 2". The bottom row of the table is the HL extension. Each HL extension has two aspects, shown as bullet points in the table. There are also two overarching topics in paper 1: Research methods and Ethics. If you look at the diagram of the course (Figure 1.2.1), you will see that these two topics form the background for all other content in paper 1.

Now that you know these starting points, here is what you should know about exam questions in paper 1.

- Both SAQs and ERQs will be formulated on the basis of the "Content" column (column 2).

- Within that column, SAQ questions can be based on the headings themselves (for example, "Neuroplasticity") and occasionally some additional terms (these are given in Table 1.2.3). Here is an example of an exam question using a heading from the Content column: "Describe one research study related to hormones and behaviour [9 marks]." Here is an example of an exam question using one of the additional terms from Table 1.2.3: "Outline how neural networks are formed, with reference to one study [9 marks]."

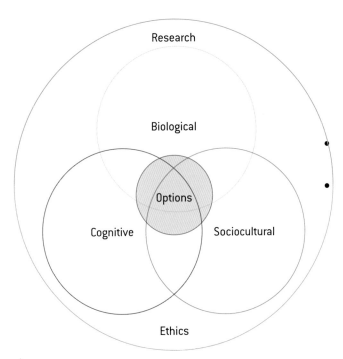

▲ Figure 1.2.1  Diagram of the IB Psychology course

- ERQs can only use the headings. Additional terms from Table 1.2.3 will not be used in ERQs.

- Exam questions targeting one of the overarching topics (Research methods and Ethics) will be formulated on the basis of the "Topic"

| Approach to understanding behaviour | Content | Additional terms that may be used in short-answer questions (SAQs) |
|---|---|---|
| Biological | Neuroplasticity | Neural networks |
| | | Neural pruning |
| | | Neuron |
| | Neurotransmitters and their effect on behaviour | Synapse |
| | | Excitatory/inhibitory neurotransmitters |
| | | Agonist |
| | | Antagonist |
| | Genetic similarity | Twin and kinship studies |
| Cognitive | Models of memory | Multi-store memory model |
| | | Working memory model |
| | Schema theory | Cognitive schema |
| | Thinking and decision-making | Rational thinking (controlled) |
| | | Intuitive thinking (automatic) |
| Sociocultural | Social identity theory | Social groups |
| | Culture and its influence on behaviour and cognition | Cultural groups |
| | Enculturation | Norms |
| | Acculturation | Assimilation / assimilate |

▲ Table 1.2.3  Additional terms that can be used in formulating SAQs in paper 1

column (column 1). This means that, for example, you can be asked to "Discuss approaches to research used in investigating genetics and behaviour", but you cannot be asked something as specific as "Discuss approaches to research used in investigating neuroplasticity".

- For the HL extension, each of the two aspects (the two bullet points) can be combined with each of the three topics from column 1. This gives you six possible combinations, but of course there is a lot of overlap between them in terms of material you can use in your response.

With this knowledge you can now predict, to a certain extent, the questions you will get in paper 1. Below are some examples of exam questions that are plausible (we are using Biological approach to behaviour as an example).

### Short-answer questions (SAQs)

- Explain one technique used to study the brain in relation to behaviour.

- Describe the effects of one hormone on behaviour.

- Outline one evolutionary explanation for behaviour.

### Extended response questions (ERQs)

- Discuss psychological research into localization of function in the brain.

- Evaluate one or more evolutionary explanations for behaviour.

- To what extent can genetic similarities be used to explore heritability of human behaviour?

### HL extension ERQs

- Discuss the value of animal models in investigating human genetics and behaviour.

- To what extent can animal research provide insight into human behaviour?

- Discuss ethical considerations involved in using animals to investigate the relationship between brain and behaviour.

### Overarching topics (Research methods and Ethics)

- Contrast two approaches to research used to investigate genetics and behaviour.

- Evaluate the use of one or more research methods in the study of the brain and behaviour.

- Discuss ethical considerations in investigating the influence of hormones and/or pheromones on behaviour.

Here is a summary.

- SAQs can be formulated using content headings (column 2), topic headings (column 1) and overarching topics (Research methods and Ethics), as well as the additional terms (see Table 1.2.3).

- ERQs can be formulated using content headings (column 2), topic headings (column 1) and overarching topics (Research methods and Ethics). Additional terms cannot be used.

- Two overarching topics will be used: Research methods and Ethics. Questions linked to these overarching topics will be formulated using the topic headings (column 1).

- HL extensions can only be formulated as ERQs.

### Additional information on the formulation of questions in paper 1

Whenever the syllabus states "study one something" (for example, "Study one example of neuroplasticity"), the formulation of ERQs will use "one or more" (for example, "Discuss one or more examples of neuroplasticity"). In other words, the syllabus requires you to study a minimum of one "something", but you can choose to study more, and the exam question will allow you to demonstrate this knowledge.

## Paper 2: Only ERQs

Paper 2 questions are ERQs assessed against the same rubric as questions in paper 1 section B (see pages 8–14).

Paper 2 questions broadly follow the same rules as paper 1 questions, except for the following.

- Only ERQs will be asked.

- The three approaches to behaviour (Biological, Cognitive and Sociocultural) serve as the overarching topics in paper 2. This is in addition to the other two overarching topics: Research methods and Ethics.

Therefore, the rules for formulating paper 2 questions are as follows.

- Questions will be formulated using one of the four command terms associated with ERQs: "discuss", "evaluate", "contrast" and "to what extent".

- Questions will be formulated on the basis of the content column (column 2).

- Exam questions targeting the overarching topics (Biological, Cognitive and Sociocultural approaches to behaviour, Research methods and Ethics) will be formulated on the basis of the Topic column (column 1). For example, you may be asked to "Discuss biological and cognitive factors in the etiology of abnormal psychology", but you cannot be asked something as specific as "Discuss sociocultural factors involved in investigating validity and reliability of diagnosis".

### Additional information on the formulation of questions in paper 2

Any material connected by the word "and" in the syllabus (for example, "validity and reliability of diagnosis") may be connected by "and/or" in examination questions (for example, "Discuss the validity and/or reliability of diagnosis"). This means that you can choose to discuss both, but you do not have to.

There are three exceptions to this:

- Childhood trauma and resilience (Developmental psychology)
- Gender identity and social roles (Developmental psychology)
- Dispositional factors and health beliefs (Health psychology).

For these exceptions, exam questions may be formulated by separating the pairing. For example, a question could be set separately on childhood trauma, or separately on resilience, or on childhood trauma *and* resilience. This means for these content headings, it is best to be ready to treat them as two separate aspects.

## Paper 3: Set questions

Paper 3 questions are selected from a fixed list of questions that you know beforehand. This is how the selection is carried out.

### Question 1

Question 1 has three compulsory parts.

a. **Identify** the research method used and outline two characteristics of the method [3 marks].

b. **Describe** the sampling method used in the study [3 marks].

c. **Suggest** one alternative or one additional research method that could be used to investigate the aim of the original study, giving one reason for your choice [3 marks].

### Question 2

The second question will be one of the following.

- **Describe** the ethical considerations that were applied in the study and **explain** if further ethical considerations could be applied [6 marks].
- **Describe** the ethical considerations in reporting the results and **explain** additional ethical considerations that could be taken into account when applying the findings of the study [6 marks].

### Question 3

The third question will be one of the following.

- **Discuss** the possibility of generalizing/transferring the findings of the study [9 marks].
- **Discuss** how a researcher could ensure that the results of the study are credible [9 marks].
- **Discuss** how the researcher in the study could avoid bias [9 marks].

In other words, the first question (with three parts) will always be the same. You will then have to answer two more questions out of a possible five. Note that you will have 1 hour to answer them all.

Questions 1 and 2 will be assessed using an analytical markscheme that will be developed separately for every exam based on the specific stimulus material. Question 3 will be assessed using a rubric. Descriptors for the highest markband in this rubric are given in Table 1.2.4.

| Marks | Descriptor |
|---|---|
| 7–9 | The question is understood and answered in a focused and effective manner with an accurate argument that addresses the requirements of the question. |
| | The response contains accurate references to approaches to research with regard to the question, describing their strengths and limitations. |
| | The response makes effective use of the stimulus material. |

▲ Table 1.2.4 Paper 3 question 3 rubric: highest markband

# 1.3   DECIPHERING ASSESSMENT CRITERIA

| Marks | Level descriptor |
|-------|------------------|
| 0 | The answer does not reach a standard described by the descriptors below. |
| 1–3 | The response is of limited relevance to or only rephrases the question. |
| | Knowledge and understanding is mostly inaccurate or not relevant to the question. |
| | The research supporting the response is mostly not relevant to the question and if relevant only listed. |
| 4–6 | The response is relevant to the question, but does not meet the command term requirements. |
| | Knowledge and understanding is accurate but limited. |
| | The response is supported by appropriate research which is described. |
| 7–9 | The response is fully focused on the question and meets the command term requirements. |
| | Knowledge and understanding is accurate and addresses the main topics/problems identified in the question. |
| | The response is supported by appropriate research which is described and explicitly linked to the question. |

▲ Table 1.3.1  SAQ marking rubric

## Short-answer question marking rubric (total 9 marks)

Paper 1 section A consists of three short-answer questions (SAQs). All three questions are compulsory. Each question is marked out of 9 marks using the rubric in Table 1.3.1, for a total of 27 marks.

As shown by the assessment criteria, **in a short-answer question you are not expected to evaluate research studies** or explicitly demonstrate critical thinking. However, the following aspects of knowledge and understanding are important:

- relevance and focus (these aspects are related; your answer needs to be relevant for the 4–6 markband and fully focused for the highest markband)

- accuracy of knowledge (knowledge needs to be accurate for the 4–6 markband and accurate and detailed for the highest markband)

- meeting the requirements of the command term (three command terms are possible in SAQs: "describe", "explain" and "outline")

- explicitly linking to the question.

Note that "knowledge and understanding" and "use of research" are separate aspects in each markband, which implies that describing relevant research is not enough to demonstrate your knowledge fully. You need to spend some time answering the question on a conceptual level, and only then use a research study to illustrate your conceptual understanding. To answer the question on a conceptual level means to "address the main topics/problems identified in the question".

For example, suppose the question asks you to "Explain how one hormone may affect one human behaviour". Suppose what you have done is:

- defined hormones

- named one example of a hormone – oxytocin

- stated that hormones can affect human behaviour

- described a research study that investigated the effect of oxytocin on behaviour – for example, Kosfeld *et al* (2005)

- repeated that, based on the results of the study, hormones can affect human behaviour.

Most likely, provided there are no inaccuracies, this response will be marked in the middle markband (4–6). Here are the reasons why it will not achieve a higher markband.

- The response does not fully meet the requirements of the command term "explain". It is only **stated** that hormones can affect behaviour, but not explained how. Although the research study serves as an example, it does not contribute to the explanation on a conceptual level.

- Similarly, knowledge and understanding are limited because the topics/problems implicit in the question are not explained.

- Research is described but not explicitly linked to the question. Although it is restated at the end that hormones affect human behaviour, this statement in itself may not be enough.

So what should you do in order to move from the middle markband to the highest markband?

- Instead of going straight into the details of the supporting research study, spend some time answering the question on a conceptual level. For example, you might want to explain how hormones function in the human body (unlike neurotransmitters, they enter the bloodstream) and how they are related to behaviour (they change the likelihood of certain behaviours by altering the physiological states linked to those behaviours). You might also make a reference to the assumption of the biological approach to behaviour that physiological structures and functions determine behaviour.

- Explain the problem implied in the question. For example, you might say that the link between hormones (biological mechanisms designed to regulate long-lasting behaviours through chemicals entering the bloodstream and targeting specialized cell receptors) and behaviour (which seems to be under our conscious control) seems distant. However, although hormones do not determine behaviour directly, they do increase the probability of a certain behaviour occurring.

- Link the research study explicitly to the conceptual points you made before.

## Extended response question marking rubric (total 22 marks)

Extended response questions (ERQs) are marked using five assessment criteria. We unpack these criteria one by one below.

Criterion A is shown on the right, but what does it mean to **explain** the problem/issue? How is this different from simply identifying the problem being raised by the question? Let us try to illustrate with an example. Suppose the question is "Discuss the theory of localization of function".

Localization of function is the idea that psychological functions are associated with specialized brain areas. There were numerous research studies that supported this idea based on the observation that damage to a brain area results in the loss of a function. The scientific challenge was to find correspondence between specific brain areas and all known psychological functions.

What we said in the previous paragraph counts as restating the question. We have identified the problem (to find correspondence between brain areas and psychological functions), but we have not explained it. Hence, we have probably earned 1 mark for criterion A, but not both marks.

Here are some of the things we could add to dig deeper and explain the problem.

- It may not be easy to find such correspondence because not all functions are localized in a specific brain area. Some brain areas are responsible for more than one function, some functions are localized in more than one area of the brain, and some

### Criterion A: Focus on the question (2 marks)

To understand the requirements of the question, students must identify the problem or issue being raised by the question. Students may simply identify the problem by restating the question or breaking down the question. Students who go beyond this by **explaining** the problem are showing that they understand the issues or problems.

| Mark | Level descriptor |
|------|------------------|
| 0 | Does not reach the standards described by the descriptors below |
| 1 | Identifies the problem/issue raised in the question |
| 2 | Explains the problem/issue raised in the question |

functions are widely distributed. This is reflected in how ideas about localization developed historically, with the theory of strict localization gradually being replaced by more flexible theories.

- Success in establishing localization of function depends on the research methods that are being used. Various methods have been used for this purpose including post-mortem autopsy in case studies, cortical stimulation, induced cortical damage (in animal studies) and research with brain imaging technology. Each of these methods has certain limitations that do not allow us to make certain inferences about localization of function.

As we see from this example, unlike simple identification of a problem, the explanation goes one or several steps further and uncovers essential aspects or dimensions of the problem.

Note that although the introduction in your essay will tell the reader a lot about how focused the essay is going to be, criterion A (focus on the question) is used to assess the whole essay, not only the introductory part.

## Criterion B: Knowledge and understanding (6 marks)

This criterion rewards students for demonstrating their knowledge and understanding of specific areas of psychology. It is important to credit **relevant** knowledge and understanding that is **targeted** at addressing the question and explained in sufficient detail.

| Mark | Level descriptor |
|------|------------------|
| 0 | Does not reach the standard described by the descriptors below. |
| 1–2 | The response demonstrates limited relevant knowledge and understanding. Psychological terminology is used but with errors that hamper understanding. |
| 3–4 | The response demonstrates relevant knowledge and understanding but lacks detail. Psychological terminology is used but with errors that do not hamper understanding. |
| 5–6 | The response demonstrates relevant, detailed knowledge and understanding. Psychological terminology is used appropriately. |

Criterion B is straightforward and does not require much deciphering. However, a few details are worth noting.

- The terms "knowledge" and "understanding" are never used independently, which emphasizes the fact that what you should demonstrate in a response is not merely knowledge of facts or details, but understanding of how and why these details are important, and in what context.

- It is important for knowledge to be relevant to the question. Relevance is the most basic concern – you need to be sure that what you use in your response is absolutely relevant to the question, otherwise you risk scoring no marks for the essay. For example, a common mistake is to use neurotransmitter research (such as into serotonin) in response to a question about hormones. No matter how good the response is, chances are it will not score anything.

- The use of psychological terminology is another facet of this criterion. Psychological concepts should be correctly defined and used precisely and in appropriate contexts. You should demonstrate that you understand what relevant concepts in psychology mean and how they are applied. For example, it would be a mistake to use the term "experiment" to identify a research study that is not experimental in nature. Similarly, it is not correct to refer to experimental research as a "case study" (this is a common mistake among students).

Criterion C, shown on the right, emphasizes the importance of using research studies to support arguments (conceptual understandings), not just for their own sake.

Here are some important points to note.

- If you use research studies that are not relevant to the question, you risk scoring no marks on this criterion.

- If you use research studies to support one and the same argument, you score low marks.

- High marks are scored if research is used to support the development of the argument.

- What matters is not the number of studies used, but the quality of their use. For example, the link between the study and the conceptual understanding that it supports must be clearly and explicitly demonstrated.

What does it mean to use research to support the development of the argument? It means answering the question on a conceptual level first and then supporting the points you have made with research studies, as opposed to answering the question descriptively by just talking about research that seems to be relevant.

A good mental exercise to see if your research is really being used to support your arguments is this: look at your essay and mentally remove all mentions of research studies and their procedural details (you can only leave the conclusions), then look at what is left. If the leftover content is in itself a well-developed argumentative answer to the question, then your essay is strong on the conceptual level and the research studies are probably used to support the arguments. For more tips on how to accomplish this, see pages 14–19.

According to Criterion D, shown on the next page, you are expected to demonstrate critical thinking about the knowledge and understanding used in your responses and the research used to support that knowledge and understanding. There are a number of areas where you may demonstrate critical thinking. Examples include:

- research design and methodologies
- triangulation
- assumptions and biases
- contradictory evidence or alternative theories or explanations
- areas of uncertainty
- strengths and limitations
- possible applications of a model or explanation
- cross-cultural, gender and age differences present in findings.

The IB Psychology Subject Guide explicitly states that these areas are not hierarchical, and neither is it necessary to give them all equal or any coverage in a response. For example, a good response may include a very limited critique of research design and methodologies, but also include a well-developed discussion of areas of uncertainty implied in the question. A holistic judgment will be made by the examiner regarding the quality of critical thinking in the essay. It must also be noted that critical thinking points will be different depending on the question and the command term, so examiners will assess evidence

## Criterion C: Use of research to support answer (6 marks)

Psychology is evidence-based so it is expected that students will use their knowledge of research to support their argument. There is no prescription as to which or how many pieces of research are appropriate for their response. As such it becomes important that the research selected is **relevant** and useful in **supporting** the response. One piece of research that makes the points relevant to the answer is better than several pieces that repeat the same point over and over.

| Mark | Level descriptor |
|---|---|
| 0 | Does not reach the standard described by the descriptors below. |
| 1–2 | Limited relevant psychological research is used in the response. Research selected serves to repeat points already made. |
| 3–4 | Relevant psychological research is used in support of the response and is partly explained. Research selected partially develops the argument. |
| 5–6 | Relevant psychological research is used in support of the response and is thoroughly explained. Research selected is effectively used to develop the argument. |

## Criterion D: Critical thinking (6 marks)

This criterion credits students who demonstrate an inquiring and reflective attitude to their understanding of psychology. There are a number of areas where students may demonstrate critical thinking on the knowledge and understanding used in their responses and the research used to support that knowledge and understanding.

| Mark | Level descriptor |
|------|------------------|
| 0 | Does not reach the standard described by the descriptors below. |
| 1–2 | There is limited critical thinking and the response is mainly descriptive. Evaluation or discussion, if present, is superficial. |
| 3–4 | The response contains critical thinking, but lacks development. Evaluation or discussion of most relevant areas is attempted but is not developed. |
| 5–6 | The response consistently demonstrates well-developed critical thinking. Evaluation or discussion of relevant areas is consistently well developed. |

of critical thinking within the context of the problem that is being addressed in the question.

The opposite to well-developed critical thinking is a descriptive response. A typical descriptive response would focus on a list of research studies, emphasizing procedural details and findings. What can you add to a typical descriptive response to get an essay that demonstrates good critical thinking skills? Let us look at it one step after another, from more basic critical thinking points to more sophisticated ones.

You can add evaluation of the research studies. This would typically include a critique of research designs/methodologies. However, you should remember that this critique needs to be well developed. There is always a large variety of aspects you can look at when evaluating a study, falling under four overarching themes: credibility, bias, sampling and generalizability. For example, in an experimental study you could consider:

- internal validity (how the variables have been controlled, and how the common threats to internal validity have or have not been avoided)

- population validity (the ability to generalize results from a sample to the target population, and issues such as using samples coming from one culture or participants of only one gender)

- ecological validity (the extent to which it is possible to generalize from experimental settings to real-life situations, from the artificial context of the experiment to the natural context of participants' lives)

- construct validity (how the variables are operationalized and to what extent is the "leap" from operationalizations to theoretical constructs justified in the study)

- issues of gender, culture and ethics.

You can link these individual research studies explicitly to the theories/models/concepts you are investigating in your response (for example, localization, neuroplasticity, models of decision-making). Consider answering questions such as the following.

- Is the jump from the empirical findings of the research study to the theoretical conclusions of the model justified?

- Does the study fully and conclusively support the theory/model/concept? If not, which parts or aspects of the theory/model/concept are supported by the study and which ones are not?

- Are there other research studies (follow-up studies) that provide a more complete support to the theory/model/concept?

You can consider alternative models or explanations, if the question allows you to do so. Examine the relative merits of alternative explanations. If you use contradictory evidence, do not just state that such contradictory evidence exists; try to demonstrate why it exists (for example, contradictory research studies are based on different assumptions, use different methods or are conducted with different samples).

You can look at the theory/model/concept in the question more generally, through the lens of research methodology. What methods are available to investigate the theoretical concept? Are the available methods imposing any limitations on the nature of theoretical inferences? To what extent is triangulation possible in this area of research?

Finally, you can summarize this discussion by identifying the conclusions that seem to be most reliable, areas that are likely to have biased results, and existing areas of uncertainty where conclusions cannot be made with confidence.

There are some "buzz words" that you are likely to use in a response that includes a variety of critical thinking points. Make sure you understand what these words mean in the context of psychological research, and try to use them whenever appropriate: evidence, findings, conclusion, inference, theory/model/concept, alternative explanation, assumption, implication, practical application, reliability, triangulation, effectiveness, bias, credibility, generalizability, sample, evaluation, significance, uncertainly, strengths, limitations.

## Criterion E: Clarity and organization (2 marks)

This criterion credits students for presenting their response in a clear and organized manner.

A good response would require no re-reading to understand the points made or the train of thought underpinning the argument.

| Mark | Level descriptor |
|------|------------------|
| 0 | Does not reach the standard described by the descriptors below. |
| 1 | The answer demonstrates some organization and clarity, but this is not sustained throughout the response. |
| 2 | The answer demonstrates organization and clarity throughout the response. |

Although Criterion E comes last and is only worth 2 marks, its significance should not be underestimated. If your answer is not clear enough, the reader (the examiner) may miss out on certain important steps in your train of thought or misunderstand certain points you are making. This, in the long run, may affect your marks for the other criteria.

Clarity and organization are connected. A well-organized response is one where it is clearly visible where one argument ends and another begins. It will have a clear introduction, key arguments will start with a new paragraph, and the conclusion will be well developed. In a well-organized response, new arguments do not appear in the conclusion of the essay because the conclusion is only a summary of all the arguments that have already been made.

Clarity is closely linked to how effectively you use terminology. It needs to be used precisely and in appropriate contexts. If you are describing a research study, it needs to be clear what argument you are supporting. Make it a rule to link back to the question after every major part of the essay, explaining to the reader how it connects to the question at hand.

For example, for individual research studies it is important to write both findings and conclusions. Findings are just empirical results of a particular study. Conclusions are theoretical generalizations based on those results. It is the conclusion that links the research study back to the question, and that is why it is important to spell out the conclusion clearly and precisely.

# 1.4   STRUCTURING AN ESSAY

In this section we will introduce two approaches that students typically use in structuring their ERQ responses. One of these (the study-based approach) may be considered a more basic approach and the other one (argument-based) may be considered more elaborate, with a heavier emphasis on critical thinking.

These two approaches certainly do not exhaust all the possibilities you have in terms of structuring your essay. They are just given here as typical examples. Experience shows that spontaneously (without specific instruction) students often use the study-based approach, as it is intuitively appealing. However, the argument-based approach gives you more scope to demonstrate critical thinking and to use research more effectively. This is not to say that the argument-based approach is preferable in all situations, but knowing the difference between the two may help you structure your responses more effectively.

Since the study-based approach is already intuitively used by most students, the focus in this chapter will be on the argument-based approach, and on demonstrating its advantages over the study-based approach. For this reason, the question that we use in the example given below ("To what extent is one cognitive process reliable?") invites the use of the argument-based approach rather that the study-based approach. A study-based response to this question will be demonstrated for the sake of contrast, to show how students often choose an inefficient way to address the question.

The structure of a typical study-based essay response is as follows.

---

### Structure of a typical study-based response

**Introduction** (where the question is restated and explained)

**Research study 1** (for example, "To investigate this question, Author and Author (1999) conducted a research study where … ")

**Evaluation** of the research study

**Research study 2** (for example, "Another study to investigate the question was conducted by … In this study … ")

**Evaluation** of the research study

Possible further research studies, leading to the …

**Conclusion**

---

Note that the number of research studies is not fixed. Typically, in an ERQ response most students using the study-based approach write about two to four research studies (usually two, but sometimes more).

Using the topic "Reliability of cognitive processes" as an example (Cognitive approach to behaviour), here is an outline of what a typical response following the study-based approach would look like.

**Question: To what extent is one cognitive process reliable?**

[Introduction] Memory is a cognitive process ... Memory has been found to be **unreliable in a variety of situations**. This has been demonstrated in a number of research studies, for example those based on **eyewitness testimony**. In this response I will ...

[First research study] **One study** that investigated unreliability of memory in an eyewitness testimony situation is **Loftus and Palmer (1974)**. They showed participants video recordings of car accidents and asked them to estimate the speed of the cars. They varied one verb in the leading question: "About how fast were the cars going when they hit each other?" ... [details of the study follow].

[Evaluation] The **strength** of this study is its internal validity, but the limitations are ... [evaluation of the study follows].

[Second research study] **Another study** that investigated a similar phenomenon is **Loftus and Zanni (1975)**. They varied the article used in the leading question: "Did you see a ... " versus "Did you see the ... ". Similarly, they found that the article "the" changes the probability that participants will recall seeing the object in question, although it was not actually there ... [details follow].

[Evaluation] The **strengths** of this experiment are ... and the **limitations** are ... [evaluation of the study follows].

[Conclusion] In conclusion, it can be said that in certain situations **memory is unreliable** because it can be changed by such small external influences as the article or the verb used in the leading question.

Several things should be noted about the study-based approach.

- Essentially both research studies used here support one and the same argument: that memory is unreliable because it can be changed by small variations in leading questions. Loftus and Palmer (1974) is a classical study that demonstrates the phenomenon of leading questions influencing the memory of an event, Loftus and Zanni (1975) replicate the finding with even smaller variations in the leading question.

- As you know, the study of Loftus and Palmer (1974) had two parts to it. In the first experiment, five groups of participants were asked leading questions with verbs of varying emotional intensity ("hit", "smashed into" and so on) and then asked to estimate the speed; in the second experiment there were three groups of participants and they were asked factual questions (for example, "Did you see broken glass in the video?"). When you use the study-based approach, these two parts of the experiment will probably be presented as one study.

- Evaluation points in this response are focused on individual research studies, but not on the phenomenon of memory reliability in general. For example, the student can talk about issues of generalizability in Loftus and Palmer (1974).

In their first experiment they used 45 students split into five equal groups, which raised at least two questions: (a) can you generalize results from undergraduate students to a wider population, and (b) is nine participants per group a large enough sample? However, although these points do bring into question the ability of Loftus and Palmer's research study to test the theory of reconstructive memory, they do not say anything about the credibility of the theory itself.

Let us compare this now with a possible structure of an argument-based response.

---

### Structure of a typical argument-based response

**Introduction** (the question is explained with a focus on the problem/issue inherent in it)

**Argument 1**, explaining one of the aspects of the problem/issue

**Supporting study 1**: findings of the study translate into a conclusion that supports argument 1

**Evaluation** of the study in the context of this conclusion, which raises an additional issue, thus leading to:

**argument 2**, explaining this additional issue

**supporting study 2**, to clarify this issue

**Evaluation** of the study in the context of argument 2, which potentially identifies the next problem/issue, leading to further arguments and supporting studies

**Conclusion**, summarizing the main flow of argumentation and linking back to the question

---

Again, note that the number of research studies is not fixed. In fact, as you will see a little later, since research studies are used in a focused way to support the arguments, it is possible to drop some irrelevant details of individual research studies. As a result, you will not need the same amount of detail and thus will be able to use more research studies than one would normally expect in a study-based response. Note that although using the argument-based approach makes it possible to use more research studies, you don't have to. Instead, you can choose to focus more on discussing the theoretical points and the arguments, or use one and the same study to bring up everal arguments.

Using the same example (reliability of memory), let us look at an outline of a possible argument-based response to the same question.

**Question: To what extent is one cognitive process reliable?**

[Introduction] Reliability of memory means its ability to store information securely and retrieve it exactly as it was encoded. Memory can be considered reliable only if we assume that it cannot be changed once it is encoded. But what if this assumption is false?

[Argument] **Reliability of memory** was brought into question when it was discovered that in a typical eyewitness situation, memory of an event may change in response to small variations in the leading question.

[Support] For example, **Loftus and Palmer (1974)** conducted a study where they showed that the emotional intensity of the verb in the leading question changes speed estimates provided by participants. [Relevant details of the study follow here.] On the basis of that, researchers formulated the theory of reconstructive memory. [Details of the theory.]

[Evaluation] However, there existed **two possible interpretations** of the findings from **Loftus and Palmer (1974).**

- There is a genuine memory change: the leading question interferes with the information about the event stored in long-term memory and changes it.
- We are dealing with a response bias: memory itself does not change, but when participants are unsure about the speed of the car the leading question may bias their response in a certain direction.

[Argument] The second interpretation is not consistent with the theory of reconstructive memory; therefore in order to accept the theory we must demonstrate that a genuine memory change is taking place.

[Support] To rule out the second interpretation (which goes contrary to the theory of reconstructive memory), **Loftus and Palmer (1974)** conducted another experiment where participants were asked the question "Did you see any broken glass in the video?" (when in fact there was no broken glass). They observed that participants who had a more intense verb in their leading question (such as "smashed into") were more likely to report seeing broken glass. This suggested that genuine memory change did in fact occur, ruling out the second interpretation and supporting the theory of reconstructive memory.

[Evaluation] However, the theory was further criticized on the basis of its applicability to real-life situations. All the experiments mentioned so far were carried out in artificial laboratory conditions.

[Argument] The theory of reconstructive memory gets plenty of support in laboratory experiments, but not so much in real-life situations.

[Support] The influence of leading questions on eyewitness testimony in a real-life situation was investigated by **Yuille and Cutshall (1986)**. [Details of the study follow.] They found no effect of leading questions on recall of the details of the robbery. This means one of two things.

- Either the theory of reconstructive memory is only applicable to artificial experimental conditions.
- Or the study of Yuille and Cutshall tapped into a separate memory phenomenon, perhaps flashbulb memory. Unlike the previous studies,

we may assume that participants in the study of Yuille and Cutshall experienced a strong emotional arousal when they witnessed the event. It is possible that this emotional arousal activated the mechanism of flashbulb memory which obscured the action of reconstructive memory.

[Conclusion] Eyewitness testimony research has demonstrated that post-event information can be integrated with the memory of the event and alter this memory. The alternative competing explanation – response bias – seems to have been eliminated. However, there are still questions regarding the applicability of reconstructive memory to real-life situations. When emotional arousal is present, it may be hard to separate the action of reconstructive memory from that of flashbulb memory, which complicates research in this area.

There are several things to note about the argument-based approach to structuring essays (and the example above).

- Different research studies in this response are used to support different arguments. Two studies are never used to support the same argument. This links directly to assessment criterion C (Use of research to support answer), which states that "One piece of research that makes the points relevant to the answer is better than several pieces that repeat the same point over and over".

- The study of Loftus and Palmer (1974) consists of two parts. In one of the parts participants were asked to provide speed estimates and in the other part they were asked a factual question ("Did you see broken glass?"). These were actually two separate experiments with two different samples. When you use a study-based approach, these two experiments will be presented as parts of a single study, supporting the thesis that misleading post-event information can alter the memory of an event. However, in the argument-based approach these parts of the study can be clearly presented as two separate experiments, as they support two distinctly different arguments: results of the first experiment have two potential explanations, and results of the second experiment are used to rule out the explanation that is not consistent with the theory of reconstructive memory.

- The arguments are arranged in a flow: first the theory of reconstructive memory and a supporting study, then two possible interpretations and a supporting study to examine one of them, then the criticism of ecological validity (and a supporting study). This is a bit like telling a story.

- With this story-like arrangement of the arguments it becomes possible to incorporate a more diverse range of critical thinking points in the essay. You may have noticed that in the study-based approach, critical thinking points were mostly limited to evaluating individual research studies. In the argument-based approach, many of the arguments themselves serve as critical thinking points; for example, suggesting two alternative explanations to the results of Loftus and Palmer (1974).

| Study-based | Argument-based |
|---|---|
| The starting point is a research study | The starting point is an argument, then a study is used to support it |
| Two or more studies are used to support one and the same argument | Different studies are used to support different arguments |
| Both parts of Loftus and Palmer (1974) are presented as aspects of the same study | The two parts of Loftus and Palmer (1974) may be used as two independent studies because they support different arguments |
| Studies are not arranged in any meaningful sequence | Arguments are arranged in a flow (story-like arrangement) |
| Critical thinking points are mainly gained from the evaluation of individual studies | Critical thinking points are embedded in the argumentation itself |
| Evaluation points are mostly related to details of individual studies | Evaluation points are mostly related to the theory/concept in the exam question |
| Description of research studies tends to be detailed | It is not necessary to describe all details of a research study (only those relevant to the argument) |

▲ Table 1.4.1 Comparison of study-based and argument-based approaches

- Many evaluation points in the argument-based example are related to the question itself (the concept of reconstructive memory) rather than individual studies.

- In the argument-based example it is possible to skip irrelevant details of a research study if they are not essential to explain the argument. This saves space and allows you to focus more on critical evaluations. (Alternatively, one can use a larger number of research studies.)

The main differences between the study-based and the argument-based approach to structuring essays (related to the example above) are summarized in Table 1.4.1.

A good exercise to see if your response follows the argument-based approach is this. Take the essay and remove all the details of all the research studies, as well as evaluation of these individual research studies. Have a look at what is left. If the leftover content is a well-developed argumentative answer to the question, you are dealing with an argument-based response. If the leftover content is an introduction, a conclusion and one simple idea in between, this is a study-based response.

Of course, a "pure" study-based and a "pure" argument-based approach are only two extremes provided here for the sake of comparison. Most actual essays will lie somewhere in between these two extremes and combine features of both approaches.

You will notice, however, that in a majority of cases the argument-based approach is preferable to the study-based approach as it is more aligned with the assessment criteria. Needless to say, in the example presented above the study-based essay would score much lower than the argument-based essay.

There may be some questions for which the study-based approach will work just fine, for example: "Discuss research studies investigating if one cognitive process is reliable". From the way the question is formulated, you can see that listing research studies one by one might do the job. However, such questions are rare and, to reiterate, you will often find that essays score higher when they follow the logic of the argument-based approach.

# 1.5 COMMAND TERMS AND HOW TO APPROACH THEM

Command terms that you can get in your exam questions, along with the explanations provided in the IB Psychology Subject Guide, are summarized in Table 1.5.1.

The differences between command terms may not always be obvious due to considerable overlap in their meanings. However, it is important to keep those nuances of meaning in mind and to stay focused on the requirements of the command term at all times, as that directly translates into marks.

To illustrate these differences, suppose you are writing an essay about a popular comedy television show, such as *Friends* or *The Big Bang Theory*. We will compare that to a typical exam question, such as a question on localization of function in the brain.

Let us start with SAQ command terms.

## Describe

To describe means to give a detailed account. Detail is the key word here. When you describe *The Big Bang Theory*, the expectation is that you provide a narrative that gives your reader a clear picture of what the show is like. To do so, it would probably make sense to say a few words about the show in general and then describe the characters and typical situations portrayed in it. You might even choose to describe a sample episode. It becomes important to convey what the main characters are like, what they do for a living, where they live and what their typical days are like. If you choose a concrete episode to describe, it is important to convey the sequence of events, the characters' reactions and maybe even the key jokes in the episode.

Similarly, exam questions using the command term "describe" will probably target one specific theory or research study. An example is "Describe one research study related to localization of function in the brain". You will need to include all the key details of the study: its aim, method, procedure, results and conclusion. Procedural information such as the sample, the nature of experimental tasks or how the variables were measured is also important.

Students often find it more challenging to describe a theory, such as "Describe one model of thinking and/or decision-making".

| SAQ or ERQ | Command term | Explanation |
|---|---|---|
| SAQ | Describe | Give a detailed account. |
| SAQ | Outline | Give a brief account or summary. |
| SAQ | Explain | Give a detailed account including reasons or causes. |
| ERQ | Contrast | Give an account of the differences between two (or more) items or situations, referring to both (all) of them throughout. |
| ERQ | Discuss | Offer a considered and balanced review that includes a range of arguments, factors or hypotheses. Opinions or conclusions should be presented clearly and supported by appropriate evidence. |
| ERQ | Evaluate | Make an appraisal by weighing up the strengths and limitations. |
| ERQ | To what extent | Consider the merits or otherwise of an argument or concept. Opinions and conclusions should be presented clearly and supported with appropriate evidence and sound argument. |

▲ Table 1.5.1 Command terms

For such questions, it is important to describe the key components of the model, how they interact with each other and the assumptions on which the model is based. Importantly, a supporting research study is still required in such questions, because assessment criteria include a requirement to use research to support the answer, and a theory or a theoretical model is not considered research. However, unlike "describe one study" questions, details of the study are not that important in this case. It is details of the theory that must be emphasized. As for the study, the crucial part is linking its findings back to the theory.

## Outline

To outline means to give a brief account or summary. How is "outlining" *The Big Bang Theory* different from describing it? When you outline, you are not interested in details of specific characters or specific episodes. Instead your aim is to provide a summary that gives the reader a general idea about the show, much like the summaries you read on websites that provide reviews of television shows. You will probably mention things like the setting (when, where, who), the category of the show (sitcom), the main overarching elements of the storyline (such as the fact that a girl moved in to an apartment across the hall from a couple of geeky physicists) and similar information.

If your question asks "Outline the theory of localization of function", you will use a similar strategy. You will put emphasis on localization as a concept and mention the key issues surrounding this idea (for example, some functions are more strongly localized than others, some functions seem not to be localized at all, methods of research that we use determine what we can say about localization of function). You are also expected to give an example research study, but in an "outline" question procedural details are not that important.

## Explain

To explain means to give a detailed account including reasons or causes. Looking at Table 1.5.1, you have probably noticed that to explain means to describe plus something extra. This does not mean that "explain" is more difficult or requires a longer time to answer than "describe". In an "explain" question, you will focus a little less on procedural details and other descriptive information. Instead the main emphasis will be on answering the question on a conceptual (theoretical) level and connecting the results of the study to that level.

If you were asked to explain one episode of *The Big Bang Theory*, you would probably not need to give a full description of an episode, but you would need to pick an example of a scene and explain how it links to the main idea of the show, why people find it funny and why they like to watch it. For example, in one of the episodes Sheldon Cooper stayed up all night to rewrite the "roommate agreement" when his roommate started dating a girl, and that links to the show's portrayal of Sheldon's character as someone who likes things to be predictable. People may find this kind of personality funny and amusing.

Similarly, if the question is "Explain the theory of localization of function", you need to start by clearly writing the thesis statements of the theory itself (conceptual level), then give an example of a research study supporting the theory or any of its parts (level of research), then link the conclusions of the study back to the theory and explain how exactly the study supports the theory (back to the conceptual level).

Now let us look at ERQ command terms.

## Discuss

To discuss means to offer a considered and balanced review that includes a range of arguments, factors or hypotheses. It is important to understand the difference between "discuss" and "evaluate". Although any extended response essay will include some evaluation as part of a demonstration of critical thinking skills, evaluation is not the main focus of a "discuss" question.

Suppose you need to discuss *The Big Bang Theory*. This is like writing a critical overview for the general audience. You should avoid one-sided opinions and you should carefully consider existing perspectives, potential arguments and counter-arguments. In a review like this you are normally expected to consider a range of aspects of the television show: screenplay, camerawork, acting, setting, originality, budget and so on. The purpose is to convey an objective, unbiased review of various aspects of the television show so that the reader can make a more informed decision about it.

Similarly, you might get a question asking you to "Discuss the theory of localization of function". Think about the question on a conceptual level first. Surely you will need to start with an explanation of the idea of localization. Then you can start exploring several aspects of this idea, including but not limited to the following.

- Limitations of the theory. Some functions are more easily localized than others, some functions seem not to be localized anywhere, localization is not static in the sense that parts of the brain may take over functions of other areas as a result of neuroplasticity.

- Dependence on research methods. When post-mortem examination of brain-damaged patients was the only available method, conclusions in this field were limited; with the invention of brain scanning technology we can now look at the structure and function of a living brain, which has boosted research, but even brain scanning technology has certain limitations (for example, spatial and temporal resolution of a scanner).

- Ethical considerations linked with the idea of localization. For example, the most reliable way to establish localization is through brain damage, but we cannot intentionally do that to participants.

- Assumptions upon which the idea of localization is based. For example, you might bring in some TOK and discuss the pros and cons of reductionism.

- Implications of the idea of localization, such as practical applications, long-term prediction of behaviour and so on.

All the arguments should be supported by relevant and appropriate empirical research. The conclusion should be clear, balanced and evidence-based.

## Evaluate

To evaluate means to make an appraisal by weighing up strengths and limitations. The main difference between this command term and

"discuss" is the focus. You will still consider various aspects/factors/
arguments linked to the question, but the emphasis is on making
an appraisal. So your conclusion should be formulated in terms of
acceptable/unacceptable, reliable/unreliable, conclusive/inconclusive.

If you were to evaluate *The Big Bang Theory*, you would be expected to
produce a value judgment. Is it good or bad? Is it worth watching or not?
This judgment needs to be supported by evidence and critical thinking.

Similarly, if you are asked to "Evaluate research into localization of
function", the focus is on the essential strengths and limitations of
research in this area, its credibility and generalizability, biases that
are difficult to avoid and so on. Just make sure to focus the response
on evaluation of research in this field in general, not standalone
research studies. For example, saying that Broca's case study is limited
in generalizability because it was conducted with a patient with
unique brain damage is acceptable, but it does not directly answer the
question. Adding that case studies were typical for research during that
period of time due to the absence of brain imaging technology solves
the problem, because you are now evaluating research in general.

## To what extent

The command term "to what extent" requires you to consider the
merits or otherwise of an argument or concept. You can usually
expect this command term in content units that include two opposing
viewpoints. For example, the content heading "Genetic similarity"
implies the nurture-nurture debate, so it is plausible to expect
questions such as "To what extent does genetic similarity explain
similarity in behaviour?"

In our television show example, a plausible question might be "To
what extent is *The Big Bang Theory's* representation of young scientists
accurate?" Obviously, you will consider some aspects in which the
representation is accurate and some aspects where it is not. You might
compare the importance of these aspects to arrive at a conclusion. You
will probably mention a range of arguments related to what should be
considered an accurate representation of the life of young scientists.

Similarly, in the question related to the content heading "Genetic
similarity", you might consider arguments to support the statement
that behaviour is genetically inherited (with supporting evidence)
as well as arguments in favour of the idea that it is the environment
that influences behaviour the most (again, with supporting evidence).
You might compare the quality of evidence from both sides of the
debate, outline essential limitations of such evidence and arrive at a
balanced conclusion. You can bring up the fact that genetic inheritance
and the environment interact with each other, making the assessment
of isolated effects difficult. Avoid answering such questions with a
superficial "to some extent". There are other ways to go about it, for
example demonstrating that in some aspects of reality one side of the
argument applies better than the other side.

For *The Big Bang Theory*, for example, the conclusion might be that
the life of young scientists is represented accurately in terms of their
typical day in the university, but not too accurately in terms of their
typical weekend. For the "genetic similarity" question, you might
try to give a quantified answer using twin studies (or other genetic
similarity research).

## Contrast

To contrast means to give an account of the differences between two (or more) items or situations, referring to both (all) of them throughout. Typically, such questions will be used when there are two clearly identifiable theories/models/perspectives implied in the content unit. For example, psychology students are required to study two models of memory: the multi-store memory model and the working memory model. One might expect a question asking students to contrast the two models. In our television show example, a typical question might be "Contrast two television shows: *The Big Bang Theory* and *Friends*".

It is important to note that the expectation for this command term is a comparison **throughout** the response. What does this mean? Suppose the student who is comparing two models of memory describes one model first (and evaluates it), then describes and evaluates the second model, and then in the concluding paragraphs contrasts the two models. This does **not** count as contrasting throughout the response; strictly speaking, the question is only being answered in the concluding paragraphs. A more effective approach would be to define some criteria for comparison at the start, then go from one criterion to the next, making references to both the models in the process. The focus should be on the differences between the two models (as opposed to similarities).

Table 1.5.2 summarizes the key features of an essay response that are expected for each of the command terms. This is not an exhaustive list. The table merely suggests some prominent differences between command terms as well as areas of overlap.

| Feature | Describe | Outline | Explain | Contrast | Discuss | Evaluate | To what extent |
|---|---|---|---|---|---|---|---|
| Using empirical research to support the answer | ✓ | ✓ | ✓ | ✓ | ✓ | ✓ | ✓ |
| Describing research studies, focusing on procedural details | ✓ | | | | | | |
| Explaining how findings of a research study link to theoretical conclusions | | | ✓ | ✓ | ✓ | ✓ | ✓ |
| Focusing on strengths and limitations of a theory/study/idea | | | | | ✓ | ✓ | ✓ |
| Focusing on contrasting explanations or approaches to the same idea | | | | ✓ | | | ✓ |
| Summarizing the important aspects of a problem or an idea | | ✓ | | | ✓ | | |
| Providing a summary that gives a general idea | | ✓ | | | | | |
| Considering existing perspectives | | | ✓ | | ✓ | | ✓ |
| Considering arguments and counter-arguments | | | | | ✓ | ✓ | ✓ |
| Arriving at a balanced conclusion | | | | | ✓ | | ✓ |
| Making a critical appraisal | | | | | ✓ | ✓ | |
| Making a judgment | | | | | | ✓ | |
| Focusing on essential limitations of research in a certain area | | | | ✓ | ✓ | ✓ | ✓ |
| Comparing the quality of evidence from two sides of a debate | | | | | | | ✓ |
| Outlining the essential limitations of empirical evidence | | | | | ✓ | ✓ | ✓ |
| Summarizing differences between theories, ideas or concepts | | | | ✓ | | | |

▲ Table 1.5.2 Command terms: differences and overlaps

An analysis of common mistakes specific to particular content headings will be given in parts 2–8 of this book. Here let us only briefly mention some things to look out for irrespective of the specific exam question.

## >> COMMON ERRORS

### Using animal studies when the exam question refers to "human behaviour"

For example, if the question is "Explain how one hormone may affect one human behaviour", you are expected to use a research study with human participants. Animal studies can be used, however, to support the arguments made about humans. We know that research with animals may inform our understanding of human behaviour because animals are in many aspects similar to humans. That said, there are some things you need to ensure.

- Whenever you are using animal research to answer a "human" question, this needs to be done in support of an argument about human behaviour.

- Animal research should also be explicitly linked to the argument about human behaviour, for example by referring to the assumption that animal research may inform our understanding of human behaviour based on physiological similarities.

- If the question on human behaviour is an SAQ (where you are normally expected to use only one piece of research in support), it would be better not to use animal research at all.

## >> COMMON ERRORS

### Ignoring details of the question such as quantifiers (such as "one", "one or more") and conjunctions (such as "and", "or", "and/or")

When the question asks you to "Explain how one hormone may influence one human behaviour", it would be a mistake to talk about two examples of hormones because the second example will not be marked by the examiner. In the same way, when you are asked about one human behaviour, you are expected to stay focused on one example. If the question says "one or more", you can choose either to focus on one example and explore it deeply (the depth approach), or to provide two or more examples and explore each of them in less detail (the breadth approach). Both these approaches in such cases are equally acceptable.

Conjunctions (such as "and", "or", "and/or") are also important. For example, suppose the question is "Evaluate research into psychological trauma and resilience". The conjunction "and" suggests that you need research concerning both trauma and resilience. Although there is some overlap, there exist separate bodies of research for these two phenomena. If the conjunction is "or", you are supposed to choose one of the two; you cannot write about both because half of your response in this case will not be marked. If the question is "and/or", it is up to you to choose between the depth approach and the breadth approach.

The IB has a clear rule on when a pairing may be separated.

- Three pairings in the syllabus may be separated so that the question is formulated using one of the concepts only: Gender identity and social roles (Developmental psychology), Dispositional factors and health beliefs (Health psychology), and Trauma and resilience (Developmental psychology).

- The other pairings in the syllabus will not be separated and one can expect questions with the "and/or" conjunction.

### Using irrelevant knowledge to support the answer

This is something that you need to be very careful about, as it may cost you a lot of marks. A typical example would be speaking about a neurotransmitter in response to a question about hormones. When this happens, the student is risking being awarded zero marks for that response, no matter how well developed it is. Another typical example is using animal research in an SAQ about human behaviour. You should be absolutely certain about which theories and research studies are relevant to which parts of the syllabus. If you have doubts, do not hesitate to consult your teacher. To further assist you, in parts 2–8 of this book where we are discussing the content headings one by one, typical mistakes will be highlighted again.

# 2 BIOLOGICAL APPROACH TO BEHAVIOUR

## 2.1 LOCALIZATION OF FUNCTION

Initially researchers tried to establish strict localization for all psychological functions. This was gradually replaced by the understanding that localization is relative. Relative localization implies that:

- some functions are indeed strictly localized

- some higher-order functions are widely distributed

- sometimes aspects of the same function may be localized differently

- several brain areas may be responsible for the same function

- one brain area may take over the function of another.

Discoveries and conclusions in this area largely depend on the methods used to establish localization. Methods and techniques used for this include: case studies with post-mortem examination of the brain, brain scanning technology, neural stimulation, induced brain damage and case studies of individuals who underwent brain surgery.

### 🔍 KEY RESEARCH STUDIES

- Penfield and Boldrey (1937): using the method of neural stimulation to map the sensory cortex.

- Lashley (1929): using induced brain damage in an attempt to find localization of memory in rats.

- Gazzaniga (1967) and Sperry (1968): research with split-brain patients.

- Maguire *et al* (2000): localization of spatial memory in the posterior and anterior hippocampus.

- Sharot *et al* (2007): localization of flashbulb memory.

- Saxe and Kanwisher (2003): localization of theory of mind.

- Chugani (1999), Giedd (2004), Kolb and Fantie (1989): investigation of structure-function relationships in the developing brain.

### ➤➤ COMMON ERRORS

If you use lateralization research in your answer (such as Sperry), explicitly recognize that lateralization is a special case of localization.

Try not to base responses (especially for SAQs) solely on 19th-century research, such as case studies of Broca and Wernicke. You can use more recent research studies to show a more complex understanding of localization.

Another common error is to use an animal study of brain damage and suggest that the findings can automatically be applied to localization of function in the human brain. An explicit recognition of the limitations of such generalizations is crucial.

Apart from the heading "neuroplasticity", the following additional terms can be used in SAQs:

- neural networks
- neural pruning
- neuron.

Any combination of one or more of these additional terms with one of the command terms is acceptable for an SAQ.

The mechanism of neuroplasticity is the restructuring of neural networks. This restructuring may be achieved through both creating new connections and breaking down the ones that are no longer used. Factors that cause such restructuring of neural networks are genetic (for example, the process of biological maturation) and environmental (for example, learning or a brain injury).

Neuroplasticity occurs on many levels, from the level of a single neuron (synaptic plasticity) to the level of large, interconnected neural networks (for example, cortical remapping). Our ability to understand neuroplasticity on various levels depends on the methods of research that are available.

Synaptic plasticity depends on the activity of the neuron. If two neurons are repeatedly activated together, it is likely that a connection between them will be formed. Similarly, lack of activation leads to neural pruning.

There are various examples of neuroplasticity occurring in response to genetic and environmental influences. For example, neuroplasticity is observed in response to brain injury. But neuroplasticity is also a brain mechanism that underlies such common processes as learning.

## 🔍 KEY RESEARCH STUDIES

- Rosenzweig, Bennett and Diamond (1972) on the influence of an enriched environment on the growth of rat brains.
- Draganski *et al* (2004), Draganski *et al* (2006), Maguire *et al* (2000): examples of neuroplasticity in response to different kinds of learning.
- Goldapple *et al* (2004): brain changes caused by psychological treatment of depression due to neuroplasticity.

**For the additional terms**

- Any study on neuroplasticity is also relevant to the concept of neural networks.
- Draganski *et al* (2004) can be used as a study illustrating neural pruning because a lack of activity led to a decrease in grey matter volume.
- Squeglia *et al* (2013) is a study demonstrating that cortical thinning (elimination of unnecessary connections) in adolescence is correlated to better performance on cognitive tasks of memory and problem-solving.

## ≫ COMMON ERRORS

Neural pruning is not the opposite of neuroplasticity. Rather it is an integral part of neuroplasticity. Fewer neural connections does not mean the network is less efficient. In fact, the opposite is often true: eliminating redundant connections may make the network more efficient.

## 2.3   NEUROTRANSMITTERS AND THEIR EFFECTS ON BEHAVIOUR

Apart from the heading "neurotransmitters and their effects on behaviour", the following additional terms can be used in SAQs:

- synapse (how these relate to excitatory and inhibitory neurotransmitters)

- agonist

- antagonist.

Any combination of one or more of these additional terms with one of the command terms is acceptable for an SAQ.

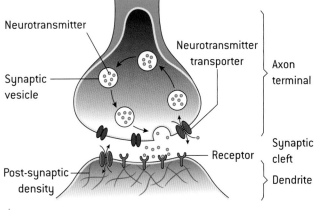

▲ Figure 2.3.1   Neurotransmission

Information transmission in the nervous system is both electrical and chemical. Electrical impulses travel from synapse to synapse, but in the synapses it is a chemical process that enables the impulse to be passed from one neuron to another.

There are more than 100 known neurotransmitters (for example, serotonin, acetylcholine, GABA and others). Neurotransmitters travel across the synapse to the post-synaptic membrane and bind onto receptors on that membrane. Some receptors are excitatory, which means that neurotransmitters binding onto them increase the probability of the neuron firing. Some receptors are inhibitory, so when a neurotransmitter binds onto them, the probability of the neuron firing decreases. A neurotransmitter may be both excitatory **and** inhibitory depending on the receptor site where it is functioning. Exceptions are acetylcholine (whose function is usually excitatory) and GABA (whose function is usually inhibitory).

Receptors on the post-synaptic membrane can also be affected by outside chemicals (such as drugs). Chemicals that bind onto receptors and mimic the effects of a neurotransmitter are known as agonists for that neurotransmitter. For example, lysergic acid diethylamide (LSD), a hallucinogenic drug, is an agonist for serotonin. It binds onto serotonin receptors and activates them, increasing the effect that serotonin normally produces.

Selective serotonin reuptake inhibitors (SSRIs), strictly speaking, do not act on a receptor site, so they can be called neither agonists nor antagonists. However, their effect is identical to that of agonists. SSRIs prevent serotonin from being taken back into the neuron that released it. As a result, there are larger concentrations of serotonin in the synaptic gap and the function of serotonin is enhanced. Hence SSRIs may be called "indirect agonists".

Antagonists have the opposite function: they inhibit the action of a neurotransmitter by blocking the receptor site. For example, atropine is a chemical that binds to acetylcholine receptors without activating them, thus suppressing the function of the neurotransmitter acetylcholine.

Neurotransmitter research is highly complex. In the simplest typical study, the researcher manipulates the level of a neurotransmitter in the participant's brain and observes the resulting change in behaviour. But even if the change is observed, it does not necessarily mean that the given neurotransmitter "influences" the given behaviour. The effect may be postponed or indirect. Behaviour may be determined by multiple factors simultaneously, and when the level of a neurotransmitter is manipulated, there are usually side effects that can have an influence on the observed behaviour too.

## KEY RESEARCH STUDIES

- Crockett *et al* (2010) on the effect of serotonin on prosocial behaviour.

- Fisher, Aron and Brown (2005) on the effect of dopamine on romantic love.

- Freed *et al* (2001) on the effect of dopamine on symptoms of Parkinson's disease.

- Caspi *et al* (2003) on the role of the serotonin transporter gene in reaction to stressful events and depression.

### For the additional terms

Crow and Grove-White (1973). In this study hyoscine – an antagonist for acetylcholine – was administered to 12 volunteers. Hyoscine is also known as scopolamine. Administration of the drug resulted in an impairment of long-term memory but not short-term memory. This study can be used to support answers on excitatory neurotransmitters and antagonists, but also to support the multi-store model of memory,

specifically the idea that short-term memory and long-term memory are two separate memory stores (see pages 47–48). The full text of the study is available online.[1]

Alcohol (ethanol) is an agonist for the inhibitory neurotransmitter GABA. There has been a lot of research on the effect of alcohol on memory impairment, and any such study will do the job of demonstrating both agonists and inhibitory neurotransmitters.

One such study is Nelson *et al* (1986), where it was found that a dose of alcohol (1 millilitre per kg) significantly impaired participants' performance on recall tasks (questions like "What is the capital of Chile?"), but had no effect on recognition tasks (for example, "Which of the following is the capital of Chile: Caracas, Lima, Santiago, Acapulco, Quito, Curacao, Valparaiso or Bogota?").[2]

## COMMON ERRORS

It is very important to make a clear distinction between neurotransmitters and hormones. Sometimes in response to a question on neurotransmitters, students write a good essay that is based on research using a hormone (for example, oxytocin is a hormone while serotonin and dopamine are neurotransmitters). Such essays will likely score no marks.

If you use animal studies in an ERQ, you should explicitly make a link between the study and human behaviour. In an SAQ, where only one research study is usually necessary, you are advised to use a human study.

---

1 Crow, TJ and Grove-White, IG. 1973. "An analysis of the learning deficit following hyoscine administration to man". *British Journal of Pharmacology.* Vol 49. Pp 322–327. doi: 10.1111/j.1476-5381.1973.tb08379.x.

2 Nelson, TO, McSpadden, M, Fromme, K and Marlatt, GA. 1986. "Effects of alcohol intoxication on metamemory and on retrieval from long-term memory." *Journal of Experimental Psychology: General.* Vol 115, number 3. Pp 247–254. doi:10.1037/0096-3445.115.3.247.

# 2.4 TECHNIQUES USED TO STUDY THE BRAIN IN RELATION TO BEHAVIOUR

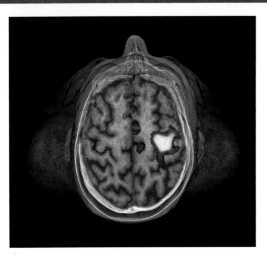

▲ Figure 2.4.1 fMRI scan

Brain imaging techniques enabled a paradigmatic change in how we approach studying the brain in relation to behaviour. Earlier methods (such as post-mortem examinations of the brains of patients with unique behavioural deviations) were crude, slow and did not provide any insight into the inner workings of the living brain. Conversely, brain imaging technology allows us to see inside a participant's brain almost in real time.

There is a variety of brain imaging techniques, and the choice is informed by such factors as the aim of the study, acceptable limitations of the technique (for example, in terms of its spatial and temporal resolution) and costs.

Spatial resolution is the smallest difference in location that the scanner can detect (in voxels). The smaller it is, the grainier the picture. Temporal resolution is the smallest time period in which changes can be detected. It is possible to increase spatial and/or temporal resolution by increasing scanning time, but:

- there is a threshold of resolution beyond which technology cannot go, no matter how long scanning takes

- it is difficult for the participant to stay still for a long time, and this adds more noise to the data (for example, due to fidgeting).

Some techniques are less accessible than others. For example, fMRI scanners are heavy, expensive and require a long scanning procedure. Other techniques may be simpler to use but may have their own limitations. For example, PET scanners can be much smaller and even portable, but PET involves administering a dose of radioactive tracer into the participant's blood. Some brain imaging techniques cannot be used with some participants due to their medical conditions, such as if they have a pacemaker or metal implant. The choice of technique depends on the aim of the study.

## 🔍 KEY RESEARCH STUDIES

Any research study that used a brain imaging technique is acceptable. A good response will demonstrate why this particular technique might have been chosen for this particular study, as well as the pros and cons of this choice in the context of the study.

Examples are:

- MRI: Draganski *et al* (2004), Draganski *et al* (2006), Maguire *et al* (2000), Giedd (2004)

- fMRI: Fisher, Aron and Brown (2005), Sharot *et al* (2007), Loh and Kanai (2004), Phelps *et al* (2000), Saxe and Kanwisher (2003)

- PET: Freed *et al* (2001), Goldapple *et al* (2004), Chugani (1999), Chugani *et al* (2001).

## ≫ COMMON ERRORS

Brain imaging techniques are not research methods. They can be used to measure variables as part of a research method – experimental, correlational or qualitative. For example, Maguire *et al* (2000) used MRI scans to investigate brain structure in relation to the taxi driving experience, as part of a quasi-experimental research study that compared taxi drivers to a control group of participants who did not drive a taxi.

Neurotransmitters and hormones have distinctly different mechanisms of action and distinctly different functions. Glands that are part of the endocrine system release hormones into the bloodstream and from there hormones reach their target cells. Since the system of blood vessels is more elaborate than the system of neurons, hormones can reach places in the body that neurotransmitters cannot. Due to this difference in the mechanism, hormones, unlike neurotransmitters, can also regulate long-term processes such as metabolism, growth or reproduction.

Each hormone has a set of target cells that it may influence because these cells have hormone-specific receptors. When a hormone binds to a receptor in the target cell, it triggers a set of changes that indirectly affect behaviour. Hormones do not influence behaviour directly, but they increase or decrease the probability that certain behaviour will occur.

There is a large variety of hormones and they influence a wide range of human behaviours. Examples include adrenaline, noradrenaline, testosterone, melatonin, thyroxine, insulin, leptin, oxytocin, androgen, oestrogen and many others.

Since hormones affect behaviour indirectly by causing a set of changes that create a certain predisposition to behaviour, many hormones may influence a wide range of behaviours, including some less obvious links. For example, oxytocin has been demonstrated to be involved in bonding behaviour and spouse fidelity. However, oxytocin has also been linked to such behaviours as ethnocentrism and intergroup conflict.

## 🔍 KEY RESEARCH STUDIES

- Ferguson *et al* (2000): an oxytocin gene knockout study on mice.

- Romero *et al* (2014) on oxytocin promoting social bonds in animals.

- Kosfeld *et al* (2005) on the role of oxytocin in interpersonal trust.

- Scheele *et al* (2012) on the role of oxytocin in fidelity in human subjects.

- De Dreu *et al* (2012), linking oxytocin to defence-motivated non-cooperation and intergroup conflict.

- De Dreu *et al* (2014), linking oxytocin to ethnocentric behaviour.

## ≫ COMMON ERRORS

Remember to be careful not to use research investigating neurotransmitters when you are asked about hormones (and vice versa).

# 2.6 PHEROMONES AND THEIR EFFECTS ON BEHAVIOUR

A pheromone is a chemical substance released by one member of a species that affects the behaviour of other members of the same species. In this sense pheromones serve the function of chemical communication. One example of how they are important in the animal world is by signalling fertility.

The existence of human pheromones is questionable and has not been conclusively established. Substances exist that have been researched as candidates for this role – putative human pheromones, such as androstadienone (AND) and estratetraenol (EST) – but such research is filled with limitations.

Biologically speaking, if pheromonal communication does indeed play a role in human behaviour, it is not clear where such chemical information is processed. The accessory olfactory bulb (involved in processing such information in the brains of animals) disappears in humans after birth, and the vomeronasal organ (another important component of this biological system in animals) is there, but it appears to be disconnected from the central nervous system. However, there is always a possibility that pheromonal information in the human brain is processed elsewhere.

The search for a human pheromone has been concentrated on discovering a sex pheromone: one that would signal gender and/or sexual attractiveness. Both laboratory and field experiments have been conducted in this area, typically involving administering a synthesized pheromone to male or female subjects. Research has reported mixed results.

Some of the main limitations of pheromone research with human subjects include:

- demand characteristics (because it may be easy for participants to guess the true aim of the study, especially since many pheromones have a specific smell, so participants may even understand which group they are in)

- issues of construct validity (because even if the smell of a certain chemical affects people's behaviour, that does not mean that the chemical is a pheromone)

- replicability and publication bias (since many of the researchers are commercially interested in the results of the research).

Additionally, the dosage of pheromones given in a typical study is much bigger than that found in real-life conditions.

## ➤➤ COMMON ERRORS

You should recognize that the fact that research on human pheromones is inconclusive does not automatically mean that they do not exist. After all, pheromones play a large role in the animal kingdom, and it is possible that humans have retained some form of chemical communication. The existence of human pheromones is debatable, but remember that good critical thinking means demonstrating where exactly doubts are coming from, rather than simply rejecting the idea.

## 🔍 KEY RESEARCH STUDIES

- Lundstrom and Olsson (2005), Hare *et al* (2017): laboratory experiments (with contradictory findings).

- Cutler, Friedmann and McCoy (1998), McCoy and Pitino (2002), Saxton *et al* (2008): field experiments with male and female subjects, by researchers who were commercially interested in the findings.

# 2.7 GENES AND THEIR EFFECTS ON BEHAVIOUR

A distinction is made between the genotype and the phenotype: characteristics that are genetically programmed and characteristics that actually manifest on the outside, for example in the form of a person's appearance or behaviour. Genotype is a code for phenotype, but the presence of this code does not guarantee that the phenotype will be in full accordance with it. Environmental factors may affect genes through epigenetic changes in gene expression. Although the DNA remains unchanged, environmental factors can suppress the expression of certain genes, thus effectively switching these genes off.

Methods of research used to study (and quantify) genetic heritability of traits and behaviour may be broadly divided into two groups:

- methods based on the principle of genetic similarity
  (twin studies, family studies and adoption studies)

- methods of molecular genetics.

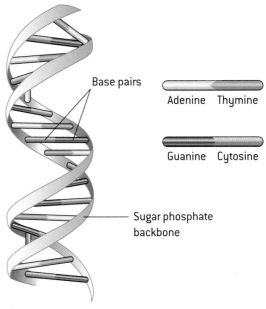

▲ Figure 2.7.1  Structure of DNA

The content heading "Genes and their effects on behaviour" focuses on the second group – methods of molecular genetics. These involve using modern technology to create maps of the individual genome and then compare these maps to behaviour. Epigenetic changes (regulation of gene expression and gene suppression) can also be studied using special techniques. This group of methods allows researchers to identify specific genes (or their expression) that are responsible for a particular behaviour.

## 🔍 KEY RESEARCH STUDIES

- Caspi *et al* (2003): used the methods of molecular genetics to identify 5-HTT (the serotonin transporter gene) as the gene responsible for vulnerability to stress and hence an increased chance of depression.

- Ferguson *et al* (2000): studied oxytocin gene knockout mice and found that "switching off" the oxytocin gene leads to a loss of social memory.

- Weaver *et al* (2004): investigated epigenetic changes in the brains of rats who had more nurturing or less nurturing mothers. Findings showed that less nurturing in early childhood leads to the epigenetic suppression of the glucocorticoid receptor gene, which in turns leads to more sensitivity to stress.

- Kaminsky *et al* (2008): a case study of two identical twins who led dramatically different lives; epigenetic mapping revealed epigenetic changes in one particular gene (DLX1).

## ≫ COMMON ERRORS

Studies based on the principle of genetic similarities (twin/kinship studies) should not be confused with studies using methods of molecular genetics.

# 2.8   GENETIC SIMILARITY

Apart from the content heading "Genetic similarity", the following additional term can be used in SAQs:

- twin and kinship studies.

Any combination of this additional term with one of the command terms is acceptable for an SAQ.

## 🔍 KEY RESEARCH STUDIES

- Bouchard and McGue (1981): a meta-analysis of 111 twin studies to quantify the genetic contribution into traits such as intelligence.

- Scarr and Weinberg (1983): a transracial adoption study. On the one hand, it found that children adopted into families with a higher socio-economic status (SES) reach larger average intelligence levels compared to children reared in their biological, lower-SES families. This shows environmental malleability of intelligence. On the other hand, the study demonstrated that the intelligence of adopted children correlates more strongly with the intelligence of their biological parents than that of their adoptive parents, even if they were adopted very early. Together these two findings demonstrate the additive influence of environment and genetics on intelligence.

### For the additional terms

- Bouchard and McGue (1981) can be used as an example for twin studies. However, it may also be used as an example for kinship studies because it compared groups of individuals with various degrees of genetic relatedness: MZ and DZ twins, siblings, children and parents, and adopted children and parents.

- Scarr and Weinberg (1983) can be used as an example for kinship studies if you look at one part of the study specifically, where they calculate correlations between adopted children and biological parents, adopted children and adoptive parents, biologically related siblings, biologically unrelated siblings and so on.

Methods of research used to study (and quantify) genetic heritability of traits and behaviour may be broadly divided into two groups:

- methods based on the principle of genetic similarity (twin studies, family studies and adoption studies)

- methods of molecular genetics.

The content heading "Genetic similarity" focuses on the first group. The idea behind these methods is that individuals who are more strongly related (thus share a larger portion of their genotype) should demonstrate more similar behaviour, provided that this behaviour is inherited. These methods allow us to quantify the relative contribution of genetic inheritance to a certain behaviour, but they do not allow us to pinpoint a specific gene (or genes) responsible for the behaviour.

The nature-nurture debate in psychology in its traditional form asks whether behaviour is primarily influenced by genetic inheritance or environmental factors. However, an implicit assumption in this debate is that the two factors (genetic inheritance and environmental influences) are independent of each other, which is not completely accurate. Another incorrect assumption is a black-and-white view where characteristics are thought to be determined by one of the two factors but not both factors simultaneously.

The modern version of this debate recognizes the following points.

- Behaviour can be determined by both factors, and the relative contributions of the two factors into observed behaviour can be quantified.

- Genetic inheritance and environment are not independent factors in the sense that they can influence each other. An example of genes influencing environment is the phenomenon of niche-picking. An example of environmental factors influencing genetic factors is epigenetic changes in gene expression.

- For these reasons it is now believed that a dynamic interaction exists between genetic inheritance and environment, with the two factors influencing each other.

## ⏩ COMMON ERRORS

Studies based on the principle of genetic similarities (twin/kinship studies) should not be confused with studies using methods of molecular genetics.

We know that the theory of evolution is a powerful explanation for the development of physical traits in the biological world. But if genes programme for behaviour as well as physical traits (which was established in genetic psychology), it should mean that evolutionary principles apply to the development of behaviour too.

The theory of evolution rests on the assumption that the need to survive and reproduce is the primary driver of genetic changes in a species population. Combined with the idea that the likelihood of survival depends on how fit an organism is for the requirements of its habitat (the environment), this gives rise to ideas of survival of the fittest and natural selection. Genes that do not enable the best fitness are gradually, generation after generation, eliminated from the gene pool, and hence behaviours that these genes are responsible for are also eliminated.

Evolutionary explanations in psychology are attractive because they can explain a range of behaviours that are difficult to explain otherwise. They have been applied in various fields, such as to explain emotions, attraction, competition, mental disorders and even behaviours such as contagious yawning. Researchers usually claim that an evolutionary basis of a behaviour can be assumed when the behaviour is universal for all people and leads to a successful adaptation. Additionally, our confidence in an evolutionary basis grows if there is a structure of the brain that is activated when the behaviour occurs.

Since we cannot directly manipulate the process of evolution, experimental research in this area seems to be impossible. Instead we can use a suggested evolutionary explanation as a model and formulate a set of predictions based on that model, then observe whether research data supports our predictions. As more and more predictions are supported, our confidence in the model grows stronger.

At the same time, there are certain limitations that are inherent in every evolutionary explanation of behaviour. These include, among others:

- testability (it is impossible to directly test these ideas so we have to rely on post-hoc explanations)

- the existence of cultural variations (which contradicts the idea that certain behaviours are a product of the evolutionary process that we share as a species)

- the assumption that evolutionary development is linear

- limitations of a reductionist argument.

## 🔍 KEY RESEARCH STUDIES

A variety of research studies may be used to demonstrate evolutionary explanations, including many studies from other parts of the syllabus. For example, Hamilton (1994) and Madsen *et al* (2007) provide an explanation for altruism based on kin selection theory (Psychology of human relationships). Fessler *et al* (2005) investigates disgust sensitivity in pregnant women in various trimesters of pregnancy.

It is advisable, however, to select at least one piece of research that would demonstrate using an evolutionary explanation as a basis for formulating a set of predictions that are then compared to observed data. One such example is Curtis, Aunger and Rabie (2004): a study that investigates a set of five predictions based on the evolutionary model of disgust.

# 2.10 THE ROLE OF ANIMAL RESEARCH IN UNDERSTANDING HUMAN BEHAVIOUR (HL ONLY)

For all three topics in Biological approach to behaviour, and with reference to research studies, HL students should study:

• the value of animal models in research to provide insight into human behaviour

• ethical considerations in animal research.

Exam questions may use a combination of the two bullet points above with the three topics from column 1 of the syllabus (The relationship between the brain and behaviour, Hormones and pheromones and their effects on behaviour, The relationship between genetics and behaviour).

▲ Figure 2.10.1 How similar are rat and human brains?

An animal model is a particular animal used to test a particular hypothesis (model) about a particular human behaviour. Hence to fully identify an animal model, one should mention three characteristics: what human behaviour is investigated, what animal species is used and what cause-effect relationship is tested. For example, "mouse gene knockout models of obesity" use the technique of switching off one particular gene to test the hypothesis that this gene is linked to obesity, and seek to apply these findings to humans.

There are many advantages of working with animal models with the purpose of generalizing findings to human subjects. First, the assumption that humans and animals would behave similarly seems justified because they do have a lot of similarities, both genetically and in terms of their brain structures. Second, it is easier to strictly control confounding variables in laboratory experiments with animals. Additionally, animal models are accessible and relatively inexpensive, allowing researchers to run multiple experiments in a short span of time.

However, there are also important limitations. The assumption that human and animal brain structures are similar is still an assumption. Even if a structural similarity does exist, it does not automatically mean that there will be a functional similarity too. For example, the fact that rats and humans both have a hippocampus does not mean that the function of the hippocampus in rats is the same as in humans. It is the intricate neural networks that the brain structure is included into that determine behaviour. In humans, the hippocampus is linked to many areas in the cortex that do not even exist in the rat brain. These areas can modify or even completely change behavioural reactions that one could predict if these links did not exist.

Additionally, animals are tested in highly controlled laboratory conditions, and many animals are specially bred to be research participants. Animal subjects may behave differently in laboratory conditions than they would in their natural habitat.

Ethical considerations in animal research are different from those in research using human subjects. Typically, an organization that publishes a code of ethics for psychologists (such as the American Psychological Association or the British Psychological Society) would have a separate code of ethics for conducting animal research. Some key ethical considerations include:

- the necessity to clearly justify animal research

- the duty to assume that procedures causing pain in humans can cause pain in animals as well

- the requirement to have clear knowledge of the species being used in order to be able to tell when the animal is in distress

- giving laboratory animals humane care and minimizing their discomfort.

All animal studies must be submitted for approval to an ethics committee.

## 🔍 KEY RESEARCH STUDIES

You need to know examples of animal research for the three topics in Biological approach to behaviour. Examples for the three topics are listed below.

**The relationship between brain and behaviour**

- Rosenzweig, Bennett and Diamond (1972) on the effect of an enriched environment on brain growth in rats; Lashley (1929) on localization of memory in rats

**Hormones and pheromones and their effects on behaviour**

- Romero *et al* (2014) on the role of oxytocin in promoting social bonds in dogs; Ferguson *et al* (2000) on the oxytocin gene knockout mouse models of social amnesia

**The relationship between genetics and behaviour**

- Weaver *et al* (2004) on epigenetics regulation of gene expression in rats; Ferguson *et al* (2000) – see above.

## ≫ COMMON ERRORS

A very common mistake among students when discussing ethical considerations in animal research is to apply human ethical considerations to the use of animals. It is important to understand that ethical considerations in animal research are unique and independent from their "human" counterparts.

# SAMPLE QUESTIONS

Below are two example SAQs and two example ERQs that you might see on Biological approach to behaviour. Read the sample student answers and the accompanying comments, which will help you to understand what the students have done well and what they could do better.

## SAQ example 1

QUESTION PRACTICE

Explain one technique used to study the brain in relation to behaviour.                                                   [9]

SAMPLE STUDENT ANSWER

The only way to investigate the brain in relation to behaviour used to be post-mortem examination of the brains of patients with unique patterns of behaviour. For example, Paul Broca examined the brain of his patient Tan to discover that there had been damage to a particular brain area in the left temporal lobe, now known as Broca's area, responsible for articulate speech. When he was alive, Tan could understand speech but could not produce any speech sounds other than the two syllables "tan tan". This approach to research was flawed in many ways, for example, there was no way to see inside the brain of a living person.

► This is an effective introduction explaining why the ability to see inside the brain of a living person is important for research, but the introduction is not specific to **one** technique. It is a little too generic.

However, that changed with the discovery of brain imaging technology, which opened a lot of new doors in terms of brain research. Brain imaging techniques include magnetic resonance imaging (MRI), functional magnetic resonance imaging (fMRI), positron emission tomography (PET), computerized axial tomography (CAT), electroencephalography (EEG) and some others. In this essay I will explain how magnetic resonance imaging (MRI) can be used to study the brain in relation to behaviour.

► There is no need to state the different brain imaging techniques; this is a waste of the candidate's time. One technique is needed only.

One research study that used MRI was Maguire et al (2000). In this study the brain structure of 16 right-handed, male London taxi drivers was investigated in comparison to the average brain (a control sample of brain scans). MRI scans for the control group were obtained from the same unit. Researchers also investigated the correlation between the number of years of taxi driving experience and the structure of the brain as shown in the MRI scans.

Results showed that taxi drivers, as compared to control group participants, had increased volumes of grey matter in the posterior hippocampus, but less grey matter in the anterior hippocampus. In other words, there was redistribution of grey matter in the brain of taxi drivers, from the anterior hippocampus to the posterior. This is explained by using our knowledge of the typical functions of these brain structures: the posterior hippocampus is involved in using previously learned spatial information, while the anterior hippocampus is involved in learning new spatial information. Finally, there was a correlation between taxi driving experience and the extent of this grey matter redistribution. Researchers concluded that neuroplasticity occurs in natural settings due to gaining navigational experience in the city.

Thus magnetic resonance imaging (MRI) was instrumental in obtaining these conclusions. Brain imaging techniques allow researchers to see the structure of the living brain, so they play a crucial role in investigating the interaction between the brain and behaviour.

▼ The research study has been explained in detail and clear knowledge is demonstrated, but there is not enough focus on MRI: why it was used, how it worked and how it linked to the conclusions. The focus here is on the study but not the brain imaging technique.

**This response could have achieved 4/9 marks.**

The response is partially relevant to the question, but the focus on the question and the requirements of the command term is not consistent. Knowledge and understanding is accurate but limited. The response is supported by appropriate research that is described but not sufficiently linked to the question. The response does not fully meet requirements of the command term.

## SAQ example 2

QUESTION PRACTICE

Describe one effect of neurotransmission on human behaviour.     [9]

SAMPLE STUDENT ANSWER

One of the principles of the biological approach to behaviour refers to the idea that human behaviour and physiology can be studied through animal (non-human) experimentation. Martinez and Kesner studied the effect of the neurotransmitter acetylcholine (Ach) on memory in rats.

In their study, Martinez and Kesner set up a T-maze that the rats had to run in order to get food that was on one of the

▶ The question explicitly asks about human behaviour. The candidate has stated that animal research can be used to understand human behaviour. This justification is acceptable, but it should have been elaborated further.

sides of the T. After that, rats were injected with three different solutions depending on the condition they were in. The first group was injected with scopolamine which blocks Ach's receptor sites, meaning that there is less Ach in their blood. The second group was injected with physostigmine that breaks down Ach, meaning that there was more Ach in the blood. The third (control) group was injected with a saline solution that had no effect on Ach levels.

The results demonstrated that the higher the Ach levels the better the T-maze was remembered, since the second group was the one that performed best. Those in the control group had better memory than those in the first group in which they had reduced levels of Ach. This suggests that higher levels of the neurotransmitter Ach have an effect on memory.

▼ The research study is accurately described, but the effects of neurotransmission on behaviour are barely described on a conceptual level.

**This response could have achieved 3/9 marks.**

The response is relevant to the question, but does not meet the command term requirements. The response is focused on the description of a research study rather than giving a conceptual answer supported by research. Knowledge and understanding is accurate but limited. Most importantly, the question explicitly requires a description of the effects of neurotransmission on **human** behaviour, but the candidate does not sufficiently address this requirement.

## ERQ example 1

QUESTION PRACTICE

Discuss one or more approaches to research in studying genetics and behaviour.    [22]

SAMPLE STUDENT ANSWER

According to one of the principles of the biological approach to behaviour, genetic inheritance can influence behaviour. This is a justified assumption because it is known that genetic inheritance directly influences biological factors like the structure and function of the nervous system and the endocrine system, and these factors in turn influence behaviour. It is therefore logical to assume that inheritance influences behaviour, either directly or indirectly. But the question is, how do we test research hypotheses regarding the influence of genetics on behaviour?

▲ The introduction is a bit lengthy, but it effectively identifies and explains the issue implicit in the question. Justification is given to the assumption that genetic inheritance can influence behaviour.

There are many methods traditionally used in research in psychology. They are subdivided into qualitative and

▲ The focus is on methods (approaches to research).

quantitative. Quantitative methods are usually used to discover universally applicable laws of behaviour, whereas qualitative methods are usually more focused on an in-depth investigation of a unique individual or a group of individuals. Quantitative methods are further subdivided into experimental research and correlational research, and qualitative methods include methods like interview, observation, case study and so on.

In the field of investigating the influence of genetics and behaviour, the most commonly used group of methods is correlational research based on the principle of genetic similarity. Another group of methods that may be used is experimental research involving direct manipulation of the genotype. However, since manipulation of genetic material is a serious ethical concern, this is possible only with animal subjects. Thus in this essay I will discuss correlational research using the example of twin studies to investigate heritability of human intelligence, and experimental research using the example of gene knockout animal models in anxiety research.

▲ The choice of methods – correlational research and experimental research – is effective and revolves around the issue of causation.

A typical twin study takes two samples of twins – monozygotic (MZ) and dizygotic (DZ) – and calculates within-pair similarities between twins in the same pair, then compares this estimate of similarity in MZ and DZ twins. The only assumed difference between MZ and DZ twins is that MZ twins share 100% of their genotype and DZ twins share on average only 50% of their genotype. So the logic is, if a behaviour is influenced genetically, this behaviour should be more similar in pairs of MZ twins than in pairs of DZ twins. Stronger heritability of a behaviour leads to greater differences between MZ twins and DZ twins.

▲ The candidate demonstrates understanding of the method.

An example of such a study is Bouchard and McGue (1981) who studied heritability of intelligence. This was an aggregate analysis of the results of 111 twin studies published previously. The mean correlation between MZ twins reared together was 0.85 and the mean correlation between DZ twins reared together was 0.58. From this, researchers could estimate that heritability of intelligence was about 50–60%. Additionally it should be noted that even MZ twins reared together did not show 100% similarity. This suggests that intelligence is influenced by factors other than genetic inheritance – most probably, environmental factors.

▶ Bouchard and McGue used median correlations, not mean correlations, but this minor mistake does not affect marks.

▲ Critical thinking points are effectively balanced: the study itself is evaluated as well as typical limitations for the whole range of studies of this type. In this way, critical thinking is explicitly linked back to the question.

This study may be considered reliable because it is based on an extensive dataset from 111 other research studies. However, one also needs to remember about some important limitations of twin studies. For example, it may be claimed that higher similarity between MZ twins reared together is partially explained by larger similarities in how parents treat MZ twins as compared to DZ twins (in other words, the common environment they share may be more common than for DZ twins). Additionally, MZ twins may trigger similar responses from the environment, making their environmental influences more similar too. If that is the case, the 50–60% estimate for heritability of intelligence may be exaggerated.

▲ Clear knowledge is demonstrated. Research is used effectively to support the argument.

An example of experimental research investigating the influence of genes on behaviour is the study of Toth (2003). This investigated genetic knockout models using mice whose $5\text{-HT}_{1A}$ receptor gene was deactivated. $5\text{-HT}_{1A}$ receptors are known to be involved in mood and anxiety disorders. A deficit of such receptors leads to discrepancies in the function of serotonin (the neurotransmitter). This is involved in increased sensitivity to stress. Researchers hypothesized that $5\text{-HT}_{1A}$ receptor gene knockout mice would be more prone to anxiety. Their experiment supported their prediction: in a variety of conditions, such mice showed a high level of avoidance of unfamiliar environments as compared to control mice. This allowed researchers to conclude that this particular gene influences anxiety behaviour, at least in mice.

▲ The conclusion is precise and focused on the question.

The study of Toth (2003) was performed in highly controlled laboratory conditions where confounding variables were carefully monitored and either eliminated or kept constant. This increases the credibility study. However, it also reduces its generalizability to natural settings (ecological validity).

▼ The evaluation of the study is somewhat limited. More critical thinking opportunities exist here.

Experimental research in the field of behavioural genetics is valuable because it is the only method that allows researchers to make cause-effect inferences. As we have seen from the example of Bouchard and McGue (1981), correlational research (such as twin studies) always includes a possibility of confounding variables that are not easily controlled. Experimentation with the genetic material of human subjects is absolutely unethical, and this imposes certain limitations on the nature of

▲ The conclusion is precise and summarizes all the points made in relation to the question. This shows clear focus and organization.

conclusions we can achieve in research from humans. However, if important discoveries are anticipated, ethics committees can grant permission for experimental genetic research with animal subjects. Such research can shed more light on the nature of causation in behavioural genetics.

**This response could have achieved 17/22 marks.**

**Focus on the question:** 2/2. The answer both identifies and explains the problem raised in the question.

**Knowledge and understanding:** 5/6. Psychological terminology is used accurately and appropriately. The response demonstrates relevant knowledge and understanding that is detailed in most cases. Discussion of experimental research is slightly less detailed, however.

**Use of research to support answer:** 4/6. Relevant psychological research is used to support the answer and different pieces of research are used effectively to support different arguments. However, research could be used to develop the argument more deeply/effectively.

**Critical thinking:** 4/6. The response contains critical thinking (both in terms of evaluating individual studies and critically discussing the conceptual claims) and some relevant areas are discussed. However, critical analysis in the essay could be further developed.

**Clarity and organization:** 2/2. The answer demonstrates clarity and organization throughout the response.

## ERQ example 2

QUESTION PRACTICE

To what extent can animal research provide an insight into the influence of hormones and/or pheromones on human behaviour?                                          [22]

SAMPLE STUDENT ANSWER

Animal research is widely used in psychology, especially in the biological approach to understanding behaviour, because the assumption is that animals and humans are similar enough for us to generalize research findings. This assumption rests on the observed biological similarity between humans and many animal species. For example, humans and chimpanzees share more than 99% of their genotype. When looking at brain structure, one can also see important similarities. For example, the theory of triune brain by MacLean suggests that the human brain broadly consists of three parts: the reptilian complex, the old mammalian brain (the limbic system) and the neocortex. At the same time, humans and animals are not completely identical so we can never be completely sure that findings

▲ The issue raised in the question is both identified (generalization of results from one group to another) and explained (with reference to the assumption of similarity as well as limitations of this assumption).

▼ The research study is relevant and explained in sufficient detail, but it is not clear what argument is being supported here because the focus is not on the issue of generalizing results from animals to human subjects.

▼ Critical analysis is presented both as evaluation of an individual research study and critical application of its results to the conceptual understanding.

from animal research are applicable to human subjects. It is interesting to estimate the extent to which this is possible. In this essay I will do so using research into the influence of hormones/ pheromones on human behaviour.

Hormones are chemical messengers that travel through the bloodstream and regulate relatively long-lasting processes, such as growth or metabolism. One example of how the hormone oxytocin may affect behaviour is demonstrated in Romero et al (2014). Sixteen dogs participated in this study. They were sprayed intra-nasally either with a dose of oxytocin or a placebo. The dogs participated in both conditions (repeated measures design). After the spray the dogs spent 1 hour in a room with their owner and one other dog, and their behaviour was recorded by video cameras and later analysed by independent observers. Observers coded for such behaviours as sniffing, licking, body contact and being in close proximity. Collectively such behaviours were called "affiliation". The owner was instructed not to initiate contact with the dogs and be as impartial as possible. Results of this study showed that, when sprayed with a dose of oxytocin, dogs demonstrated significantly more affiliation behaviours than when sprayed with a placebo. Researchers concluded that oxytocin plays the role of promoting social bonding in animals.

This conclusion goes well together with the known functions of oxytocin. This hormone has been called "the love chemical" and "the bonding hormone" because it is known to be released in situations of social bonding, for example during hugs or kisses or between a mother and her child.

Romero et al's (2014) study had high internal validity because potential confounding variables were carefully controlled (for example, owners were instructed not to initiate contact). Also independent coders were used to encode behaviours in the video footage. At the same time, ecological validity may be low because dogs were placed in an artificial environment. But the largest focus in the context of this essay is generalizability of results – how can we be sure that findings from Romero's study can provide insight into human behaviour? Perhaps human beings react to oxytocin differently. For example, humans have a lot of social conventions and norms that will disguise the effect of oxytocin even when it is present. There are reasons to believe that oxytocin has the same effect in the human body at least biologically, but to see if it actually promotes social bonding the only option seems to be conducting replication studies with human subjects. Such studies have been done, for example Kosfeld et al (2005) showed that a dose of oxytocin increases the amount of trust in human subjects between each other.

In a different study, Ferguson et al (2000) used 42 oxytocin gene knockout mice and 42 comparison mice with a normal genotype to show that oxytocin is involved in recognizing familiar social cues. In the experiment a female mouse was put in the cage of the participant mouse for the duration of 1 minute four times in a row. On the fifth time, a new female mouse was put in the same cage. Researchers investigated if the male mouse would understand that the female mouse was new, which would manifest in longer time spent in nasal contact with the new mouse. Results showed that oxytocin gene knockout mice did not spend more time in nasal contact with the new mouse as compared to the old mouse. Control mice did indeed spend more time with the new female mouse when she was introduced into the cage on the fifth trial. Researchers concluded that oxytocin in mice is involved in recognizing familiar members of the same species. Although not directly applicable, this suggests a potential role for oxytocin in the formation of autism in human subjects.

Another example is research into pheromones. Pheromones, like hormones, are chemical messengers, but they are transmitted from one organism to another via the sense of smell. So pheromones are a form of chemical communication between members of the same species. A pheromone is a specific chemical that triggers a specific reaction. For example, in the animal world it is usual to have pheromones signalling fertility; sensing such pheromones triggers flirting behaviour in the male members of the species.

It is tempting to find similar pheromones that may affect human behaviour. However, the problem is that human physiology is not exactly the same. The two main organs involved in pheromonal processing in animals are the vomeronasal organ and the accessory olfactory bulb. The former

▲ Some valid arguments are made including a reference to a human study, although the argument could be further developed.

▼ This is a good example of research with clear and accurate details, but the link to the question is somewhat obscure. The study seems to make the same point as the previous one.

▲ The example of pheromone research is used effectively to develop the argument, namely to introduce the idea that some biological structures in humans and animals are not exactly the same.

is present in some but not all humans, and the latter is present in human fetuses but disappears after birth. At the same time, it is still a possibility that pheromonal information is processed in the human brain but elsewhere.

This triggered the search for a human pheromone. Substances like androstadienone (AND) were extensively investigated as putative human pheromones. However, the results of such research are very debatable and inconclusive due to multiple flaws and limitations in the methodology.

In conclusion, animal research can provide some insight into the influence of hormones and pheromones on human behaviour. This is more applicable to hormones, however, because research on putative human pheromones has not so far brought any consistent results.

▶ Pheromone research is not given as much attention as hormone research, but that is not a requirement.

▼ The conclusion is not effective enough. The candidate could have summarized the main conceptual arguments that were made in the essay, with a clear focus on the question.

**This response could have achieved 15/22 marks.**

**Focus on the question:** 2/2. The answer both identifies and explains the problem raised in the question.

**Knowledge and understanding:** 4/6. The response demonstrates relevant knowledge and understanding, but lacks detail. Psychological terminology is used accurately and appropriately, although the question does give the opportunity to demonstrate broader knowledge.

**Use of research to support answer:** 3/6. Relevant psychological research is chosen to support the answer. There is an attempt to use different research studies to support different points, but at times research is still used to reiterate the same point. Links to the question are not always explicitly present. The research selected partially develops the argument.

**Critical thinking:** 4/6. Evaluation or discussion of most relevant areas is attempted but could be further developed. The response contains critical thinking, but it comes mostly in the form of individual evaluation points, not as a systematic analysis of the problem raised in the question.

**Clarity and organization:** 2/2. The answer demonstrates sufficient clarity and organization, although the conclusion lacks development.

## 3.1 MODELS OF MEMORY

Apart from the heading "Models of memory", the following additional terms can be used in SAQs:

- multi-store memory model

- working memory model.

Any combination of these additional terms with one of the command terms is acceptable for an SAQ.

Memory is a cognitive process used to encode, store and retrieve information. Just like any other cognitive process, it cannot be directly observed and hence in order to study it scientifically we need to design and test memory models. Based on a model, researchers formulate a set of predictions and then compare these predictions to empirical data. If the model fits the observed data, our trust in the model increases. If, however, the model does not match the observed data too well, researchers either reject or modify the model.

A well-known classical model of memory is the multi-store memory model proposed by Atkinson and Shiffrin (1968). This model suggests the following.

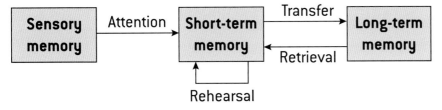

▲ Figure 3.1.1  Multi-store memory model

- Memory consists of three separate stores: sensory memory, short-term memory store (STM) and long-term memory store (LTM).

- Each store is characterized by a specific duration (how long information may be held there) and capacity (how many units of information may be held).

- In order for information to transfer from one store to another, a key condition has to be met. For sensory to STM transition, this is attention. For STM to LTM transition, the condition is continuous rehearsal.

It is impossible to test a memory model in a single study. Support for the multi-store memory model comes in the form of multiple research studies testing various predictions based on specific aspects of the model.

The multi-store memory model has been criticized for its emphasis on structure over function, for rote rehearsal as the only mechanism of STM to LTM transfer, for viewing memory as a unidirectional process, and for generally being too simplistic and not being able to explain some phenomena.

Another well-known model of memory is the working memory model, proposed by Baddeley and Hitch (1974). It identifies additional components in short-term memory and uses them to explain some phenomena that could not be accommodated by the multi-store memory model. Components of the working memory model are:

- the central executive

- the phonological loop

- the visuospatial sketchpad

- the episodic buffer.

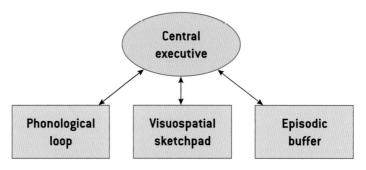

▲ Figure 3.1.2 Working memory model

The model effectively explains results of experiments using the dual-task technique (where participants need to perform two tasks simultaneously). The model also explains observations such as the phonological similarity effect and the word length effect. Thus the strength of the model (compared to the multi-store memory model) is its explanatory power. However, this comes at the cost of the model being too complex. This complexity makes it difficult to test the working memory model empirically.

## ≫ COMMON ERRORS

It is not advisable to use schema theory as a model of memory. Schema theory is a very generic explanatory principle rather than a specific model of a specific cognitive process. Moreover, schema theory is not limited to memory. The focus is on how pre-existing mental representations can affect a variety of cognitive processes.

It is not necessary to learn any models of memory other than the multi-store memory model and the working memory model.

## 🔍 KEY THEORIES AND RESEARCH STUDIES

**Support for the multi-store model of memory**

- Atkinson and Shiffrin (1968): the multi-store memory model.

- Sperling (1960): support for the existence of sensory memory.

- Glanzer and Cunitz (1966): support for STM and LTM being separate memory stores.

- Crow and Grove-White (1973): a study of the effect of acetylcholine antagonist on memory. This can be used to support STM and LTM as two separate stores.

- Craik and Tulving (1975): criticism of the idea that rote rehearsal is the only mechanism of information transfer from STM to LTM.

**Support for the working memory model**

- Baddeley and Hitch (1974): the working memory model.

- Murray (1968), Baddeley, Lewis and Vallar (1984): effects of articulatory suppression on the phonological similarity effect.

- Baddeley, Thomson and Buchanan (1975): effects of articulatory suppression on the word length effect.

- Baddeley (1996): experiments with the generation of random sequences; support for the central executive.

Apart from the heading "Schema theory", the following additional term can be used in SAQs:

- cognitive schema.

Any combination of this additional term with one of the command terms is acceptable for an SAQ.

Cognitive schemas are mental representations that organize our knowledge, beliefs and expectations. This is a broad concept denoting a subset of "mental representations" that have a substantial effect on how we process information. Schemas are not directly observable (their existence is hypothesized), but they can be studied through their observable effects on mental processes such as memory. Schemas have been shown to influence memory at all stages: encoding, storage and retrieval.

Schemas are derived from prior experience. On the one hand, they may result in certain biases, such as stereotypes. On the other hand, they save mental energy, so their existence may be useful from an evolutionary perspective. They help us to interpret and predict events and they guide our behaviour in social situations.

Researchers differentiate between various types of schemas, such as social schemas, self-schemas and scripts. Social schemas influence our interpretation of others. Self-schemas organize our knowledge about ourselves. Scripts help us make sense of sequential data (such as a sequence of events).

Jean Piaget (who coined the term "schema") spoke about two opposite but interrelated processes in the formation of schema: accommodation and assimilation. Assimilation occurs when we modify new information to better fit into our existing schemas. Accommodation is the opposite process of adjusting existing schemas to newly discovered information.

## KEY RESEARCH STUDIES

- Bransford and Johnson (1972): schemas may influence memory at the stage of encoding.
- Anderson and Pichert (1978): schemas also influence memory at the stage of retrieval.
- Darley and Gross (1983): showing the effects of social schemas.
- Bower, Black and Turner (1979): showing how participants fill in the gaps in sequential information using scripts.
- Bartlett (1932): the "War of the Ghosts" study showing the influence of cultural schemas on the memory of a Native American story.

## >> COMMON ERRORS

Schema theory is very generic. It can be used to try to explain such diverse phenomena as reconstructive memory, biases in thinking and decision-making, stereotypes, biases in diagnosis (in abnormal psychology), gender identity and social roles (in developmental psychology), and so on. However, the fact that schema theory may be used to explain these phenomena does not mean that research studies supporting schema theory can always be used when answering questions about these phenomena. You should be careful in selecting research that tests the concept in the question (reconstructive memory, biases in thinking and so on) directly.

## 3.3    THINKING AND DECISION-MAKING

Apart from the heading "Thinking and decision-making", the following additional terms can be used in SAQs:

- rational thinking (controlled)

- intuitive thinking (automatic).

Any combination of these additional terms with one of the command terms is acceptable for an SAQ.

All models of thinking and decision-making can be divided into two groups: normative and descriptive. Normative models explain thinking the way it should be. Examples of normative models are formal logic, the theory of probability and utility theory. Descriptive models explain thinking the way it is. These models take into account limited time, limited computational resources and elements of irrationality.

Examples of descriptive models include the theory of planned behaviour and the adaptive decision-maker framework.

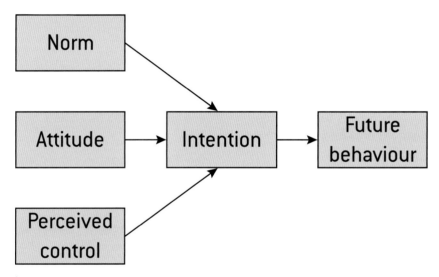

▲ Figure 3.3.1  Theory of planned behaviour

The theory of planned behaviour (Ajzen 1985) aims to predict observable behaviour from attitudes and beliefs. In this model, an individual's choice of a particular behaviour is based on behavioural intention (the expectation that this behaviour will lead to a desired outcome). Behavioural intention is influenced by three factors: attitudes, subjective norms and perceived behavioural control.

The adaptive decision-maker framework (Payne, Bettman, Johnson 1993) was designed specifically to account for the influence of emotion on decision-making. This model suggests that people have a toolbox of strategies that may be used in decision-making tasks.

Depending on which of the goals is perceived as most important in a given situation, one of the strategies will be preferred. For example, if minimizing the experience of negative emotion is important, individuals will prefer attribute-based strategies and avoid alternative-based ones (because attribute-based strategies avoid emotionally difficult trade-offs).

Empirical support for models of thinking and decision-making comes in the form of looking for evidence of predictive validity. Predictive validity of a model is the extent to which components of this model can be used to predict observable behaviour in a variety of situations.

Another commonly used distinction in thinking and decision-making research is between system 1 thinking (intuitive, automatic) and system 2 thinking (rational, controlled).

- System 2 thinking is based on careful rational analysis that takes into account all available information. Its advantage is the ability to arrive at rational decisions, and its disadvantage is that it requires a lot of cognitive effort.

- System 1 thinking is based on cognitive shortcuts – heuristics – that use limited information to arrive at a quick decision.

System 1 and system 2 thinking are commonly used to characterize heuristics and cognitive biases, where the cognitive shortcuts actually used by people in a certain situation (heuristics, system 1) are compared to what would be a rational decision in this situation (normative model, system 2).

## 🔍 KEY THEORIES AND RESEARCH STUDIES

- Fishbein (1967): the theory of reasoned action.

- Ajzen (1985): the theory of planned behaviour.

- Ajzen and Fishbein (1973): a meta-analysis of research studies investigating predictive validity of the theory of reasoned action.

- Albarracin *et al* (2001): a meta-analysis of studies investigating predictive validity of the theory of planned behaviour in the domain of condom use.

- Payne, Bettman and Johnson (1993): the adaptive decision-maker framework.

- Luce, Bettman and Payne (1997): a study of decision-making strategies in charity work involving emotionally difficult trade-offs.

**For the additional terms**

It is advisable to use a research study that demonstrates a pattern of intuitive thinking, but at the same time discusses how this pattern deviates from rationality (the normative model). A lot of studies of heuristics and cognitive biases may be suitable here (see page 53).

One example is Tversky and Kahneman (1981) on the framing effect. Here the framing effect is an example of intuitive (automatic) thinking, and it is characterized by a deviation from expected utility (which is the normative, rational decision). The framing effect is a descriptive model, and it is related to system 1 thinking. Expected utility theory is the normative model, and it is related to system 2 thinking.

## 3.4   RECONSTRUCTIVE MEMORY

One of the pertinent research questions concerning cognitive processes is the question of how reliable they are. Taking memory as an example, to be reliable means to be able to retrieve information exactly the way it was encoded.

The theory of reconstructive memory suggests that memory is an active process of reconstruction rather than passive retrieval of information from the long-term memory store. In other words, every time we remember something, we actively reconstruct it. The results of this reconstruction depend on both the originally encoded information and information available at the time of retrieval. As applied to episodic memory, the theory takes the form of the following statement: post-event information may alter memory of the original event.

This has been tested in a variety of experiments modelling the situation of eyewitness testimony. It has been shown, for example, that manipulating the emotional intensity of the key verb in the leading question (which is a form of post-event information) influences the reported estimate of the speed of the car in the witnessed car accident (that is, memory of the original event).

The theory of reconstructive memory, and in particular eyewitness testimony research, has been criticized on the grounds that an alternative explanation of the findings exists – response bias. Participants' reports might deviate from what they actually witnessed for one of two reasons: (a) genuine memory change, or (b) a change in response itself with the memory of the event remaining unaltered. Much of the research in this area has attempted to eliminate the second explanation, which goes contrary to the theory of reconstructive memory.

### 🔍 KEY RESEARCH STUDIES

- Loftus and Palmer (1974): two experiments that change the emotional intensity of the verb in the leading question.

- Loftus, Miller and Burns (1978): a modification of the experiment with a visual recognition task.

- McCloskey and Zaragoza (1985): support for response bias; no evidence for memory change when misleading information is not an option on the test.

- Payne, Toglia and Anastasi (1994): a meta-analysis of studies using the same procedure as McCloskey and Zaragoza (1985).

- Yuille and Cutshall (1986): a study with witnesses to a real-life gun-store robbery.

- Bartlett (1932): the "War of the Ghosts" study showing the influence of cultural schemas on the memory of a Native American story.

# 3.5 BIASES IN THINKING AND DECISION-MAKING

Biases in thinking and decision-making may be identified by designing a typical decision-making situation and comparing the decisions people actually make in these scenarios to normative decision-making models – in other words, comparing decisions as they are to decisions as they should be.

System 2 thinking is rational and deliberate, and in this sense it approximates normative models much more closely. System 1 thinking is intuitive and automatic. It is based on past experiences and allows for quick decisions to be made on the basis of limited analysis. System 1 thinking therefore uses heuristics (cognitive shortcuts). The interesting thing about cognitive biases that makes them so pertinent for research is that biases themselves are predictable.

Multiple heuristics and cognitive biases have been identified in research, and an attempt has been made to categorize them based on their hypothetical causes. Examples of such hypothetical causes are:

- the tendency to focus on a limited amount of available information (examples of cognitive biases include asymmetric dominance and the framing effect)

- the tendency to seek out information that confirms pre-existing beliefs (examples are confirmation bias, congruence bias and illusory correlation).

All these causes of intuitive thinking, however, are merely theoretical speculations. To study a cognitive bias empirically, one must recreate a typical decision-making scenario in experimental conditions and compare individuals' decisions in these scenarios to normative models (such as logic, probability theory or utility theory). For example, the normative model for framing effect is expected utility theory.

>> **COMMON ERRORS**

A bias is a systematic deviation from a certain standard. Therefore, when discussing biases in thinking and decision-making, it is important to identify the "standard". It could be a normative model of thinking and decision-making. Identifying a bias as a deviation from this normative model then becomes more meaningful.

🔍 **KEY RESEARCH STUDIES**

- Huber, Payne and Puto (1982): the asymmetric dominance effect.

- Tversky and Kahneman (1981): the framing effect.

- Snyder and Swann (1978): confirmation bias in a study of hypothesis testing in social interactions.

- Wason (1968): the four-card problem experiment; an illustration of confirmation bias.

- Tschirgi (1980): congruence bias.

- Hamilton and Gifford (1976): a study of illusory correlation as the mechanism of the formation of stereotypes.

- Chapman and Chapman (1969): illusory correlations in implicit personality theories; research with the Rorschach ink-blot test.

- Englisch and Mussweiler (2001), Strack and Mussweiler (1997): anchoring bias.

- Palmer and Peterson (2012): halo effect of attractiveness.

- Zebrowitz and McDonald (1991): halo effect; a study of the influence of facial appearance on judicial decisions.

# 3.6   THE INFLUENCE OF EMOTION ON COGNITIVE PROCESSES

The influence of emotion on memory is commonly studied through the phenomenon of flashbulb memory. Flashbulb memories are vivid memories of the circumstances in which one first learned of a surprising and emotionally arousing event.

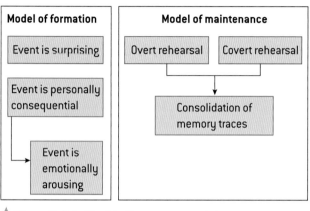

▲ Figure 3.6.1  Flashbulb memory model

The theory of flashbulb memory (Brown, Kulik 1977) is a model that includes the following components.

- The mechanism of formation (which explains how flashbulb memories are created): if the event is perceived as surprising and personally consequential, it will elicit emotional arousal.

- The mechanism of maintenance (which explains how flashbulb memories remain vivid over long periods of time): overt rehearsal and covert rehearsal both contribute to consolidation of memory traces.

Scientific investigation into flashbulb memories has been focused on the following three areas:

- looking for a special neural mechanism responsible for flashbulb memories

- finding out if the vividness of flashbulb memories is mainly due to the event itself or to subsequent rehearsal

- investigating the accuracy of flashbulb memories (while not questioning their vividness).

Brain imaging research in the first area has shown that there is indeed a special neural mechanism that is activated when flashbulb memories are triggered (selective activation of the amygdala).

Research in the second area suggests that rehearsal after the event makes a significant contribution to the vividness of flashbulb memories. This means that flashbulb memories are not, after all, like photographic snapshots of an event. They need to be regularly "updated".

Finally, research in the third area suggests that flashbulb memories, despite their vividness, are not entirely accurate. Like reconstructive memory, the more they are rehearsed, the more they are likely to be altered along the way. Flashbulb memories are special in their perceived accuracy but not their actual accuracy.

## 🔍 KEY THEORIES AND RESEARCH STUDIES

- Brown and Kulik (1977): the theory of flashbulb memory.

- Brown and Kulik (1977): study of factors leading to the formation of flashbulb memories.

- Sharot *et al* (2007): fMRI study of personal memories of the 9/11 attacks.

- Neisser *et al* (1996): the role of rehearsal in flashbulb memories of the Loma Prieta earthquake.

- Bohannon (1988): the role of rehearsal in flashbulb memories of the Challenger space shuttle disaster.

- Neisser and Harsh (1992): study of flashbulb memory accuracy (Challenger space shuttle disaster).

- Talarico and Rubin (2003): study of flashbulb memory accuracy (9/11 attacks).

# 3.7 COGNITIVE PROCESSING IN A TECHNOLOGICAL (DIGITAL/MODERN) WORLD (HL ONLY)

For all three topics in Cognitive approach to behaviour, and with reference to research studies, HL students should study:

- the influence (positive and negative) of technologies (digital/modern) on cognitive processes
- methods used to study the interaction between technology and cognitive processes.

> Exam questions may use a combination of the two bullet points above with the three topics from column 1 of the syllabus (Cognitive processing, Reliability of cognitive processes, Emotion and cognition).

We know that experience shapes the physical structure of the brain through neuroplasticity. It is therefore reasonable to expect that digital technology – which many people spend most of their typical day in contact with – will have an impact on the brain and consequently on cognitive processes. However, it seems possible to justify opposing viewpoints, as follows.

- Digital technology enhances our cognitive processes, making them more reliable and efficient. For example, the use of online search engines and hyperlinks may create an information-rich environment with plenty of interconnections. Hypothetically this should be useful for the formation of elaborate semantic networks and a better understanding of ideas.

- Digital technology has a detrimental effect on our cognitive processes. Easy accessibility of information in search engines may cause us to rely less on memory, thus weakening memory as a cognitive process. Thinking may also suffer because ready-made answers are too easily available.

Research has attempted to work out which of the two explanations is true.

Some studies have shown that interaction with digital technology (such as playing video games) improves certain cognitive processing skills, especially when it comes to relatively simple skills such as spatial orientation, mental rotation and motor coordination. The criticism that skills acquired playing video games may be artificial and not transferrable to real-life situations has been addressed and partially refuted. It has been shown, for example, that spatial skills acquired in the process of playing first-person shooters are transferrable to a wider domain of science learning; see for example Sanchez (2012).

Some types of digital technology appear to be more beneficial than others. For example, using virtual-reality simulations to train real-life coordination skills has been shown to be effective, especially if the learner is motivated and the simulation is realistic. Conversely, excessive video-game playing has been linked to reduced attention and associated learning problems.

▲ Figure 3.7.1 Do video games improve or limit cognitive processes?

>> **COMMON ERRORS**

For this content heading, it is especially important to clearly and explicitly explain the link between study findings and the essay question or the argument that is being supported. For example, if a study demonstrates the effect of media multitasking on students' GPA scores, it must be explained that multitasking serves as an indicator of the presence of digital devices (technology) and that GPA scores serve as an indicator of reduced attention (cognition). For every study, you should explicitly identify what in this study counts as "technology" and what counts as "cognitive processing".

## KEY RESEARCH STUDIES

- Kaspersky Lab (2005): the "Digital Amnesia" report on the phenomenon of forgetting information that you trust a digital device to remember for you.

- Rosser *et al* (2007) on the improvement of hand-eye coordination skills among surgeons who played video games.

- Sanchez (2012) on the transferability of skills acquired in video games to the domain of learning abstract scientific concepts.

- Fery and Ponserre (2001) on the positive effects of training on a virtual-reality simulator on real-like skills (playing golf).

- Rosen, Carrier and Cheever (2013): an observational and correlational study of media multitasking in its relation to learning (GPA scores).

- Rosen *et al* (2011) on the ability of metacognitive strategies to neutralize the negative effects of multitasking on attention and learning.

- Carrier *et al* (2015): a longitudinal correlational study showing a decline in empathy scores from the start of the digital era; an attempt to explain the observed patterns through whether or not online activities lead to face-to-face communication.

- Swing *et al* (2010): a longitudinal correlational study on the relationship between gaming, reduced attention and ADHD.

One of the aspects of digital technology especially linked to reliability of cognitive processes is induced media multitasking. This means being surrounded with digital technology that constantly triggers switching between tasks. Induced media multitasking may compromise reliability of attention, which in turn has a detrimental effect on other cognitive processes involved in learning, such as memory.

It has been demonstrated that induced media multitasking is a widespread phenomenon, especially among young people. At the same time, it has been shown that using appropriate metacognitive strategies may neutralize the negative effects. However, these metacognitive strategies are not easy to develop.

One of the areas relevant to emotion and cognition is empathy. Empathy has both cognitive and emotional components. Research in this area has yielded conflicting results; there is a tendency for earlier studies to demonstrate a negative association between online activities and real-world empathy, while later studies do not find any such relationship.

A possible explanation is that the effect of social networks on empathic abilities may depend on how exactly social networks are used. If they are used to support existing relationships, the influence may be positive: social networks allow us to stay in touch with our friends and be exposed to their personal stories, which enhances perspective-taking and enriches our real-life interaction. If they are used to develop new friendships that are limited to online environments, on the other hand, these personal stories may be found less relatable, thus leading to the development of pseudo-empathy.

Methods used to study the interaction between digital technology and cognitive processes are quite diverse, which reflects the complex nature of the cognitive process under study.

The key challenges that research in this area presents include the following.

- In real life we are surrounded by all sorts of digital technology and our pattern of interaction with it is very complex. It is difficult to reproduce in artificial experimental conditions, so it makes sense to conduct studies in natural settings. But this means using tools such as questionnaires, observation, the experience sampling method and so on.

- Such research relies on self-reporting, which has its limitations. In natural settings it is also difficult to isolate variables and work out what influences what.

- To overcome these limitations, we can use experiments where the independent variable is isolated and confounding variables are controlled. While this allows us to reliably make cause-effect inferences, it leads to a number of inevitable limitations of a different nature: only a limited number of variables may be investigated, attention must be focused on specific types of digital technology and specific cognitive processes and so on.

- A wider focus may be achieved by using correlational studies, but this comes at the cost of losing the ability to make cause-effect inferences.

- Triangulation of methods and evidence is the key to a full understanding of the interaction between cognitive processes and digital technology.

# SAMPLE QUESTIONS

Below are two example SAQs and two example ERQs that you might see on Cognitive approach to behaviour. Read the sample student answers and the accompanying comments, which will help you to understand what the students have done well and what they could do better.

## SAQ example 1

Describe one study investigating the reliability of one cognitive process. [9]

Memory is an important cognitive process, and is one that allows us to both learn and store our thoughts and knowledge. The reliability of memory refers to how much we can trust our memory and whether our memory is reliable or not in its recall, which refers to the ability to correctly state past events and knowledge that are stored in the memory.

One study that investigates this reliability of memory is Loftus and Palmer. The aim of the study was to see whether the usage of diction could affect eyewitness memory. In doing so they conducted two experiments. In the first one they got five groups of people to watch live footage of a car crash. They were then prompted to estimate the speed of the car. The independent variable was the verb they used in this question, ranging from "How fast were the cars going when they contacted each other?" all the way to "How fast were the cars going when they smashed into each other?"

The idea behind this was to have a range of five words in increasing severity, and see whether this affected the estimate of the speed. In the first experiment they found that the more forceful the verb, the higher the group estimated the car's speed to be, even though they had all been shown the same clip.

In the second experiment conducted a few weeks later, they sent a questionnaire to the different groups, with the key question asking if there had been broken glass. It was found that the groups exposed to the more forceful verbs answered yes to that question at a higher rate than the groups with less forceful words. The reality was that there was no broken glass in the clip. This showed that eyewitness testimony is unreliable, and can

▲ Some key terms are defined in the introduction, which is fine for a "describe" question.

▼ The aim is inaccurate ("diction"), but this could be due to the use of English as another language.

▲ The study is clearly described with sufficient detail, and all key elements (such as aim, procedure, results and conclusion) are present and clearly separated.

be affected by external factors such as diction. The explanation given by Loftus and Palmer supported the idea of schema theory, in that we have preset notions linked to certain words or actions, and these affect our memory recall.

This study is a good example of a study that investigates the reliability of memory (a cognitive process) because it directly manipulates variables in order to test the memory of its participants. In this case, the manipulated variable was the verb used in the question, which ranged in terms of forcefulness. Loftus and Palmer clearly showed that the verb not only affected the subject's estimate of the initial speed of the car, but also affected subject's memory recall when asked whether or not there was broken glass. They concluded that memory was not as reliable as previously thought, and attributed this unreliability to the presence of schema theory.

▼ The final part of the essay would be more suitable for an "explain" question and does not affect marks for a "describe" question.

**This response could have achieved 7/9 marks.**

The response is fully focused on the question and the focus on the command term is sustained most of the time. Knowledge and understanding is accurate apart from a minor inaccuracy. The topic in the question is directly addressed. The research study is relevant, well described and clearly linked to the question. To meet the requirements of a "describe" question even further, some more details about the study could be presented, and the unnecessary explanations at the end of the essay could be avoided.

## SAQ example 2

QUESTION PRACTICE

Describe one research study related to schema theory. [9]

SAMPLE STUDENT ANSWER

The world and the environment is very complex and is a lot to handle for the brain. Therefore, information gets categorized into groups with similar characteristics so the brain can better assess things. This is known as a schema. The schema theory suggests that people will remember things that fit into a certain schema or category, or attribute things to the schemas they know.

A study that relates to this is Bartlett's "War of Ghosts". In this study, Bartlett told a Native American story to Western participants and then later asked them to retell it. Bartlett found that when participants retold the story, they had changed aspects

► This explanation of the concept is acceptable, but not the key point for a "describe" question.

▼ This is a very short, underdeveloped description (although mostly accurate).

of it to fit their Western schemas. Words such as "canoe" were changed to "boat". This is because people put these things into already existing schemas in their mind in order to remember them. This supports the schema theory.

**This response could have achieved 2/9 marks.**

Knowledge and understanding is accurate and relevant to the question, but the response is basic and underdeveloped. Only the second half of the essay explicitly addresses the requirements of the command term. It is only a superficial description of the study. The response is very limited in detail and in how the study is related to schema theory.

## ERQ example 1

Discuss positive and negative effects of digital technology on cognitive processing. [22]

The advent of the technological age has led to an increased use of digital technology. Due to neuroplasticity, environmental interactions can strengthen or weaken neuronal connections. In this manner, the use of digital technology can have various influences on cognitive processes like attention, visuospatial skills, reaction time and more. There has been contradictory research indicating both positive and negative influences of digital technology, which can be attributed to its complexity. Some of the positive influences of the use of digital technology were indicated in a study by Rosser et al (2007). They measured the amount of time spent playing video games by laparoscopic surgeons, and their video game mastery. Those that played video games for more than 3 hours a week performed surgeries 27% faster and made 37% fewer errors, measured using standardized drills. This correlation between video game play and faster and better surgery skills was attributed to the positive influence of video game play on attention, fine motor skills and reaction time. However, the study was limited to a specific narrow population, which is not representative of other populations. Furthermore, being correlational, the direction of causality cannot be inferred – those with the aforementioned skills could be more inclined towards playing video games.

▲ The introduction effectively identifies a problem implicit in the question and clearly explains this problem.

▲ Good knowledge is shown, with a concise report of the study's key details.

▲ Evaluation points are not numerous, but the ones used are crucial/essential.

▲ Good detail is given and there is a clear connection between results and conclusions.

The positive effect of visuospatial games on visuospatial learning was studied by Sanchez (2012). He conducted an experiment where the experimental group was made to play a visuospatial game and the control group was not. After this, both groups had a complex passage on group tectonics (without diagrams) and were asked to write an essay on it, which was scored by independent raters. The dependent variable, the level of understanding, was found to be higher in the experimental group. This indicated the positive influence of digital technology (visuospatial games) on cognitive processing of visuospatial information. The operationalization of the dependent variable as the understanding of the text was well done, since other similar experiments used performance on a visuospatial test, which was in itself similar to the game. However, the study only indicated short-term effects of the technology, and was specific to only visuospatial games.

▼ This study seems to be addressing the same argument as the previous study.

▲ This is a new argument, and the new study clearly addresses this new argument.

It is important to note whether the skills acquired due to digital technology can be transferred to other situations. This was tested in an experiment by Fery and Ponserre (2001). In this study, participants were divided into three groups. The first group played a golf-putting video game with the intention to learn, the second played with the intention of enjoyment and the control did not play it. None of the groups had any prior experience in golf-putting. The researchers then measured actual golf-putting skills and found that playing the game had improved them, more so when the intent was to learn. They concluded that there are two conditions required for the transfer of skills acquired through digital technology: credibility of the game in terms of real life and the motivation of the person to learn. This study indicated that the positive influence of digital technology usage on cognitive processes and other skills can be transferred to other situations, under certain conditions. However, the study was reductionist, being an experiment, and was focused on one narrow skill, hence the findings cannot be easily generalized to other situations. Despite various findings on the positive influences of digital technology on cognitive processes, there have also been many studies indicating the negative influences of the use of digital technology on various cognitive processes. This can be attributed to the complexity and variety of technology available, which

▲ The conclusions from the study are organized in a way that contributes to the discussion.

▼ Some evaluations/critical thinking points could be further elaborated.

▲ There is balanced consideration of positive and negative influences, plus an attempt to explain the existence of both by the complexity of the technology.

affects the impact. For example, VR simulations have beneficial impacts like learning new skills.

Some of the negative influences of digital technology on judgment and decision-making, and the capacity for delayed gratification, were indicated by Small and Vorgan (2008). Digital technology has also been shown to have an adverse impact on attention as it induces multitasking. This was indicated in a study by Rosen, Carrier and Cheever (2013). They conducted surveys assessing the GPAs and attitudes towards technology of university students. The students were then observed in a naturalistic environment while studying, by an observer, who noted the presence of technology, the number of tabs open and conducted a minute-by-minute assessment of behaviour.

They found through their observations that the average time spent on-task before switching to off-task was 6 minutes, and off-task behaviour increased when there was more digital technology present. Those who accessed Facebook at least once in the 15 minutes had lower GPAs. This task-switching behaviour was also not induced when studying for an exam, indicating that it was intentional. This study supported the negative influence of digital technology on the cognitive process of attention. It was holistic and conducted in natural settings, but the use of observation could have led to a change in behaviour of the participants. Furthermore, being correlational, the direction of causality cannot be inferred. A preference for multitasking could lead individuals to surround themselves in technologically abundant areas or vice versa.

> ▲ Relevant evaluation points for individual studies are presented and explained.

The negative influence of the use of digital technology was also indicated through neurological correlations found by Loh and Kanai (2014). They found a negative correlation between scores on the Media Multitasking Index (indicating the amount of multitasking due to technology) and the density of grey matter in the anterior cingulated cortex (ACC). The ACC has been known to play a role in cognitive processing, selective attention and motivation. This indicated the negative influence of an increased use of digital technology on these cognitive processes, like attention, due to multitasking. However, this study was also correlational, hence the direction of causality cannot be

> ▲ This response uses a large number of research studies, and they are used relatively effectively in an argument-based way, where each following argument deepens the discussion and each study supports a new argument (with the exception noted above).

inferred. It is possible that the decreased grey matter in the ACC results in a predisposition for multitasking. Furthermore, the sample was educated adult men with access to technology, which is not generalizable as multitasking patterns can differ across populations.

This negative influence of digital technology on attention was also indicated in a longitudinal study by Swing et al (2012). They found that teachers reported decreased attention over a period of 13 months for those students who used more digital technology (had more than 2 hours a day of screen time). This further indicated the negative influence of digital technology on the cognitive process of attention, over an extended period of time. However, being longitudinal, there could be many confounding variables affecting the internal validity of the study, despite high ecological validity.

In conclusion, there are both positive and negative influences of digital technology on cognitive processes, depending on the type of technology, the amount of usage, and the cognitive process under consideration. There are usually positive influences of technology on reaction time, visuospatial skills and so on. However, there is a large negative influence on attention since digital technologies induce multitasking.

▼ Closer to the end the essay feels more like a list of factors related to the influence of technology on cognition. In addition, the evaluation points could be further developed.

▼ The conclusion could be a little better developed, perhaps summarizing the key arguments or sub-conclusions from the body of the essay.

**This response could have achieved 19/22 marks.**

**Focus on the question:** 2/2. The answer identifies and explains the problem raised in the question (mostly in the introduction, but also throughout the essay).

**Knowledge and understanding:** 5/6. The response demonstrates relevant, detailed knowledge and understanding. Psychological terminology is used appropriately and in suitable contexts.

**Use of research to support answer:** 5/6. A large number of relevant psychological research studies are used to support the answer. Importantly, different studies largely support different arguments, and the sequence of arguments and studies provides a deep exploration of various aspects of the problem. Selected research is effectively used to develop the argument.

**Critical thinking:** 5/6. The response demonstrates well-developed critical thinking, and this is consistent throughout the essay. However, although concepts and theoretical generalizations are also analysed, critical thinking is still somewhat limited to evaluation of individual research studies.

**Clarity and organization:** 2/2. The answer demonstrates organization and clarity throughout the response, with a good structure and a clear central argument in each paragraph.

# ERQ example 2

Evaluate one theory of how emotion may affect one cognitive process. [22]

Emotions are "a combination of feelings and 'cognitive interpretations' which occur in response to stimuli" (Damasio, 2000). They have the ability to influence memory; an active cognitive process of encoding, storing and retrieving information. Flashbulb memory theory can be used to show how emotion can influence memory. The theory proposes that memories of traumatic or highly emotional experiences or events are more easily retained. It also suggests that the flashbulb memories obtained from these traumatic experiences are more vivid and highly detailed.

▶ Key terms are introduced and identified, but the problem raised in the question is only indirectly explained.

Brown and Kulik proposed the flashbulb memory theory, and that six pieces of information from these events are remembered: what the people were doing at the time, where they were, how they felt, their own response, the response of others, and what the event entailed. Brown and Kulik tested their own theory in 1977, aiming to investigate flashbulb memory theory. Participants were 30 African Americans and 30 Caucasian Americans. They were interviewed on the assassinations or attempted assassinations of popular American personalities. Results found that African-American participants were more likely to remember details regarding the deaths of personalities such as Martin Luther King, whereas Caucasian Americans remembered more details of events concerning people such as John F. Kennedy. The study supports flashbulb memory theory based on the assumption that Martin Luther King's assassination was of high emotional significance, because more details were remembered in regards to this event. However, it is important to consider that the results were retrospective and the accuracy of the memories cannot be commented on based on the study, as African-American communities may discuss certain events more than others, meaning participants may have learned the details from others as opposed to remembering the details themselves.

▲ Clear and detailed knowledge of the study is demonstrated.

▲ This is a good, non-trivial evaluation point that is relevant not only to this individual study, but also to the theory of flashbulb memory in general.

Despite not being able to determine exactly the accuracy of the results from Brown and Kulik's study, it still provides primary support towards the theory. One strength of flashbulb memory theory is that there are biological approaches in terms of its explanations. McGaugh suggested that the activated amygdala sends messages to the brain to alert it of a dangerous or important event. It suggests that if the amygdala is activated during the making of a memory then the memory will be stronger.

Cahill and McGaugh (1995) also tested flashbulb memory theory. Participants were split into two groups and told different stories; all participants were shown 12 slides (which contained pictures) of their respective stories. The first group listened to a story about a mother and son going to visit the boy's father at the hospital and watching nurses. The second group listened to a story about a boy having his feet severed in a car accident and being sent to the hospital to reattach them, then being sent home several weeks later. Participants were asked to recall details of their respective stories. Results showed that participants in the second group were able to recall more information than the first group, showing that flashbulb memory was evident due to the heightened emotion experienced in the second story. This provided more support towards flashbulb memory theory.

Flashbulb memory theory is limited in that real-life studies are not always consistent. Cahill and McGaugh (1995) showed flashbulb memory was evident in their experiment, however it lacks ecological validity due to the artificial environment. Yuille and Cutshall (1986), on the other hand, conducted a study on flashbulb memory in naturalistic real-life conditions. Twenty-one participants of real-life cases of eyewitness testimony were interviewed. Thirteen participants were re-interviewed five months later. Researchers even included two misleading questions to see if participants' memory would be influenced. Their results showed that despite the misleading questions, participants accurately recalled what had happened through comparison with their first interview. This shows that participants' memories of the event were vivid, thus supporting flashbulb memory theory. It is still important to consider that complete accuracy cannot be tested, as details were again retrospective.

Although multiple studies support flashbulb memory theory, some real-life studies go against the theory, showing that more

▲ A relevant additional study with a good amount of detail is used.

▼ The study seems to be linked to the same argument that has already been discussed (the argument is not being developed here).

▶ More explanation of this evaluation point is needed.

▲ Development of the argument continues. A new study is used effectively to support the new argument about real-life applicability of the theory.

research needs to be conducted. Neisser and Harsch (1992) investigated flashbulb memory and interviewed 106 participants on the Challenger disaster. Participants were re-interviewed several weeks later and were also asked to rate their confidence. The researchers found that there was a discrepancy between accuracy and confidence. Despite a high average confidence of 4.17 out of 5, the average accuracy was quite low at 2.95 out of 7. This means that participants were under the assumption that they were mostly correct, despite the low accuracy results. Neisser and Harsch's study shows that traumatic events do not always result in more accurate and vivid details, as participants did not give the same responses, thus going against the idea that flashbulb memories are more accurate.

It is important to evaluate flashbulb memory theory to show how emotion may affect cognition. In terms of comprehensiveness, the theory does provide details regarding the type of events and memories obtained. However, it does not necessarily explain explicitly why the memories are more vivid or accurate. The theory does have a biological approach that attempts to explain how memories are stronger, though there is a lack of research supporting this specific explanation. Moreover, much of the research already conducted does not align, with different studies suggesting different reasons or showing different results to one another, making it somewhat difficult to comment on whether the theory is reliable.

Overall, flashbulb memory theory is a vital theory to evaluate as it provides a basis for explaining why some memories may be more vivid than others because of emotion as a factor. Brown and Kulik's original study is important as it shows primary evidence supporting the theory, leading to other research conducted by Cahill and McGaugh to further test the theory. Moreover, real-life and more ecologically valid studies, such as Yuille and Cutshall, also support the theory, making it somewhat supported. Despite this, it is still vital to evaluate the theory because not all studies agree with it, like Neisser and Harsch, who found opposing results in terms of memories being more accurate. Hence, more research should be conducted to further evaluate Brown and Kulik's flashbulb memory theory.

▲ This shows good knowledge of detail.

▲ An additional dimension of flashbulb memory is introduced and discussed (vividness versus accuracy). This contributes to the development of the argument.

▲ There is an attempt to explain contradictory results.

▲ The conclusion recaps all the key points being made and summarizes the key controversy between laboratory and field studies of flashbulb memory.

**This response could have achieved 17/22 marks.**

**Focus on the question:** 2/2. The answer explains the problem raised in the question (this explanation is not sufficient in the introduction, but it is later elaborated on in the body of the essay).

**Knowledge and understanding:** 5/6. The response demonstrates relevant and detailed knowledge and understanding. Psychological terminology is used appropriately. There are no factual mistakes.

**Use of research to support answer:** 4/6. Studies are effectively used in support of the response and are well explained. Research is mostly used to develop the argument and this is done effectively, with some exceptions where studies may be used to support the same argument. Both sides of the argument are considered and supported by research.

**Critical thinking:** 4/6. The response contains relevant critical thinking that is mostly seen in the evaluation of the theory and some studies. Evaluation of the most relevant areas is attempted but could be further developed.

**Clarity and organization:** 2/2. The answer is well organized and clearly presented.

# 4 SOCIOCULTURAL APPROACH TO BEHAVIOUR

## 4.1 SOCIAL IDENTITY THEORY

> Apart from the heading "Social identity theory", the following additional term can be used in an SAQ.
>
> - social groups.
>
> Any combination of this additional term with one of the command terms is acceptable for an SAQ.

Social identity theory aims to explain the occurrence of conflict and discrimination on the basis of psychological variables (such as the sense of belonging to a certain group). This is in contrast to explanations based on external variables (such as limited resources that the groups compete over).

The theory is based on the following propositions.

- Competition over resources is not necessary for the development of intergroup conflict.

- Social categorization (the perception of being part of different social groups) is sufficient to trigger ingroup favouritism and outgroup discrimination.

- Social categorization becomes the basis of an individual's social identity.

- It is important for people to have a positive social identity because that links to their self-esteem.

- Positive social identity is based on group distinctiveness (social identity is positive if I perceive my group to be positively different from other groups). This involves the process of social comparison.

- In an attempt to support their own social identity and self-esteem, individuals try to maximize the positive distinctiveness of the group to which they belong. This may be the cause of discriminatory behaviour towards outgroups.

Research to support social identity theory has been based on the minimal group paradigm – an experimental procedure where participants are assigned into different groups based on a very trivial/ superficial criterion. The idea is that if this trivial criterion is sufficient to trigger ingroup favouritism and outgroup discrimination, social identity is indeed responsible for discriminatory behaviour.

## 🔍 KEY THEORIES AND RESEARCH STUDIES

- Tajfel *et al* (1971): two experiments using the minimal group paradigm to test social identity theory.

- Locksley, Ortiz and Hepburn (1980): follow-up research investigating the limitations of the minimal group paradigm.

- Festinger (1954): social comparison theory.

- Maass (2003): a study of the role of social identity on gender harassment.

- Abrams *et al* (1990): a study of the role of social identity in conformity.

- Cialdini *et al* (1976): a study of the phenomenon of "basking in reflected glory" and its relation to social identity.

**For the additional term:** any research that demonstrates how human behaviour is affected by belonging to social groups will do. Tajfel *et al* (1971) will be suitable for this purpose.

## ≫ COMMON ERRORS

As is always the case with closely linked topics, there is a fine line between two topics being connected (conceptually and empirically) and two topics being the same.

For example, many students write about Tajfel's research in comparison to Sherif's "Robber's Cave" studies. While this may be appropriate when discussing origins of conflict (because the two approaches provide distinctly different explanations of why conflict emerges), Sherif's research is not directly relevant to questions focused on social identity theory because it did not use the minimal group paradigm.

Social cognitive theory is a theory that explains the mechanism of cultural transmission. It tries to explain how social and cultural norms and behaviours are transmitted from one individual (or generation) to another. In this sense, together with theories such as behaviourism, social cognitive theory is a theory of learning.

Social cognitive theory is a development of its preceding simpler version, social learning theory. Both theories were developed by Albert Bandura.

At the core of the theory is the idea of observational learning. Observational learning is learning by observing the behaviour of others and the consequences of that behaviour. It implies that, in opposition to what behaviourists thought, trial and error is not the only way to learn new behaviours. Learning can occur implicitly even if the individual has not yet demonstrated the learned behaviour.

Another key component of social cognitive theory is the idea of reciprocal determinism in the system of three interacting factors: personal factors, behaviour and environment. According to reciprocal determinism, the three factors influence each other mutually, in a bidirectional way.

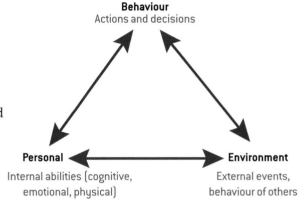

▲ Figure 4.2.1  Reciprocal determinism

For example, if we focus on the idea of learning and how observing the behaviour of others influences one's own behaviour, we note the following.

- There may be a direct influence (the arrow from environment to behaviour).

- However, there may also be an influence mediated by cognition (from environment to cognition, then from cognition to behaviour). Some of the mediating variables closely researched in social cognitive theory include identification, self-efficacy and human agency.

## 🔍 KEY THEORIES AND RESEARCH STUDIES

- Bandura (1986): social cognitive theory.

- Bandura, Ross and Ross (1961): the Bobo doll experiment.

- Perry, Perry and Rasmussen (1986): a study of self-efficacy as a cognitive determinant of behaviour.

- Williams and Williams (2010): a study of reciprocal determinism in schoolchildren between self-efficacy (believing they can do well) and academic achievement in mathematics.

- Sheridan et al (2011): a study of the perceived effectiveness of "Skillstream", a programme following social cognitive theory principles to model prosocial behaviour in kindergartens.

## ≫ COMMON ERRORS

Although social cognitive theory grew out of social learning theory and observational learning is its important component, social cognitive theory should not be reduced to social learning theory. Social cognitive theory is a much broader theory, with the idea of reciprocal determinism being the overarching philosophical principle.

# 4.3 FORMATION OF STEREOTYPES AND THEIR EFFECTS ON BEHAVIOUR

▲ Figure 4.3.1  A stereotypical Englishman

Stereotypes are preconceived notions about a group of people. They are essentially schemas that distort the perception of social groups. Stereotypes are generalized, in the sense that individual differences are ignored and all members of a certain group are perceived as having the same stereotyped qualities. Unlike prejudice (attitudes) and discrimination (behaviour), stereotypes are cognitive.

Two research questions that have been the focus of attention are how stereotypes are formed and how they affect behaviour.

Some of the most prominent theories about the formation of stereotypes are as follows.

- The grain of truth hypothesis (Campbell 1967) suggests that stereotypes are based on reality; that is, differences that actually exist between groups. When a person first experiences a member of a certain group, this experience gets generalized to the whole group.

- Illusory correlation (Hamilton, Gifford 1976) claims that the origin of stereotypes is a cognitive bias where the co-occurrence of rare events (such as belonging to a minority group and negative/unacceptable behaviour) is overestimated, leading to a perception of correlation where none exists.

- Social categorization and social identity theory (Tajfel, Turner 1979) claims that when categorization occurs, it is accompanied by the phenomena of ingroup favouritism and outgroup discrimination. Individuals want their group to be positively distinct from other groups, and this leads them to attribute negative characteristics in a generalized manner to members of outgroups.

All these theories are supported by empirical research, so stereotypes may be a multi-determined phenomenon.

Stereotypes affect behaviour in a variety of ways. Examples are as follows.

- The self-fulfilling prophecy (Rosenthal, Jacobson 1968). This is the phenomenon where people holding the stereotype influence the behaviour of members of the stereotyped group. This is especially true if the individual has some influence on the group in other aspects too (for example, when a teacher holds a stereotype about a group of students he or she teaches).

- The stereotype threat (Steele, Aronson 1995). This is the phenomenon where members of the stereotyped group change their behaviour (unintentionally) to better fit the stereotype. Activation of the stereotype in their mind causes them to enhance behaviours that are in line with the stereotype.

## KEY RESEARCH STUDIES

- Hamilton and Gifford (1976): a study supporting the concept of illusory correlation as a mechanism of stereotype formation.

- Johnson, Schaller and Mullen (2000): a study on the effects of social categorization on illusory correlation.

- Rosenthal and Jacobson (1968): a study of self-fulfilling prophecy in a group of students.

- Steele and Aronson (1995): a study of stereotype threat.

## >> COMMON ERRORS

The formation of stereotypes and the effects of stereotypes on behaviour are two separate aspects, and you should keep in mind the difference between them. It would be incorrect to present a study showing how stereotypes are formed, such as Hamilton and Gifford (1976), as something supporting the idea that stereotypes can influence behaviour, and vice versa. Additionally, when discussing the effects of stereotypes on behaviour, you should clearly identify the behaviour that is being affected.

Apart from the heading "Culture and its influence on behaviour and cognition", the following additional term can be used in SAQs:

- cultural groups.

Any combination of this additional term with one of the command terms is acceptable for an SAQ.

Culture is a combination of beliefs, attitudes and behaviours that manifest themselves in cultural norms and are passed from generation to generation. Cultural norms therefore are certain expectations regarding the behaviour of individuals belonging to a cultural group.

Cultural transmission is the process of passing cultural norms from one generation to another. Enculturation is the process of acquiring these cultural norms. Acculturation is the process of internalizing cultural norms of new cultural groups (for example, when someone moves into a different country).

Psychological differences associated with culture are captured in a set of cultural dimensions proposed by Geert Hofstede. These include seven underlying dimensions of differences, such as:

- individualism versus collectivism

- masculinity versus femininity

- short-term orientation versus long-term orientation.

When we investigate the influence of culture on behaviour and cognition in psychology, essentially we are looking at the correlation between these underlying dimensions and a certain behaviour.

Research in this area has identified many correlations like this. For example, it has been found that individualism-collectivism is associated with conformity (individualistic cultures show less conformity), volunteering behaviour (people from collectivistic and individualistic societies volunteer for different reasons), styles of doctor-patient communication, compliance, reporting mental disorders and many more.

These cultural differences have also been shown to be associated with cognition (how people process information). For example, it has been demonstrated that there are marked differences in decision-making strategies depending on which language a bilingual individual speaks in the course of the experiment. Similarly, representatives of different cultures seem to employ different cognitive styles in reasoning (analytic for individualistic societies, holistic for collectivistic societies).

## KEY RESEARCH STUDIES

- Chiu (1972): a study of cognitive styles in Chinese and US students.

- Briley, Morris and Simonson (2005): a study of decision-making in bilingual individuals.

- Hofstede (1973): research on cultural dimensions.

- Berry and Katz (1967): the influence of individualism and collectivism on conformity.

- Meeuwesen, van den Brink-Muinen and Hofstede (2009): a study of cultural differences in patterns of patient-doctor communication.

**For the additional term:** any of the studies in the list above will be suitable because it is through belonging to cultural groups that culture influences behaviour.

## >> COMMON ERRORS

This content heading overlaps considerably with the next one, "Cultural dimensions". Although many of the same studies may be used in questions coming from both these content headings, they should not be treated as the same question. The different focus will be evident in how conclusions from the studies are drawn. "Culture" is a broader term than "cultural dimensions", and the focus in this content heading is on the effects culture has on behaviour and cognition rather than the cultural differences as such.

# 4.5   CULTURAL DIMENSIONS

▲ Figure 4.5.1 Japan is considered to be a collectivistic society

Cultural dimensions are the general factors underlying cross-cultural differences in values and patterns of behaviour. One can think of cultural dimensions as coordinates or axes along which all individual cultural groups may be placed. For example, on the axis "individualism-collectivism", all cultures in the world may be placed at some point between the two extremes.

Cultural dimensions have been identified in large-scale research involving surveys of representative samples from numerous cultural backgrounds. Such surveys were started by Geert Hofstede, in his research with IBM employees from more than 70 countries. Results of the surveys were statistically analysed to identify the main dimensions of differences. There are six dimensions, including the following.

- Individualism versus collectivism. Identity in individualistic societies is linked to personal success and independence, while in collectivistic societies identity is linked to group membership.

- Masculinity versus femininity. Masculine societies emphasize values of success, achievement and competitiveness; feminine societies emphasize values of compassion, cooperation and taking care of each other.

- Power distance index. In societies with large power distance, authority figures are more respected and treated as superior.

There have been multiple research studies looking at correlations between these cultural dimensions and various other behaviours. These studies show that cultural dimensions influence behaviour in a variety of ways (although cause-effect inferences are limited due to the correlational nature of research).

## 🔍 KEY RESEARCH STUDIES

- Berry and Katz (1967): the influence of individualism and collectivism on conformity.

- Finkelstein (2010): the influence of individualism and collectivism on volunteer behaviour.

- Meeuwesen, van den Brink-Muinen and Hofstede (2009): the influence of power distance on patterns of patient-doctor communication.

- Eylon and Au (1999): the influence of power distance on the reaction of workers to empowerment in the workplace.

- Lynn, Zinkhan and Harris (1993): a cross-country study of the relationship between power distance and tipping across 33 service professions.

- Vunderick and Hofstede (1998): a study of masculinity versus femininity in a survey of work goals for an ideal job, in a sample of Dutch and American university students.

# 4.6 ENCULTURATION

Apart from the heading "Enculturation", the following additional term can be used in SAQs:

- norms.

Any combination of this additional term with one of the command terms is acceptable for an SAQ.

Cultural norms are sets of attitudes, beliefs and behaviours unique to a particular culture. They also function as expectations regarding the behaviour of members of the culture. Cultural transmission is the process of passing on cultural norms from one generation to the next, and enculturation is the process of internalizing cultural norms. Enculturation is a kind of learning.

One of the crucial research questions in this area is the mechanism of enculturation (exactly how enculturation occurs). It has been suggested that enculturation occurs through active learning: children actively engage with elements of the culture and interact with adults, gradually internalizing cultural norms. For example, supporting research has demonstrated that musical enculturation (preference for the music of one's own culture) is more obvious when parents actively engage in musical activities with their children. The idea that the mechanism of enculturation is active learning is based on Vygotsky's approach in developmental psychology.

This idea has been challenged, however, by showing that at least in some cultures the predominant mechanism of enculturation is passive observation of adults without actively engaging in joint activities. Ideas of observational learning can be traced back to social learning theory (Bandura 1977).

Enculturation can be observed on many levels, from obvious behaviours regulated by explicit cultural norms (for example, norms of politeness) to deeply rooted unobservable patterns of cognition. An example of the latter is memory: enculturation affects schemas in a way that changes our memory so that elements that fit better with the culture will be remembered better.

Enculturation also interacts with acculturation (acquiring norms of a host culture), and this process has a great influence on individual identity. In its turn, identity is linked to such phenomena as attitudes to social groups and self-esteem.

## KEY RESEARCH STUDIES

- Trainor *et al* (2012): a study of musical enculturation demonstrating that the mechanism of enculturation is active learning in cooperation with an adult.

- Odden and Rochat (2004): an ethnographic study in rural Samoa demonstrating that at least in some cultures the predominant mechanism of enculturation is observational learning (passive observation).

- Demorest *et al* (2008): a study of musical memory showing that enculturation deeply affects cognitive schemas.

- Kim and Omizo (2006): a correlational study demonstrating the association between acculturation, enculturation and personal identity.

**For the additional term:** since enculturation by definition is internalizing cultural norms, any study on enculturation will also be relevant to cultural norms. However, it must be phrased accordingly with explicit reference to the concept of cultural norms.

## >> COMMON ERRORS

Enculturation has close conceptual links to acculturation and globalization. In fact, in line with Berry's theory, enculturation and acculturation in certain contexts can be seen as two dimensions of the same phenomenon (internalizing the norms of a host culture and preserving the norms of one's culture of origin).

If you think about globalization as acculturation to the global culture, these links become even more obvious.

However, while recognizing these links, it is also important to keep the focus on the concept that is used in the exam question. Enculturation is the process of learning a culture, and it is this process of learning that should be addressed in exam responses, with the conceptual understandings and debates focused on the mechanism of enculturation.

# 4.7    ACCULTURATION

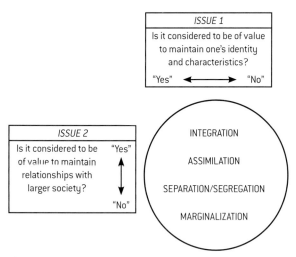

**Figure 4.7.1** Berry's (1997) two-dimensional model of acculturation

- Berry (1997): two-dimensional model of acculturation (theory).

- Shah *et al* (2015): the influence of acculturation on unhealthy eating (a study of South Asian migrants in the UAE).

- Ishizawa and Jones (2016): a study of acculturation effects on obesity in Asian migrants in the USA.

- Da Costa, Dias and Martins (2017): a study of acculturation and obesity in migrants in Portugal.

- Delavari *et al* (2013): a study of the relationship between acculturation and obesity among migrants from low to high income countries.

**For the additional term:** any study that demonstrates assimilation as one of acculturation strategies will be relevant, such as Shah et al (2015).

Apart from the heading "Acculturation", the following additional term can be used in SAQs:

- assimilation/assimilate.

Any combination of this additional term with one of the command terms is acceptable for an SAQ.

Acculturation is the process of psychological and cultural change as a result of contact and interaction between cultures. It is recognized that the effects of contact between a dominant and a non-dominant culture are bidirectional, but most research in this area has concentrated on the effects of the dominant culture on non-dominant ones.

Berry (1997) described two independent dimensions of acculturation, the combination of which, according to him, results in one of four possible acculturation strategies. The two dimensions are: acquiring the cultural norms of the host culture, and maintenance of heritage culture. The possible strategies are: assimilation, integration, separation and marginalization (Berry 2008).

While research into acculturation is important, it also suffers from limitations. The following are the most obvious of these.

- Correlational designs (it is impossible to manipulate cultural variables).

- Dependence on self-report data (effects of acculturation span across multiple behaviours and characteristics, including personal identity, attitudes and self-esteem; many of these variables are not directly observable).

- Most research, for practical purposes, simplifies the concept of acculturation by looking at changes experienced by migrants when they move to a different country. The reverse effects are ignored because it is very difficult to study them.

Despite these limitations, research in this area has yielded some important results, including the following.

- The process of acculturation has been shown to have an influence on migrants' behaviour and identity. Even the length of residence in the host country, although a very crude measure of acculturation, has been shown to correlate with the degree of behavioural and psychological changes.

- The effects of acculturation seem to be moderated by the effects of preserving links with the heritage culture. For example, living in a neighbourhood with many representatives of one's culture of origin may compromise some effects of acculturation on behaviour.

- The country itself may also be significant. Effects of acculturation are weaker in some cultures than others. It probably depends on the similarity between the heritage culture and the host culture.

For all three topics in Sociocultural approach to behaviour, and with reference to research studies, HL students should study:

- the effect of the interaction of local and global influences on behaviour

- research methods used to study the influence of globalization on behaviour.

> Exam questions may use a combination of the two bullet points above with the three topics from column 1 of the syllabus (The individual and the group, Cultural origins of behaviour and cognition, Cultural influences on individual behaviour).

Globalization is the increasing web of connections between people in the world. It is the inevitable result of economic processes. Psychology is concerned with studying psychological phenomena caused by this process – changes in individual identity and behaviour. Obviously, globalization and individual behaviour influence each other bidirectionally, but the influence of globalization on individuals is much more obvious than the influence of individuals on globalization.

Globalization may be viewed as acculturation to the "global culture". In this sense, some theoretical claims about acculturation may be applicable in the context of globalization.

Broadly and on a large scale, there are two opposing views on the possible ultimate effects of globalization.

- According to one prediction, the process of globalization and increasing interconnectedness will make people more cosmopolitan, which means that individuals will be gradually becoming "citizens of the world", prioritizing global interests over immediate local interests.

- According to another prediction, globalization will feel more and more intrusive and individuals will become more protective of their local cultures and local interests. This will trigger reactionary movements, such as anti-globalism and perhaps even nationalism.

Research in this area is difficult because there are too many factors to consider, but attempts have been made. One of the approaches is to model globalization processes in laboratory simulations where participants play with (or against) each other. This research uses principles of behavioural game theory.

Behaviour and identity are influenced by both global and local cultures. In line with Berry's (1997) two-dimensional model, it is the interaction of these two influences that determines the strategy individuals use to adapt to the global culture, and it is the strategy that is used that determines the outcome of globalization.

Supporting this reasoning, research has shown that assimilating the values of the global culture and gradually losing links with one's culture of origin is not the only phenomenon that is observed in today's world. For example, if losing ties with one's culture of origin and assimilating values of the host culture was the most common outcome, one would expect to observe gradual convergence of values in the globalized world. However, this is not the case. In fact, in some instances over time the economic links between two cultures become closer, but cultural values become more distinctly different.

Similar phenomena are observed with identity. Depending on the acculturation strategy chosen, globalization may lead to the formation of different types of identity: bicultural identity, identity confusion or the formation of self-selected subcultures (Arnett 2002).

Methods used to study the influence of globalization on behaviour are mostly limited to correlational research and cross-cultural comparisons. Occasionally researchers make use of interviews (to understand deeply the experiences of certain groups of individuals) and natural experiments (for example, investigating the behaviour of participants on a remote island before and after television was introduced).

Regardless of what method is chosen, techniques used to measure the variables are more diverse. They include self-report questionnaires, computerized simulations and value inventories.

Success in globalization research largely depends on the availability of metrics that allow cross-cultural comparisons. This in itself is not an easy task. We need to have a concept that is equally applicable to all cultures, and a measurement that reliably quantifies this concept in each culture without biases (the etic approach). A good source of such constructs is Hofstede's research on cultural dimensions, as well as the surveys developed by Hofstede to measure these cultural dimensions in individuals and whole nations. One of the ways in which surveys may be used in globalization research is to see how nations' scores change over time as the society gets involved in more and more globalization processes.

Another challenge in globalization research is generalizing findings from samples to target populations. Since target populations in such research are large (entire nations), it is not easy to ensure that the sample used in research is entirely representative.

## KEY RESEARCH STUDIES

- Buchan *et al* (2011): the influence of globalization on cooperation behaviour (a simulation based on behavioural game theory was used to measure global and local influences on cooperation).

- Berry (2008) on the possible outcomes of globalization (continuation of his model of acculturation strategies).

- Adams (2003): a longitudinal study of the convergence of cultural values in Canada and the USA over time.

- Arnett (2002) on the influences of globalization on adolescents' identities.

- Grimalda, Buchan and Brewer (2015): a study of self-reported globalization and cooperation.

# SAMPLE QUESTIONS

Below are two example SAQs and two example ERQs that you might see on Sociocultural approach to behaviour. Read the sample student answers and the accompanying comments, which will help you to understand what the students have done well and what they could do better.

## SAQ example 1

Explain how stereotypes may affect behaviour.                    [9]

Stereotypes are generalized cognitive representations of members of a particular social group, based on their group membership. In other words, it is generic judgment of a person's personality based solely on the fact that this person belongs to a certain group. Stereotypes are very often distorted in the sense that they do not reflect real interpersonal differences. However, it would be incorrect to claim that stereotypes are always a negative phenomenon. In fact, stereotypes are important because they save us mental energy. They allow simplified decision-making regarding individuals with whom we have minimal experience, and this simplified cognitive mechanism may have evolutionary roots. When correct predictions about the behaviour of others is linked to survival, having simplified, quickly accessible (mis)representations of others may prove beneficial. Stereotypes have been explored through the lens of such theories as illusory correlation and social identity theory. From the perspective of illusory correlation, stereotypes are essentially a cognitive bias where the mind sees a connection between phenomena that in reality are not connected.

Hamilton and Gifford (1976) explained that illusory correlations emerge easily between unevenly distributed variables. For example, take two variables – "group membership" and "positive/negative behaviour". Make both variables unevenly distributed, so that in "group membership" one of the groups is a majority and the other one is a minority, and in "positive/ negative behaviour" negative behaviours are less frequently encountered (which is usually the case in real life, too). So the probability of coming into contact with a member of the

> ▼ Stereotypes are defined and explained through the idea of "cognitive shortcuts". This shows understanding, but it is not directly relevant to the question.

> ▼ The study is well explained, but irrelevant to the question – it focuses on origins of stereotypes, not their effect on behaviour.

minority group is relatively low, and similarly the probability of observing a negative behaviour is lower than the probability of observing a positive behaviour. According to Hamilton and Gifford, this makes such unlikely events more salient (once witnessed, they stand out in our memory). When two unlikely events co-occur, the frequency of such co-occurrence is overestimated, and that is how a stereotype is born.

Another theory to explain the emergence of stereotypes is social identity theory (Tajfel and Turner). According to this theory, when you belong to a certain group you seek to maximize positive distinctiveness of your group from other groups (because your self-esteem depends on that). Seeking positive distinctiveness results in exaggerating certain negative characteristics of the outgroup and making them absolute.

Stereotypes can affect behaviour in a variety of ways. For example, through the process known as self-fulfilling prophecy, stereotypes can actually change the behaviour of the stereotyped group. In his research, Rosenthal (the researcher who coined the term self-fulfilling prophecy) told a group of teachers that the class they were going to teach scored really high on an IQ test, and another group of teachers that their class scored average. In fact both the classes had average IQ levels at the start of the experiment, but after one year when IQ was measured again, it was found that the students of teachers who believed their students' IQ was high actually scored higher on the IQ test compared to the control group. The explanation is that, intentionally or not, believing that their students were smart changed the behaviour of the teachers in subtle ways, which in turn affected how focused and attentive those students were in class.

▼ Social identity theory is another explanation for the origins of stereotypes, but it is not directly relevant to the effects of stereotypes on behaviour.

▶ Rosenthal's study is relevant to the question.

▼ This part of the response lacks detail and development.

**This response could have achieved 4/9 marks.**

The response is of limited relevance to the question. It meets the command term requirements, but only the last study is directly relevant to the key problem raised in the question. Knowledge and understanding of the effects of stereotypes on behaviour is accurate but limited.

## SAQ example 2

QUESTION PRACTICE

Outline the influence of one cultural dimension on human behaviour. [9]

SAMPLE STUDENT ANSWER

Hoefstede identified a list of cultural dimensions that may be used to describe how cultures are different from each other. Cultural dimensions are underlying factors that can explain the observed cultural variation, much like "personality traits" are generalized factors that summarize observed interpersonal differences.

One of the cultural dimensions identified by Hofstede is individualism-collectivism. This dimension is a bipolar continuum, with some cultures being closer to one extreme and other cultures closer to the other. Individualistic cultures are the ones that prioritize the individual over the group. They emphasize values of independence, personal achievement and success. In contrast, collectivistic cultures prioritize the group over individuals. They emphasize values of belonging to a group, extended families, continuing traditions of the past, being attentive to the opinions of others and so on. Examples of typically individualistic societies are the USA and Europe. Examples of collectivistic societies are China, India and Japan. People belonging to different extremes of this continuum have been shown to behave differently in similar situations. This exemplifies the influence of a cultural dimension on behaviour.

Examples of behaviours that have been shown to be influenced by individualism-collectivism are conformity, compliance, abnormal behaviour, prosocial behaviour and many more. I will focus on the example of conformity.

Berry and Katz (1967) conducted a study comparing the Temne and the Inuit people. The Temne are a collectivistic society of farmers who depend on collective harvesting and sharing of food. In contrast, the Inuits are an individualistic society of hunters whose survival mostly depends on personal skills. Food is not accumulated hence there is no need to share. Representative samples from both societies were given a conformity task (following the one designed by Asch in his studies of conformity). Participants had to look at cards with one target line and three comparison lines of different lengths, and they had to

▲ One cultural dimension is clearly identified and sufficiently explained.

▲ One example of behaviour is clearly identified, which shows focus on the question.

▲ The research study is relevant to the question and to the behaviour identified earlier (conformity); the study is sufficiently explained with relevant details.

pick one of the three that they thought was the same length as the target line. Additionally, participants were led to believe that most of the other members of their society had picked a different line (which was obviously incorrect). After obtaining this knowledge participants were given an opportunity to change their answer. If they did change their answer to fit with the perceived majority, this was taken as an indication of conformity.

Results of the study showed that the Temne demonstrated significantly more conformity than the Inuits. This can be related to individualism-collectivism. Thus, we can see that the cultural dimension "individualism-collectivism" influences conformity, which is an example of behaviour.

▼ Linking findings of the study back to the question is done in a superficial way. A conceptual explanation of the link between individualism-collectivism and conformity is lacking.

**This response could have achieved 6/9 marks.**

The response is fully focused on the question and for the most part meets the command term requirements. Knowledge and understanding is accurate and addresses the main problem identified in the question. The response is supported by appropriate research that is described and explained. However, the link between the research evidence and the problem identified in the question is not fully explicit. If the link to the question in the last paragraph had been better explained, the essay would have moved into the highest markband.

## ERQ example 1

QUESTION PRACTICE

Discuss the effect of the interaction of global and local influences on behaviour.  [22]

SAMPLE STUDENT ANSWER

Globalization is the process of combining all local cultures in the world into one global culture. Globalization is driven by economic factors; economic exchanges between countries are profitable, and this creates favourable conditions for exchange, joint business enterprises, more transparent borders and so on. Psychological changes, such as changes in values, attitudes and identity, are an inevitable result of these processes.

A debatable question is what the outcomes of globalization will be. On the one hand, it is reasonable to believe that the links of individuals with their cultures of origin will weaken or transform to enable seamless adaptation to the values of the new global culture. This is the view suggesting that globalization should result in cosmopolitan values and attitudes where people

▲ The problem/issue raised in the question is clearly explained and presented as a debate between two opposite viewpoints.

become "citizens of the world", and although they may still preserve strong links with their heritage culture, these links do not come into conflict with their global identity.

On the other hand, the onset of the global culture may be perceived by some individuals as a threat to their identity and their heritage culture. The global values may be in direct contradiction to the values of some local cultures. So it is possible that globalization will engender reactionary movements, such as radical nationalism. Elements of this can be observed today, for example in the anti-immigration movement becoming stronger in Europe and the USA.

It is obvious that in order to understand how globalization influences individual behaviour we should take into account both global and local influences, as well as the interaction between the two.

A popular approach to combining these two influences within a single theoretical framework is the work of Berry (1997) on strategies of acculturation. In this model there are two independent dimensions of acculturation:

▲ A theoretical model is clearly explained (and later linked to globalization).

- assimilation of values of the host culture (seeking contact with the new culture and so on)
- preserving links to the culture of origin.

The particular acculturation strategy that an individual chooses is decided by the combination of these two dimensions, giving four possibilities:

- assimilation (when individuals adjust their values and behaviour to those of the host culture and do not care about losing connection to their culture of origin)

▶ The essay is getting a little descriptive when it comes to details of the theoretical model, but good knowledge and understanding is demonstrated.

- integration (when individuals internalize the new values of the host culture, but at the same time preserve links with the culture of origin – a constructive combination)
- separation (when individuals hold on to the values of their heritage culture to the extent of avoiding contact with the host culture)
- marginalization (when individuals neither preserve the values of the heritage culture nor acquire the new values of the host culture, so they become "cultureless").

As applied to globalization, Berry (2008) claims that the two axes represent the influences of the global culture and the local culture.

▲ Berry's theoretical model is made relevant to the concept of globalization. Some critical thinking is demonstrated through the application of Berry's model of acculturation strategies to globalization.

▶ An element of critical thinking is presented here through reflecting on the difficulties of globalization research, but this could be further developed.

▲ A relevant research study is considered and its link to the theoretical model is clearly explained. Some critical thinking is shown through explaining the rationale behind the study and the leap from empirical findings to theoretical conclusions.

Accordingly, the choice of acculturation strategy pre-determines the outcome of globalization. If assimilation dominates, globalization will lead to a homogeneous global culture, and local cultural values will be gradually lost. If integration dominates, the outcome of globalization will be a well-connected society that at the same time preserves the cultural uniqueness of its constituent groups (glocalization). If separation dominates, non-dominant groups will start reactionary movements and reject the influences of the global culture (anti-globalist movements). Finally, if marginalization dominates, local cultures will be destroyed but no culture will be created to replace them, effectively resulting in a cultureless society. To figure out which of the four outcomes is most likely, and what factors contribute to the selection of acculturation strategies, is a research task. What makes it difficult is the complex nature of social development: if we observe a certain culture over a period of time and observe changes, there are multiple explanations that may be consistent with these changes, the influence of globalization being only one of such possible explanations. Researchers have to make certain inferences based on the explanations that seem most likely in the given context.

An example of such research is Adams (2003): a longitudinal correlational study that looked at the convergence of cultural values between Canada and the USA. The rationale behind this study is that the USA is the dominant culture and Canada is the non-dominant one. Culturally the USA exerts a huge influence on Canada. For example, most of the films shown in Canada are American films. With the course of time, as economic and other relations between the two countries become stronger, such influences grow. If the predominant acculturation strategy used by Canadians is assimilation, one may expect the values of the average Canadian to become similar to the values of the average American over time.

Researchers used a survey consisting of 86 value statements, administered to representative samples in both countries. The total number of participants exceeded 14,000. The surveys were administered at three points of time: in 1992, 1996 and 2000. Results of the study went contrary to predictions (based on the assumption that assimilation would be the predominant acculturation strategy). The cultural value profiles of the two countries (based on the 86 value statements) did not become more similar over time. In fact, some of the values became more different. For example, one of the statements on the survey was, "The father of the family must be master of his own house." In 1992, this statement was endorsed by 26% of Canadians and 42% of Americans. This changed by 2000: the statement was endorsed by 18% of Canadians and 49% of Americans. So it looks like the initially existing differences became more pronounced, as if the two cultures were emphasizing their uniqueness.

Of course the study should be considered with an element of skepticism. It was correlational, so cause and effect cannot be reliably established. Although the number of participants was quite large, researchers wanted to generalize to whole nations, and for that even 14,000 participants may not be enough. The time span of the study was not large enough to capture long-term changes in cultural values.

▼ Evaluation of research could be further developed.

However, the study does support Berry's model of globalization (and acculturation) in that assimilation of values is not the only possible strategy and not the only possible outcome of globalization. Local influences play a major role as well, sometimes creating the situation where local cultural values are actually strengthened and reinforced in the process of globalization.

▲ The study is linked back to the problem/issue raised in the question.

**This response could have achieved 17/22 marks.**

**Focus on the question:** 2/2. The answer clearly explains the problem/ issue raised in the question.

**Knowledge and understanding:** 5/6. The response demonstrates relevant knowledge and understanding. The theory and research included in the response are carefully linked to the key concept (globalization) as well as the idea of the interaction between local and global influences. Psychological terminology is used appropriately. However, the response could be more detailed and use more supporting research.

**Use of research to support answer:** 5/6. Relevant psychological research is used in support of the response and is thoroughly explained. Selected research is relevant to the central argument of the essay, but further research could be used to develop the argument more. Psychological research is well presented; research studies are clearly described and used to address different issues.

**Critical thinking:** 3/6. The response contains critical thinking but lacks development. Evaluation or discussion of most relevant areas is attempted but is not well developed. The focus in the essay is on "explanation" rather than "discussion".

**Clarity and organization:** 2/2. The answer demonstrates organization and clarity throughout.

## ERQ example 2

Evaluate social identity theory.            [22]

▼ The problem/issue raised in the question is vaguely identified. The introduction states that identity is more complex than simply belonging to a group, but it does not specify any problem with the social identity theory. The focus on the command term (evaluate) is not maintained – the essay starts descriptively.

The sociocultural approach to behaviour underlies the principle that humans have a social self and a need to belong, to form part of a group. Sometimes individuals are born into these groups, whether it is because of ethnicity or religion of their family. But that does not mean that they automatically feel identified within the group, it is more complex than that. This is what Tajfel and Turner explained as social identity theory.

According to their theory there are four conditions or stages in social identity. In the first stage called social categorization, an individual divides an environment into two groups: ingroup and outgroup ("us" and "them" respectively). There is a reduced perceived variability between the individual and other members of the ingroup as the individual feels that they are all similar or share similar beliefs, attitudes, values and so on. There is also a reduction in the perceived variability between members of the outgroup, since those in the ingroup think that those in the outgroup are all the same, and at the same time they feel that their ingroup is different to the outgroup. In other words, the idea that "we are different from them". This leads to a category accentuation effect which is what influences the transition to the next stage: social identification.

▲ The theory is clearly outlined.

Social identification occurs when individuals feel even more overtly connected to those in their ingroup and they even begin to act in similar ways to reinforce this identification. Then individuals tend to look for a sense of self in their surroundings, as most humans do, and happen to find that their identity is more and more linked to their belonging in a group. In order to find a sense of self or identity they use outgroup members as a reference point on which to compare themselves and reassure their membership in the ingroup. Known as the stage of social comparison, these comparisons generally lead to members of the ingroup criticizing those in the outgroup or having negative opinions about them. This leads to the last stage of Tajfel and Turner's theory, known as positive distinctiveness. Here positive aspects of the ingroup are highlighted and special focus is given to the negative aspects of the outgroup, not allowing them to see any positive features in the outgroup and any negative features in their own group (ingroup). Or if they do see them, they try to reject and/or avoid them.

Tajfel then conducted a study on 14–15-year-olds (meaning it is not generalizable to the entire population) to show if a random allocation of participants to two groups could lead to the formation of an ingroup and outgroup and demonstrate social identity theory. Participants were asked to choose between 12 paintings of the Expressionist painters Klee and Kandinsky. The children did not know which painter was which, but they were told that they were allocated to the given group according to their preferences for the paintings, when actually researchers randomly allocated them to those conditions.

That led to the creation of two literal groups: the Klee group and the Kandinsky group. Members of each group were told that they had to allocate points to a member of their ingroup and a member of the outgroup. However, the initial point allocation system developed by Tajfel established that the sum of the points being allocated had to be 15, and therefore the more points participants chose to give to the ingroup member, the fewer they gave to the outgroup member. Then, he changed the point allocation system to the points equating money (1–10 pennies) and established that a high value given to a team member would give an even higher value to the outgroup member; that a mid-range value for an ingroup member would give the same number of points and therefore pennies to the outgroup member; and that a low value for the ingroup member meant that the outgroup would only receive one point.

Results show that in the first point allocation system, participants gave consistently more points to the ingroup and fewer to the outgroup, showing that they preferred giving more points to those who were more similar to them. Also in the second system, participants were willing to sacrifice points and thus higher profits to members of their ingroup in order to maximize the difference between the two groups. Despite the experiment not being generalizable to the entire population (they were

> ▶ Sufficient level of detail in describing research procedures.

▼ The first study is well described, but there is very minimal evaluation.

teenagers) and it being artificial due to the fact that it was done in a laboratory setting, the results do demonstrate social identity theory.

Another study that showed the effect of social identity theory more implicitly by studying what is known as the stereotype threat was Steele and Aronson. They studied how the existence of a stereotype about one's culture would lead to one assuming that stereotype and performing as would be expected according to the stereotype. Stereotypes are created when people start dividing an environment into ingroups and outgroups. The division between African-American and Caucasian people into groups is based on ethnicity. In particular, when the study was conducted there was a stereotype about black people being academically inferior that had been shown by the use of IQ tests and then disproved due to the fact that they were not applicable to their culture and were not measuring intellectual capacity as initially thought.

Steele and Aronson decided to test this by using black and white participants and telling them that they were either going to be tested on verbal ability or on problem-solving skills. The test was the same but a different label was given to it depending on the condition. Results showed that black participants in the "problem-solving skills" condition performed just as well as their white counterparts, whereas when told that it was a test on their intellectual and verbal abilities they performed worse than white participants. This showed that the stereotype threat meant that African Americans were assuming what white people had once assumed by using positive distinctiveness.

▼ This second study had the potential to be relevant, but this was not really accomplished. It must be concluded that this study is irrelevant to the question.

In evaluation, this might have harmed or discomforted black participants, particularly when the study was published. They might have felt angry about themselves for accepting the stereotype. Also, the results might vary nowadays since the world is more globalized and people are less prejudiced about an ethnicity's intelligence. In conclusion, social identity theory manages to explain ingroup favouritism and the formation of stereotypes through the different stages, however it does not fully explain why social identity might lead to violence against the outgroup.

▼ There is very limited evaluation. Also there is no clear evaluation of the theory itself.

**This response could have achieved 10/22 marks.**

**Focus on the question:** 1/2. The problem/issue raised in the question is briefly identified, but not explained.

**Knowledge and understanding:** 4/6. The response demonstrates reasonably relevant knowledge and understanding, but lacks detail and not all research evidence is directly relevant to the question. Psychological terminology is used accurately in most contexts.

**Use of research to support answer:** 2/6. Limited relevant psychological research is used in the response. There is an attempt to use research studies to support different conceptual understandings, but stereotype threat is not convincing as support for social identity theory. Research is mostly used with a focus on explanation rather than evaluation of social identity theory.

**Critical thinking:** 2/6. There is limited critical thinking in the response. While critical thinking is indeed demonstrated by linking research findings to theoretical conclusions, this is not enough in light of the requirements of the command term. Evaluation of research findings is superficial and mostly limited to issues of generalizability to wider populations.

**Clarity and organization:** 1/2. The answer demonstrates some organization and clarity, but this is not sustained throughout the response.

# 5 ABNORMAL PSYCHOLOGY

In discussing topics and content headings related to Abnormal psychology, you are allowed to look at several mental disorders or focus on one, and both approaches are equally acceptable. The chosen disorders should come from the categories:

✔ anxiety disorders

✔ depressive disorders

✔ obsessive compulsive disorder

✔ trauma and stress related disorders

✔ eating disorders.

For this book we have chosen to focus mainly on major depressive disorder (MDD). This is done in order to demonstrate a variety of conceptual understandings relevant to a single phenomenon. However, you should remember that other mental disorders may also be chosen.

## 5.1 NORMALITY VERSUS ABNORMALITY

By definition, abnormal psychology is a study of behaviour that deviates from the norm. This automatically raises the problem of defining the norm and finding a demarcation criterion between normal and abnormal.

There have been multiple approaches to solving this problem. Some of the most prominent are listed here.

### 🔍 KEY THEORIES AND RESEARCH STUDIES

- Rosenhan and Seligman (1989): criteria of abnormality.

- Jahoda (1958): criteria of ideal mental health.

You can also use various studies from later parts of this option. For example, any study demonstrating how classification systems are used to arrive at a diagnosis (and what problems are associated with their use) will be suitable. The content heading "Clinical bias in diagnosis" can also be a useful source of research studies, for example Langwieler and Linden (1993). Another popular option is Rosenhan (1973) "on being sane in insane places".

- Abnormality is a deviation from social norms accepted in a given society at a given time.

- Abnormality is inadequate functioning – Rosenhan and Seligman (1989).

- Abnormality is a statistical infrequency.

- Abnormality is a deviation from ideal mental health – Jahoda (1958).

- Another approach is the medical model of abnormality.

### ≫ COMMON ERRORS

Try to avoid excessively descriptive responses that focus on unpacking each of the approaches to defining normality and abnormality. A better strategy would be to identify two to three approaches and then provide empirical support and evidence of critical thinking.

The medical model looks at disorders separately and lists the set of symptoms that defines each disorder. In this sense, the problem of defining abnormality based on its hypothesized causes is avoided. Instead the medical model's approach is descriptive: describe the symptoms that characterize a disorder and you will be able to recognize it.

A strength of the medical approach is its independence from theoretical views about the causes of disorders. Even if two clinicians have opposing views about what causes a disorder, they should agree that the disorder is present. Identifiable sets of symptoms form the basis of classification systems widely used in diagnosing mental illness.

Classification systems are structured diagnostic manuals that typically provide:

- a list of mental disorders grouped into a hierarchy of categories

- a list of symptoms for each of the disorders

- criteria for diagnosis – for example, how many symptoms of which types should be observed and for how long in order for the disorder to be diagnosed.

There are several widely known classification systems that are used today. Some of them are:

- DSM-5 (the Diagnostic and Statistical Manual, 5th edition)

- ICD-10 (the International Classification of Disorders, 10th edition)

- CCMD-3 (the Chinese Classification of Mental Disorders, 3rd edition).

The main purpose of a classification system is to enable reliable diagnosis; that is, to ensure that if two clinicians (even with very different theoretical backgrounds) use the same manual to diagnose the same patient, they will likely arrive at the same diagnosis. The history of the development of classification systems shows that this has not always been fully achieved, and neither is it completely achieved now.

Using DSM as an example, history shows the following.

- The first editions were theoretically focused and emphasized identifying the hidden cause of a mental illness. This made diagnosis dependent on a clinician's interpretation of the patient's behaviour. At first DSM was more explanatory than descriptive.

- This approach was criticized for using unobservable constructs like "motivation" and "trauma". Critics doubted that this approach is scientific.

- A movement started to make diagnostic categories more observable and less dependent on the clinician's interpretations.

- This resulted in DSM being more descriptive than explanatory. Studies showed an increase in the reliability of diagnosis, but this might have come at the cost of its validity.

- Further editions of DSM saw further attempts to increase reliability, but also better integration of cultural aspects into the diagnostic process.

Based on this example, the major challenges in designing a classification system may be summarized as:

- delineation between overlapping sets of symptoms

- explanation versus description

- validity versus reliability

- cross-cultural applicability and cultural syndromes.

▲ Figure 5.2.1  DSM-5

### 🔍 KEY RESEARCH STUDIES

Key research studies for this content heading can be found under "Validity and reliability of diagnosis" (page 92). Research into validity and reliability of diagnosis is typically carried out using one of the established classification systems, so the results of this research are equally applicable to that classification system and the concept of diagnosis in general.

### ≫ COMMON ERRORS

Try to avoid descriptive responses focused on the structure and content of diagnostic manuals. The focus in this content heading is on the problems and challenges surrounding the creation and application of a typical classification system. One or more specific classification systems may be used as an illustration of these ideas, but it is not the details of specific classification systems that are the focus here.

# 5.3 PREVALENCE RATES AND DISORDERS

Epidemiology is the study of the spread of diseases in populations. Among the main indices used in epidemiology are prevalence rate and incidence rate. Prevalence rate is the proportion of people in a given population diagnosed with a given disorder, either currently (point prevalence) or at any point during a time interval (period prevalence, for example 12-month prevalence or lifetime prevalence). Incidence is the rate of development of a disorder in previously healthy individuals in a specified time period.

Epidemiology faces a lot of challenges in terms of ensuring that the estimates are accurate. Here are some examples.

- Prevalence rate estimates depend on diagnostic criteria.

- Prevalence rate estimates depend on patient biases such as reporting bias. A related problem is somatization (presenting mental illness as physical symptoms).

- Prevalence rate estimates also depend on issues of validity and reliability of diagnosis, including biases associated with the inability of clinicians to recognize cultural variations of the norm.

- Prevalence rate estimates are generalized inferences about whole populations. Such estimates must be based on large representative samples, but getting access to such samples may be problematic.

- There will always be certain differences in prevalence rate estimates across genders, ages, cultures and other demographic variables. The question is, do these changes reflect genuine differences in symptoms in these populations or do they merely reflect biases in the diagnostic process? It is not easy to eliminate the second explanation and accept the first.

Given all the arguments above, it is important to keep in mind certain limitations of epidemiological indices. For example, national-level estimates are probably more reliable than cross-national comparisons (especially if the two countries use different classification systems).

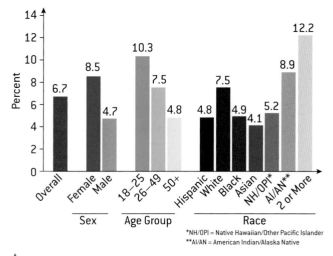

*NH/OPI = Native Hawaiian/Other Pacific Islander
**AI/AN = American Indian/Alaska Native

▲ Figure 5.3.1  12-month prevalence of MDD among American adults (data from 2015)

Depending on the specific mental disorders you are focusing on, you should also know the current prevalence rate estimates for these disorders. For example, the 12-month prevalence rate of major depressive disorder (MDD) among adults in the USA in 2015 was estimated at 6.7%. Women had a higher prevalence (8.5% against 4.7%). Prevalence rates of depression also show considerable cross-cultural variation.

## KEY RESEARCH STUDIES

There are several aspects that you can possibly focus on for this content heading. The choice of aspect will determine the choice of supporting research studies. The aspects are as follows.

- Prevalence rates of a disorder may be different for males and females, different ages, different cultures and so on. You can report on several studies that show this discrepancy. Examples include Kessler and Bromet (2013) – a study comparing prevalence rates of MDD cross-culturally – and the National Survey on Drug Use and Health (2015): an American epidemiological study that estimated prevalence rates of depression as well as differences between males and females.

- Factors that influence prevalence rate estimates should be considered. This aspect links to clinical bias in diagnosis and culturally specific expression of symptoms. Both these factors will influence prevalence rate estimates in different populations even if "objectively" their symptoms are the same. For example, Payne (2012) showed that clinicians insensitive to culturally specific expression of depression may overdiagnose it in certain cultural groups.

- Factors that influence the disorder itself should be considered (for example, why is it that depression is more prevalent in one group than other groups). This aspect links to content such as biological explanations for depression. For example, Silberg *et al* (1999) showed that females are more vulnerable to stressful life events, and this vulnerability may contribute to depression.

## COMMON ERRORS

Do not confuse prevalence rates with heritability coefficients. Higher heritability of depression in a certain social group, for example, does not automatically mean a higher prevalence of depression in that group. Where heritability studies are used and such links are made, they must be explained from the perspective of prevalence (as this is the focus of the content heading), not heritability.

# 5.4 VALIDITY AND RELIABILITY OF DIAGNOSIS

Validity and reliability are characteristics that define the quality of diagnosis. Reliability means consistency across clinicians. Diagnosis is reliable if two (or more) clinicians observing and interviewing the same patient arrive at the same conclusion.

There are two ways to estimate this inter-rater reliability of diagnosis.

- Recording method: one clinician conducts the clinical interview and the patient's answers are recorded. Another clinician then listens to the recording of the session and arrives at a diagnosis based on this recording. The limitation of this method is that it can inflate estimates of reliability because in real life different clinicians ask the patient different questions and therefore elicit different responses.

- Test-retest method: two clinicians conduct clinical interviews with the same patient independently. The limitation with this method is that if two clinicians arrive at different diagnoses, this may be due to the fact that the patient's behaviour actually changed between the two interviews. So this method may underestimate reliability of diagnosis.

Reliability of diagnosis is well illustrated by the history of research accompanying the development of classification systems. Using the Diagnostic and Statistical Manual (DSM) as an example: from its first edition to the fifth, reliability estimates were improving, but not consistently across all diagnostic categories.

Validity refers to the accuracy of diagnosis. Diagnosis is valid if it is "correct"; that is, it corresponds to the actual mental illness that the patient is experiencing.

Unlike reliability, validity of diagnosis cannot be directly quantified. Instead research in this area has used two approaches.

- Trying to identify systematic biases in diagnosis. If biases are found, this automatically means validity of diagnosis is low (even if we do not know what the "real" disorder is). This approach has led to the identification of a number of typical clinician biases in diagnosis (see page 93).

- Investigating the ability of clinicians to arrive at the correct diagnosis when the "real" disorder is objectively known. This approach was used, for example, by Rosenhan (1973) in his field study where healthy confederates faked symptoms and tried to get admission into mental health institutions.

There is an inverse relationship between validity and reliability of diagnosis. In order to make diagnosis more reliable, it should be based entirely on observable behaviour. But if we limit diagnosis to observable symptoms only, we might ignore the patient's subjective experiences, thus making diagnosis less valid.

## 🔍 KEY RESEARCH STUDIES

- Beck *et al* (1962): agreement between two psychiatrists (inter-rater reliability) using DSM-I.

- Williams *et al* (1992): test-retest reliability of a range of diagnostic categories using DSM-III.

- Chmielewski *et al* (2015): comparing reliability estimates obtained using the test-retest method and the audio-/video-recording method (DSM-5).

- Regier *et al* (2013): a summary of reliability trials in DSM-5.

- Rosenhan (1973): "Being sane in insane places", a study investigating validity of diagnosis.

Validity of diagnosis can be investigated in two ways: directly in studies involving pseudo-patients (such as Rosenhan's) or indirectly in studies of clinical biases in diagnosis. Should you wish to discuss clinical biases in this context, there are a number of additional studies that can be used: see page 93.

## ≫ COMMON ERRORS

Remember to delineate clearly the concepts of validity and reliability. Some supporting research studies are relevant for illustrating issues of reliability, some are relevant to validity, but these aspects should be clearly identified and not mixed up.

# 5.5 THE ROLE OF CLINICAL BIASES IN DIAGNOSIS

Clinical biases in diagnosis are systematic deviations of diagnosis from what the actual disorder is. How do we know that such biases exist, given than the only way for us to know the "actual disorder" is through diagnosis itself? If two groups of clinicians (for example, clinicians with different cultural backgrounds) diagnose the same patients and the results of this diagnosis are different between groups, we know that at least one of the groups is biased in its diagnosis.

Typically, two broad groups of biases are distinguished in diagnosis: those associated with "clinician variables" and those associated with "patient variables".

Clinician variables are systematic biases introduced by the psychiatrist. They may be linked to the clinician's theoretical orientation, abilities and cognitive biases. Depending on their training and life/professional experiences, clinicians may form certain explicit and implicit beliefs about mental disorders, and these may function as schemas in the process of the diagnostic interview, causing such phenomena as confirmation bias.

▲ Figure 5.5.1 Promoting mental health awareness gradually helps to overcome reporting bias

Patient variables are biases introduced by patients themselves. These are systematic group differences that have no relation to the disorder but that nevertheless affect the diagnosis. Examples include reporting bias, somatization and culturally specific expression of symptoms. Some of these biases (such as reporting bias) are largely unavoidable; the only way to overcome reporting bias is to slowly educate society about stigmatization of mental disorders. Some other biases, such as somatization and culturally specific expression of symptoms, may be accounted for and at least partially overcome by a professional clinician.

This poses a challenge, however, because it requires the clinician to be extremely culturally sensitive and reflective about the influence of his or her own culture on the diagnostic process. Today, classification systems (such as DSM-5) include more and more instruments to assist clinicians in establishing the cultural background of a patient and its possible influence on the symptoms. DSM-5 includes a "cultural formulation interview" and also defines a list of "cultural syndromes" (sets of symptoms that are only recognized as illness in a specific culture).

## 🔍 KEY RESEARCH STUDIES

- Langwieler and Linden (1993): a study demonstrating that the theoretical background of the clinician may be a source of bias in diagnosis even when the same classification manual is used.

- Chapman and Chapman (1969): the role of confirmation bias and illusory correlation in diagnosis.

- Furnham and Malik (1994): reporting bias in British Asians.

- Lin, Carter and Kleinman (1985): somatization in refugees and immigrants by choice (demonstrating that some social groups are prone to bias in expressing symptoms due to social stigmatization).

- Payne (2012): demonstrating that clinicians may be insensitive to the fact that participants from different cultural backgrounds express the same symptoms differently.

## 5.6 EXPLANATIONS FOR DISORDERS

Biological etiology of mental disorders includes aspects such as genetic inheritance and the role of chemical messengers (neurotransmitters and hormones). For example, research into the etiology of depression has revealed these points.

- Genetic heritability of depression is estimated to be around 37% (Sullivan, Neale, Kendler 2000).

- Women are more genetically predisposed to depression than men (Kendler *et al* 2006).

- Depression is the result of gene-environment interaction (GxE) rather than a direct effect of genes. Genetic inheritance creates a predisposition to depression, but symptoms manifest themselves only if the environment is "favourable" for that.

- Increased vulnerability to stressful life events may be traced back to a specific gene: 5-HTT (Caspi *et al* 2003).

- However, this increased vulnerability may be mediated by cultural variables. For example, values of collectivism may have been developed in response to this increased vulnerability, providing a buffer against stress in the form of social support (Ciao, Blizinsky 2010).

Cognitive etiology of mental disorders includes aspects such as patterns of information processing, cognitive styles and cognitive biases. For depression, the most influential theory explaining cognitive etiology is Beck's (1967) cognitive theory of depression.

Cognitive behavioural therapy (CBT) is an approach to the treatment of mental disorders that is based on the idea that if you change the patient's automatic thinking patterns, his or her behaviour will also change. The effectiveness of cognitive-based treatment indirectly supports the idea that disorders have cognitive etiology.

Research has revealed the following.

- Negative cognitive styles predict the development of depressive symptoms.

- Negative attention biases are correlated with symptoms of depression.

- Patients with depression make more logical errors in their reasoning.

Sociocultural etiology of mental disorders includes aspects such as systems of social support, employment, education and many others. Some researchers, such as Brown and Harris (1978), have tried to investigate the whole system of sociocultural factors and propose models of vulnerability, pinpointing the small number of factors that are especially responsible for the development of a disorder. A special area of research is investigating real-life social networks of friends and seeing if symptoms of disorders can spread across such networks (much like information spreads on social media). It has been shown, for example, that individuals are more likely to have depression if their friends also have depression.

## KEY THEORIES AND RESEARCH STUDIES

- Sullivan, Neale and Kendler (2000): a meta-analysis of twin studies to estimate heritability of major depression.

- Kendler *et al* (2006): comparing heritability of depression in men and women.

- Silberg *et al* (1999): investigating gene-environment interaction in developing depression in adolescent girls.

- Caspi *et al* (2003): the role of the 5-HTT gene in moderating the influence of stressful life events on depression.

- Chiao and Blizinsky (2010): culture-gene co-evolution theory (and research).

- Beck (1967): cognitive theory of depression.

- Alloy, Abramson and Francis (1999): a longitudinal study of negative cognitive styles predicting the development of depression.

- Caseras *et al* (2007): an eye-tracking study of negative attention bias in participants with depression.

- Hammen and Krantz (1976): a study showing that the reasoning of depressed people contains more logical errors.

- Brown and Harris (1978): a study supporting the vulnerability model of depression (working-class women from London).

- Rosenquist, Fowler and Christakis (2011): a study of a social network of friendships in relation to depression, demonstrating that depression may "spread" along the social network like a virus.

## 5.7  ASSESSING THE EFFECTIVENESS OF TREATMENT

Assessing the effectiveness of treatment is a pertinent task because ineffective treatment may be detrimental to the well-being of a patient. However, the task is not easy. Common challenges include the following.

- Depending on its severity, a disorder may respond to one treatment but not respond to another.

- Effectiveness may be operationalized differently, depending on what outcomes are considered the most important.

- Research should take into consideration the difference between long-term and short-term effectiveness.

- Treatment effects should be separated from placebo effects.

Apart from finding out whether treatment is effective or not, we also need to understand why it is effective. For this we need to identify the mechanism of treatment.

### 🔍 KEY THEORIES AND RESEARCH STUDIES

- Eysenck (1952): the first review comparing the effectiveness of various non-medical methods of psychotherapy.

- Smith and Glass (1977): the same meta-analysis with the same goal.

- Jacobson *et al* (1996): investigating the effectiveness of CBT in a "dismantling design".

- Lambert (2013): explaining the phenomenon of "sudden gains".

- Wampold (2007): proposing the key non-specific factors of psychotherapy.

### ›› COMMON ERRORS

Be careful not to write an answer focused on establishing the effectiveness of one particular treatment. The question "How can the effectiveness of treatment be assessed?" is different from, for example, "To what extent is biological treatment effective?". This content heading deals with broader issues surrounding assessing the effectiveness of treatment (although particular forms of treatment and relevant supporting studies may obviously be used as examples to back up arguments).

Three approaches have been commonly used to assess effectiveness of treatment in abnormal psychology:

- randomized controlled trials (RCTs)

- qualitative research studies

- meta-analyses.

One of the burning questions that can be answered with meta-analyses is the generic "Does psychotherapy work?". Eysenck (1952) found that psychotherapy was not effective beyond what is expected from normal spontaneous recovery. This finding inspired further development of randomized controlled trials and meta-analyses. As the quality of data increased, new estimates of effectiveness were obtained, and these were more optimistic.

Later on more answers were sought to more specific research questions, such as: Are some approaches to psychotherapy more effective than others? What elements of psychotherapy are responsible for its effectiveness?

A lot of initial research showed little difference between various psychotherapeutic approaches in terms of effectiveness. This raised the question of specific and non-specific factors of psychotherapy. Examples of non-specific factors include the trusting relationship between the therapist and the client, the possibility of cathartic experiences, placebo effects and so on. Specific factors are the ones associated with the concrete techniques used in one psychotherapeutic approach but not others.

One experimental approach to studying specific and non-specific factors of psychotherapy is known as the "dismantling design". In this design different (randomly allocated) groups of participants undergo either a complete course of treatment or various incomplete versions. A puzzling finding in this area is that incomplete treatment programmes are often as effective as the complete one. This has been attributed to the influence of non-specific factors of psychotherapy.

Biological treatment of disorders implies prescribing medication. The idea behind this approach is that since we know behaviour has a physiological basis, influencing physiology may result in a change in behaviour.

Using the example of depression, the search for effective biological treatments has taken the form of finding the most effective antidepressant.

One of the most widely used antidepressants – Fluoxetine (trademark Prozac) – belongs to the class of SSRIs (selective serotonin reuptake inhibitors). By inhibiting the reuptake of serotonin, this drug increases its concentration on the synapse.

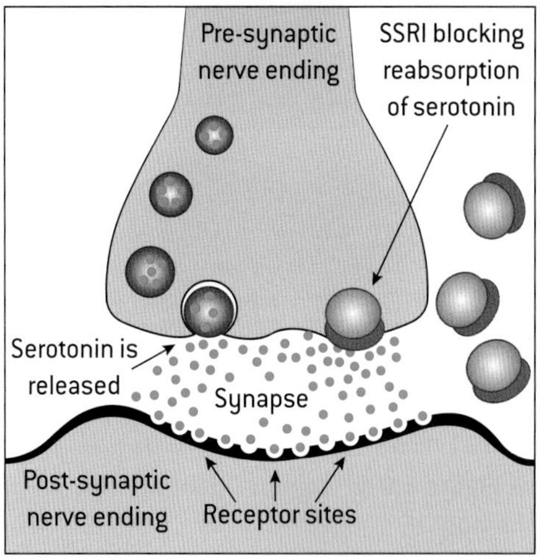

Three treatment outcomes are typically used to characterize the effectiveness of medical treatment:

- response rate: the percentage of patients who demonstrated
  a 50% or higher decrease in symptoms

- remission rate: the percentage of patients who reached considerable improvement, with few or no symptoms

- relapse rate: the percentage of patients who developed the symptoms again after the treatment was discontinued.

An effective treatment would have high response and remission rates and a low relapse rate.

Research with antidepressants has yielded mixed results. On the one hand, medication has been shown to be effective against severe depression, especially when urgent treatment is needed (such as in the presence of suicidal thoughts). On the other hand, for less severe cases, non-medical treatment has been shown to have a more lasting effect. Additionally, there have been claims that the effectiveness of antidepressants is overestimated due to publication bias.

Examples of non-antidepressant biological treatments include electroconvulsive therapy and transcranial magnetic stimulation.

▲ **Figure 5.8.1** SSRIs prevent reuptake of serotonin from the synapse

## 🔍 KEY RESEARCH STUDIES

- March *et al* (2007) ("Treatment of adolescents with depression study", or TADS): comparing CBT, medication, CBT with medication, and placebo in the treatment of depression in the short term and the long term.

- Kirsch *et al* (2002): meta-analysis of published and unpublished data on the effectiveness of antidepressants claimed that positive results in earlier studies can be attributed to publication bias.

- Hollon *et al* (2002): investigation of the effectiveness of antidepressants for weak, moderate and severe depression.

- Elkin *et al* (1989): comparing drugs, placebo and CBT for severe and very severe depression.

# 5.9 PSYCHOLOGICAL TREATMENT

▲ **Figure 5.9.1** Cognitive behavioural therapy

The psychological treatment of mental disorders consists of various non-medication approaches. Results are achieved through cognitive analysis, behavioural tasks and interpersonal interaction.

The most widely accepted psychological treatment of depression is CBT (cognitive behavioural therapy). This approach has also accumulated the largest amount of empirical evidence.

The two major goals of CBT are cognitive restructuring and behavioural activation (hence the name). Cognitive restructuring is achieved through analysing automatic thoughts and making them more logical. Behavioural activation is achieved through tasks where the client has to try out new behaviours and reflect on their effectiveness.

CBT requires the client to take an active role in the therapy process, by setting goals, defining criteria of achievement, engaging in tasks and reflecting on results. Compared to other forms of psychological treatment, CBT is short and focused on highly specific goals.

Response and remission rates of CBT have been shown to match those of antidepressant treatment in the long term. Some studies show that CBT "catches up" with medication after 16 weeks of treatment or more. From this perspective, CBT might be preferable to medication because the side effects associated with antidepressants are not desirable. However, medication is preferable when the problem is severe and urgent (for example, resulting in suicidal thoughts). Additionally, some patients find it difficult to invest the kind of effort that is required in a 16-week therapy course (taking a pill is much easier).

Another huge argument in favour of CBT over medication is that relapse rates are lower. This means that the effects of CBT last longer than the effects of medication after treatment is discontinued. This also suggests that CBT targets the cause of the problem rather than just the symptoms.

The effectiveness of therapy may also depend on which symptoms in particular are targeted. Even within MDD the symptoms that respond best to treatment may be different for CBT and antidepressant medication.

## 🔍 KEY RESEARCH STUDIES

- DeRubeis *et al* (2005): comparing CBT and antidepressant medication in terms of response and remission rates in the short term (8 weeks) and the long term (16 weeks).

- Hollon *et al* (2005): comparing CBT and antidepressant medication in terms of relapse rates after the treatment is discontinued.

- Fournier *et al* (2013): investigating clusters of MDD symptoms that are most responsive to CBT versus medication.

- Goldapple (2004): investigating brain changes in patients undergoing CBT.

As we know from a previous content heading ("The role of clinical biases in diagnosis"), culture influences how a mental disorder is experienced, presented and perceived. In the long term, this also has an effect on treatment.

Cultural factors can influence a patient's compliance with treatment. As a result, sufficient rapport between the patient and the therapist may not be established, and the patient may not take the procedures seriously or may not fully follow the procedures prescribed by the therapist. For example, a therapist may prescribe medication, but the client may fail to take it regularly and at the same time fail to admit this non-compliance to the therapist.

Cultural variables can also influence the patient's internal model of illness. This internal model of illness is responsible for how patients interpret their symptoms, how favourably they view the treatment, the extent to which they believe treatment targets the cause and so on. The internal model of illness mediates all therapeutic efforts. For this reason, the therapist must take the internal model of illness into account, by first understanding it and then adjusting the interventions accordingly. But this also raises the question: is it better to change the patient's internal model of illness, or is it better to change the therapy to fit the client's internal model?

Real-life solutions usually lie somewhere in between these two extreme options. Culturally sensitive treatments may use a top-down or bottom-up approach to designing the interventions. In a top-down approach, the core of the therapy stays intact, but superficial changes are made to better accommodate for cultural specificity (for example, changing the language of delivery). In a bottom-up approach, more fundamental changes are made. These usually start with a qualitative research programme designed to get an insight into the nature of patients' interpretations of their symptoms, and treatment is then based on these research findings. Sometimes this results in considerable modifications to the original treatment being made, such as using the support of local healers or the language of religious beliefs.

## KEY RESEARCH STUDIES

- Kinzie *et al* (1987): compliance with antidepressant treatment in Asian patients.

- Naeem *et al* (2012): investigating the internal model of illness in patients in Pakistan and designing a culturally sensitive version of CBT.

- Griner and Smith (2006): a meta-analysis investigating the effectiveness of culturally adapted treatments of mental disorders.

## >> COMMON ERRORS

Although there are close links between this content heading and cultural biases in diagnosis, be careful about the selection of research studies. Studies that are relevant to treatment may not be relevant to diagnosis, and vice versa. Although it can be argued that diagnosis affects treatment, studies that demonstrate that a cultural bias exists in diagnosing mental disorders are not directly addressing the role of culture in treatment.

# SAMPLE QUESTIONS

Below are two example ERQs that you might see on Abnormal psychology. Read the sample student answers and the accompanying comments, which will help you to understand what the students have done well and what they could do better.

## ERQ example 1

QUESTION PRACTICE

To what extent do biological factors influence abnormal behaviour?      [22]

SAMPLE STUDENT ANSWER

Abnormality is a concept that is hard to define due to differences in culture and time, but overall it is behaviour that is not deemed normal. A variety of factors come into play in abnormal behaviour or psychological disorders. Within this essay, major depressive disorder and PTSD will be discussed with regard to the extent to which biological factors influence the disorders. Major depressive disorder is an affective disorder, which according to Kessler (2003) has a lifetime prevalence of 23.1% in women and 12% in men. Post-traumatic stress disorder, or PTSD, is an anxiety disorder which according to Davidson (2007) affects 15–24% of those exposed to trauma. Overall, this essay will argue that biological factors influence abnormal behaviour by laying a foundation that is vulnerable to stress.

In depression, some psychologists have suggested a genetic predisposition. Nurnberger (1985) found a 65% concordance rate of experiencing depression in monozygotic twins (who share 100% of the same DNA), but for dizygotic twins there was a 20% concordance rate. As a twin study was used, this study has some reliability and suggests a genetic predisposition. Caspi et al (2005) also studied genetic predisposition to depression based on a theory that a mutated 5-HTT gene could lead to the disorder. The researchers found that individuals with the mutation were more likely to experience depression after a stressful event. This study demonstrates a genetic predisposition, but researchers have criticized it as there are so many people with the mutation who are not depressed. Both of these studies suggest that individuals may have a predisposed vulnerability to disorder, which could then make the likelihood of becoming depressed more likely.

▲ The problem implied in the question is clearly delineated in the introduction by stating the main argument that will be defended throughout the essay.

▲ Very detailed knowledge is demonstrated.

▶ This essay follows the breadth approach: many examples are given from various aspects of the topic, with less detailed analysis of each aspect. It is an acceptable approach.

In both depression and PTSD, researchers have looked into the role of neurotransmission. Coppen (1967) suggested the serotonin hypothesis, claiming that depression is caused by low levels of the mood-altering neurotransmitter. This is supported by Janowsky (1991), who gave a drug to a group of participants to lower their serotonin levels. This led to suicidal thoughts, demonstrating how changes in serotonin could affect an individual's mood. This theory is heavily criticized as many psychologists claim they have never seen any strong evidence supporting it and that it is not possible to change serotonin levels in living humans. The theory has some flaws, but it could help to increase our understanding of depression.

In terms of PTSD, the neurotransmitter noradrenaline is often researched as it is secreted in stressful events, as demonstrated by Cannon's 1914 fight or flight theory. Geracioti (2001) investigated the role of noradrenaline and adrenaline by stimulating the adrenal gland of individuals with PTSD and a control group of people without the disorder. In the PTSD group, 40% experienced flashbacks and 20% had a panic attack. This did not occur in the control group. This study demonstrates how the neurotransmitters affect individuals with PTSD and can produce the presence of PTSD symptoms. The study offers insight into the role of noradrenaline, however, it does not necessarily suggest that it causes the disorder but rather triggers symptoms of it. The study has some ethical issues as it negatively affected a percentage of the sample, but it does have a cause-and-effect nature so it can be deemed reliable. It does not however truly reflect the nature of neurotransmission in real life. Both this study and Janowsky's demonstrate how biological factors may create a vulnerability to stress.

Biological factors lay the framework for an individual, potentially leaving the person vulnerable to stress. Sociocultural factors demonstrate how social stress can affect abnormal behaviour and build on biological factors. Brown and Harris (1976) found that working-class mothers in Britain were six times more likely to experience depression than middle-class mothers. Working-class mothers had a 24% rate of depression while middle-class ones had a 4% rate. This study demonstrates how social standing may affect the likelihood of becoming

▼ Evaluation is relevant but superficial. For example, claiming that some psychologists criticize a theory is not an effective evaluation point.

▲ Research is effectively used to support arguments. In fact, for every individual research study the student only explains the key, most relevant details that are important for the conclusion.

▶ The question is about biological factors. Considering other factors is acceptable to address the requirements of the command term ("to what extent"), but one must be careful to ensure that these other factors are used in the context of comparison to biological factors.

depressed, as the working-class mothers were more likely to experience stress due, for example, to having more children or being in poverty. The study only made use of British women, so the results may not be generalizable enough, but it could still apply to women in other cultures. The method required surveys and interviews, therefore the data may have been affected by the fact that the individual's own reflections were recorded.

Lower social positions can lead to more experiences of depressive moods as people in lower social positions are faced with more challenges. This is also seen in PTSD, where race and gender can affect the likelihood of having PTSD. Roysircar (2000) found that vets of different races had different rates of PTSD. Hispanic vets had a 27.6% prevalence rate, while black vets had a 20.6% rate and white vets had a 13% rate. This demonstrates how race can affect the likelihood of having a disorder. The individuals may have experienced racism and prejudice that made them more susceptible to PTSD.

Kamirer (2000) found that girls in Bosnia had a 75% prevalence rate of PTSD while boys had a 35% rate. He argued this was because of the fear of rape. Sociocultural factors leave individuals with different challenges and can make them more vulnerable to a disorder as a result. Working-class mothers, people of colour and girls, according to these studies, are more vulnerable and more likely to become depressed or have PTSD. This demonstrates how sociocultural factors influence abnormal behaviour.

Cognitive factors also play a role in influencing depression and PTSD. Beck (1976) suggested that depression is caused by the negative thinking triad, consisting of negative thought about the self, the world and the future. Negative thinking can influence depression, but is depression caused by negative thinking or is it a symptom of the disorder? Alloy et al (1999) conducted a longitudinal study where a group of young adults were assigned to a positive thinking group or a negative thinking group. Six years later they were reassessed. It was found that in the negative thinking group, 17% had become depressed while in the positive thinking group, only 1% became depressed. The study demonstrates a potential link between negative thinking and the likelihood of being depressed.

▼ The connection between these other factors and biological factors is made to some extent, but not always explicitly. Sometimes sociocultural and cognitive factors are considered on their own outside of the context of biological factors.

In PTSD, Brewin suggested that the disorder is affected by cue-dependent memory, where cues to the stressor can trigger symptoms such as flashbacks. It has also been found that differences in attribution can affect abnormal behaviour. Child abuse victims who see that their abuse was not their own fault are more likely to recover from PTSD. The way we think affects abnormal behaviour to a large extent, but is abnormal behaviour caused by faulty cognitions or are faulty cognitions a result of the abnormal behaviour? It can be argued both ways but either way it is evident that cognitive factors influence behaviour. It is difficult to determine the factors that have the greatest influence on abnormal behaviour when it comes to disorders such as major depressive disorder and PTSD. Abnormality itself is difficult to define. Overall, however, it can be argued that biological factors play a role in building a foundation that leads to vulnerability to stressors. Biological factors create a framework that can then be affected by sociocultural or cognitive factors. Sociocultural factors lead to a social vulnerability, where people are presented with more challenges that can increase their likelihood of gaining a disorder. Cognition affects symptoms of the disorder and is affected by biological and sociocultural factors. To conclude, the main influence of biological factors on abnormal behaviour is creating a genetic vulnerability to potential stressors, for example social challenges such as race, and increasing the likelihood of developing a psychological disorder.

▲ The conclusion partially restores the focus on biological factors and more explicitly explains their role in relation to other factors.

**This response could have achieved 19/22 marks.**

**Focus on the question:** 2/2. The essay identifies and explains the problem implicit in the question. The focus is mostly sustained throughout the essay, and although there is a digression into a discussion of cognitive and sociocultural factors, they are related to the requirements of the question in the conclusion.

**Knowledge and understanding:** 6/6. The essay demonstrates clear knowledge and understanding with lots of detail. Terminology is used abundantly and appropriately in various contexts.

**Use of research to support answer:** 5/6. Research is used to support relevant arguments and is not repetitive. Research results are clearly linked to conclusions, and conclusions are related to the essay question and used to develop the argument. However, research could also be used more effectively to support various sides of the argument as to why biological factors do or do not influence abnormal behaviour (for example, diathesis-stress model, niche-picking, adoption studies).

**Critical thinking:** 4/6. Critical thinking is visible in the essay through an outline of the key limitations of research studies as well as clear links of research evidence to generalized inferences. However, critical thinking could be further developed by presenting other aspects of the nature-nurture debate in abnormal behaviour, and the evaluation of studies and theories could be better developed.

**Clarity and organization:** 2/2. The answer is clear and well organized, with every paragraph clearly focused on one key argument and its empirical support (alternating between depression and PTSD).

## ERQ example 2

QUESTION PRACTICE

To what extent is diagnosis valid and/or reliable?      [22]

SAMPLE STUDENT ANSWER

Reliability of diagnosis can be described as the consistency of diagnoses made by clinicians when using the same classification systems on the same patient. It can also be referred to as inter-rater reliability. There are two main methods by which inter-rater reliability can be established: test-retest method and audio/visual recording. The test-retest method allows multiple psychologists to interview the same patient independently, and come to a diagnosis afterwards. Audio/visual recording on the other hand involves only one clinician interviewing a patient and sending this recording to another clinician, where both will diagnose the patient individually. Over time, both methods have been used in classification systems such as the DSM, although in later editions the test-retest method has been favoured as it is more representative of real-life behaviours. When looking at the evolution of the DSM, it is important to understand that reliability has increased over time, although still varies greatly from one diagnostic category to another. Despite this, reliability in diagnosis has improved to an extent and this is shown in various research studies using different editions of the DSM that highlight this improvement. Another point of consideration is that validity and reliability are inversely related: when reliability increases, validity will often decrease. This is because in order to increase reliability, symptoms were made more observable, hence leaving less room for consideration of an individual's subtle differences and compromising validity. But by creating more structured and observable classification systems, overall reliability has been maximized as of now (though there is still much room for improvement).

▲ Clear knowledge of concepts and terminology is demonstrated.

▲ This introductory section clearly explains several problems with reliability of diagnosis in conceptual terms. These are the main arguments that will be later supported by research.

Firstly, reliability of diagnosis became strengthened as a result of introducing structured procedures. For example, the creation and implementation of the Structured Clinical Interview for the DSM allowed for DSM-III to have higher reliability than its predecessors. This was because misdiagnosis was prevalent in both DSM-I and II, so reliability was therefore shockingly low. In Kendall's study, psychiatrists were required to rediagnose patients with either schizophrenia or depression. As there was no structured or clear manner in approaching diagnosis at the time, many of the psychiatrists misdiagnosed patients who had depression with schizophrenia and vice versa, demonstrating low reliability as consistency was very low. Moreover, misdiagnosis with these two disorders should not have been prevalent, as they are very distinct and have different symptoms. As a result of this, the Structured Clinical Interview was released to go hand in hand with the DSM III to increase the reliability of diagnosis. By ensuring clinicians approached diagnosis in the same way universally, reliability would improve, as the same questions would be asked to patients and less freedom would be given to clinicians to create confounding variables or variation in their interviews.

Despite reliability having improved after implementing more structured approaches to diagnosis, it still varies largely between different diagnostic categories. This was highlighted by Di Nardo et al, who found that correlation was higher in disorders such as OCD in comparison to others including MDD. To explain this phenomenon of the decreased consistency of diagnosis of some categories, Williams demonstrated that only disorders where symptoms were highly observable would have increased inter-rater reliability. For example, social phobia was shown to have a low correlation of 0.47 whereas GAD had one over 0.8, because symptoms could be more observable to psychiatrists attempting to diagnose their patients. This demonstrates that although reliability of diagnosis is relatively good (having improved over time), there are still areas that can be improved, such as finding ways in which all diagnostic categories can have increased inter-rater reliability and ensuring that diagnosis is reliable across all disorders.

Furthermore, diagnosis is reliable depending on what method of distinguishing inter-rater reliability is used. When solely

▲ Evaluation of research and critical thinking about reliability in diagnosis are built into the flow of arguments. The candidate chose to present research chronologically from old to new editions of the DSM, presenting the main limitations of each stage and discussing how these challenges were addressed in later editions.

▲ Research clearly supports the arguments, and the arguments themselves are not repetitive.

seeking to achieve a high correlation, audio/visual recording is the suitable approach to take. This is because psychiatrists are able to experience the same situation (and hence behaviour) of the patient to come to a diagnosis. By being subjected to the same behaviour, consistency of diagnosis will increase as similar symptoms may be picked up by the psychiatrists. Therefore, audio/visual recordings may indicate that diagnosis is reliable to a high extent, because clinicians are offering more consistent diagnoses. On the other hand, test-retest will not always portray diagnosis as reliable, because clinicians do not observe the same behaviours and may approach the interview with the patient in slightly different ways. As a result of this, reliability is often underestimated and if the test-retest method was used in diagnosis it would not always suggest high reliability (Chmielewsky: audio/visual recording had a 0.8 correlation, test-retest had a 0.4 correlation.)

> ▲ Sufficient knowledge of research is shown. The selection of research supports the development of the main argument related to reliability of diagnosis.

Having said this, just because the correlation might be higher does not necessarily mean reliability of the diagnosis is better. This is because the audio/visual recording method is much more artificial than the test-retest method and therefore results are not representative of a real-life situation, where symptoms and behaviours may change over time. Therefore, the more recent DSM editions use the test-retest method to measure inter-rater reliability, as it reflects real-life symptoms in a patient much better. To say that reliability is low because of this would be wrong (in the case for DSM-5), because the diagnosis obtained would be a more realistic representation of what the disorder is in real life.

> ▲ Critical thinking is shown through consideration of the key challenges in assessing reliability of diagnosis.

Overall, it can be concluded that despite there being fluctuations in reliability of diagnosis in varying diagnostic categories, reliability as a whole has increased greatly over time as demonstrated in the DSM editions and studies based on them. The extent to which diagnosis is reliable is high, although it can be agreed that there is still room for improvement.

**This response could have achieved 19/22 marks.**

**Focus on the question:** 2/2. The essay is clearly focused on the question, making references to the concept of reliability of diagnosis at various key points. The problem is explained and each aspect of the explanation is unpacked.

**Knowledge and understanding:** 5/6. The essay shows clear knowledge and understanding. Terminology is used effectively in appropriate contexts. Sufficient details of supporting research are reported, but further detail could be discussed.

**Use of research to support answer:** 5/6. Although supporting research is not explained in great detail, the selection of supporting research is effective. The argument in the essay is organized chronologically, and when the main challenges and limitations of each stage are discussed, a research study is used that is relevant to this stage and illustrates it appropriately. In this way, research in the essay is clearly used to support the developing argument.

**Critical thinking:** 5/6. Critical thinking is evident from the way research evidence is linked to the conceptual level (the concept of reliability of diagnosis). Different aspects of the problem are considered, giving a holistic account of it. In terms of evaluation of research, diverse points are mentioned.

**Clarity and organization:** 2/2. The essay is clear and effectively organized.

# 6 DEVELOPMENTAL PSYCHOLOGY

## 6.1    BRAIN DEVELOPMENT

There are four linked physiological processes in the course of brain development: neurogenesis, migration, differentiation and pruning. Neurogenesis is the birth of new cells. Migration is when newly formed cells travel to pre-designated positions in the brain. Differentiation is developing new synaptic contacts, and pruning is the opposite process of eliminating synaptic connections that are not being used.

Developmental neuroscience studies show the biological process of brain development corresponds to changes in behaviour and cognition. This is a challenging task because there are many confounding variables that are impossible to separate from one another. In broad terms this is known as the problem of structure-function relationships. The problem is to investigate how changes in the structure of the brain, in the course of human development, affect corresponding changes in behaviour and cognition. If structural and functional changes coincide in time, this may be taken to mean that brain development and cognitive development are related.

However, making such inferences from empirical research is extremely difficult for several reasons. First, the evidence is correlational. To establish cause-effect relationships, one needs to manipulate brain development and observe the effects on cognitive development, but a research study like that would be entirely unethical.

Second, even if we observed a correspondence between brain development and cognitive development, there could be multiple explanations for this, such as: a coincidence, brain development influencing cognitive development (maturation), cognitive development influencing brain development (neuroplasticity) and so on.

Additionally, localization of function can change over time, making inferences along the lines of "development of brain area X is responsible for development of behaviour Y" extremely difficult. The only way to eliminate alternative explanations is the triangulation of evidence from multiple studies and sources of data.

### >> COMMON ERRORS

The content heading "Brain development" is not to be confused with the content heading "Cognitive development". Cognitive development is the development of cognitive functions (such as memory, thinking and decision-making), while brain development is the biological process of the maturation of brain structures.

### 🔍 KEY RESEARCH STUDIES

- Chugani (1999): investigating brain development in the first year of life and comparing it to corresponding changes in infant behaviour.

- Werker *et al* (1981): a study of Hindi phoneme discrimination in infants; evidence of pruning.

- Kolb and Fantie (1989): a study of the development of linguistic skills; an example of triangulation of evidence from multiple sources.

# 6.2 COGNITIVE DEVELOPMENT

It is now widely recognized that children are not just "small adults", and that children undergo certain stages of cognitive development where their intelligence is qualitatively different from that of adults. Scientists have attempted to create theories that describe the stages through which children progress (what happens, when and how?) as well as explain what drives cognitive development (why?).

Two of the most prominent theories in this area are the theories of Jean Piaget and Lev Vygotsky.

Piaget viewed cognitive development as a type of adaptation, within which he differentiated two processes: assimilation (changing one's perception of the world to better fit into already existing schemas) and accommodation (changing the existing schemas to better fit the world). According to his theory, children progressively move through a series of clear-cut stages in their cognitive development.

The stages are: sensorimotor stage (birth to 2 years), pre-operational stage (2–7 years), concrete operational stage (7–11 years) and formal operational stage (11–16 years). Each stage is characterized by age-specific cognitive phenomena. For example, the pre-operational stage is characterized by centration, irreversibility, lack of conservation and cognitive egocentrism. Piaget believed that progression from one stage to the next is driven predominantly by biological maturation.

The theory is supported by a large number of research studies that exposed children of varying ages to typical tasks and noted at what age children acquire the ability to solve these tasks. For example, the "three mountains task" was designed as a measure of cognitive egocentrism.

Vygotsky's sociocultural theory views cognitive development as a process of internalizing culture. Vygotsky draws a distinction between lower-order cognitive functions (such as rote memorization, involuntary attention, basic forms of reasoning) and higher-order cognitive functions (such as semantic memory, voluntary attention regulation and abstract reasoning). He admits that lower-order cognitive functions may be predominantly influenced by biological maturation, but higher-order cognitive functions are influenced by social and cultural variables to a much larger extent. According to his theory, every psychological function appears first in interpersonal communication between the child and someone else (for example, the parent), and then gets gradually internalized and becomes intrapersonal. For example, external control (when a parent tells the child what to do and what not to do) gradually becomes self-control.

Vygotsky views the role of education quite differently from Piaget. For Piaget, the role of education is to support the natural maturation process. For Vygotsky, education is the leading factor of development, and for this reason education must always stay one step ahead of development. In relation to this, he coined the terms "more knowledgeable other", "zone of proximal development" and "scaffolding". This has been widely used in the design of educational programmes (including the IB).

▲ Figure 6.2.1 Interpersonal communication is an important element of Vygotsky's theory

## 🔍 KEY RESEARCH STUDIES

- Piaget and Inhelder (1956): the three mountains task, demonstrating children's cognitive egocentrism.

- Borke (1975): a replication of Piaget and Inhelder (1956), demonstrating that a change in instruction can lead to a different result.

- Leontyev (1931): a study demonstrating the zone of proximal development for schoolchildren in a memorization task.

- Nedospasova (1985): a study demonstrating that interaction with a "more knowledgeable other" leads to a faster cognitive development in children.

# 6.3 DEVELOPMENT OF EMPATHY AND THEORY OF MIND

Empathy and theory of mind are interrelated. Empathy is the ability to experience what another person is experiencing. It has both cognitive and emotional components. Theory of mind is a purely cognitive ability. However, it is wider than empathy because it includes a wider range of cognitive abilities; most notably, understanding intentions, understanding perspectives and understanding false beliefs. Theory of mind is the cognitive ability to attribute mental states (such as beliefs and intentions) to others. It is a prerequisite of many other important human abilities, such as understanding deception or being able to navigate complex social situations.

Animal studies provide an insight into theory of mind. Research with higher apes shows that they can understand both intentions and false beliefs, although this conclusion comes with certain reservations. With pre-linguistic creatures we cannot ask them how they understand the intentions of others, so we must infer this from their observable behaviour. But it is difficult to separate behaviour that builds upon understanding of intentions from behaviour that builds upon a simple reproduction of previous experience. For example, if a chimpanzee selects the picture of a key in response to seeing a video of a person trying to get out of a locked cage, is that because the chimpanzee (a) understands the intention of the person is to get out, or (b) simply remembers from previous experience that the key is used when the cage is locked? Eliminating one of these explanations has required the design of novel research procedures, such as the "rational imitation paradigm".

Another aspect of researching theory of mind in pre-linguistic creatures is using modern technology such as eye-tracking. It appears that conclusions are different depending on whether the study uses eye-tracking or simple observation. For example, the ability of chimpanzees to understand false beliefs could be discovered only once researchers started using eye-tracking to measure their anticipatory behaviour.

Research with human children shows that children develop an understanding of intentions and an understanding of false beliefs by roughly the age of four years. Autistic children do not pass theory of mind tests as successfully as others, which points to the central role of this cognitive ability in autism.

## >> COMMON ERRORS

If you use animal research in your essay, you should make sure that you thoroughly discuss the possibility of applying the findings to human behaviour and development. It would be better to use a mixture of animal and human studies, especially because many of them are, in a sense, "parallel" to each other. For example, Buttelman *et al* (2007) and Meltzoff (1995) use a similar experimental procedure, one with chimpanzees and one with human children.

## 🔍 KEY RESEARCH STUDIES

- Premack and Woodruff (1978): a study of understanding intentions in chimpanzees.

- Buttelman *et al* (2007): a study with the same purpose, using the rational imitation paradigm.

- Krupenye *et al* (2016): an eye-tracking study to understand false beliefs in chimpanzees.

- Meltzoff (1995): investigating the ability of human children to understand the intentions of others.

- Baron-Cohen, Leslie and Frith (1985): investigating the ability of human children to understand false beliefs (Sally-Anne task).

- Ruffman, Garnham and Rideout (2001): the Sally-Anne task coupled with eye-tracking on normal children and children with autism.

This content heading is one of the three exceptions to the rule that any content connected by "and" cannot be decoupled.

In this particular case, "gender identity and social roles" can be decoupled in exam questions. This means that the question may refer to gender identity only, or to social roles only, or to both.

Social roles are societal expectations regarding someone's behaviour based on his or her social group membership. For example, you belong to the social group of "students", and there are certain expectations in society regarding how you should behave (that is, your social role of a student). Gender roles are a type of social role based on gender group membership.

Identity is an internalized social role. When social expectations get internalized, they become a part of who you are, and you start not only conforming to these expectations, but defining yourself in terms of these roles. Gender identity is one's self-perception as male, female or something else.

Various factors influence the development of gender identity: biological, cognitive and sociocultural.

An example of a biological factor playing a role in the formation of gender identity is sex-determining hormones, such as testosterone. It was demonstrated in research that prenatal exposure to abnormal levels of sex-determining hormones results in sex-atypical behaviour when the child is born and as the child grows up. However, an identity reversal was never observed. This leads us to conclude that biological factors influence but do not fully determine gender identity.

▲ Figure 6.4.1 Being in sex-segregated groups leads to behaviour that is more sex-typical

Cognitive factors of gender identity include self-perception, gender constancy and gender labelling – all characteristics of how we cognitively process the world. Two prominent theories in this area – Kohlberg's gender developmental theory and Bem's gender schema theory – disagree on two main questions: what is the trigger of gender identity, and what is the mechanism of development of gender identity? According to Kohlberg, the trigger of gender identity is the idea of gender constancy, and the mechanism is cognitive dissonance. By contrast, in Bem's theory the trigger of gender identity is gender labelling, and the mechanism is schematic processing.

Social factors in the development of gender identity include gender socialization by peers and gender socialization by parents. Gender socialization by parents may occur either through direct instruction or vicarious learning. Gender socialization by peers depends on how sex-segregated the peer groups are. In sex-segregated groups there are fewer opportunities to interact with the opposite gender, so the behaviour of children in such groups tends to be more sex-typical.

## 🔍 KEY THEORIES AND RESEARCH STUDIES

- Kohlberg (1966): cognitive developmental theory.

- Slaby and Frey (1975): a study showing that children with high scores on gender constancy prefer paying attention to same-sex adult models (supports Kohlberg).

- Bem (1981): gender schema theory.

- Martin (1989): a study demonstrating that rigid information processing based on gender schemas is a consequence of simple gender labelling (supports Bem).

- Draper and Cashdan (1988): gender identity in the children of !Kung bushmen (foraging groups versus farming groups).

- Mead (1935): an anthropological study of three tribes in Papua New Guinea.

- Whiting and Edwards (1973): a qualitative cross-cultural study of gender roles of children in relation to household chores.

# 6.5    ATTACHMENT

▲ **Figure 6.5.1** Harlow's research involved giving rhesus monkeys artificial surrogate mothers

Attachment is an emotional bond between an infant and a caregiver. Attachment is associated with a specific complex of behaviours, such as separation distress and seeking physical contact with the caregiver in a situation of danger.

At first, attachment behaviours were seen as a result of an association between the caregiver and food. This was challenged by Harry Harlow, who conducted an ethically ambiguous series of studies with rhesus monkeys and suggested an alternative explanation for attachment behaviour: contact comfort. Contact comfort is the state of physical and emotional comfort that the infant experiences when in contact with the caregiver.

Additionally, Harlow's research suggests that attachment provides a "secure base" for the organism to undergo cognitive development. This is known as the secure base hypothesis. According to this hypothesis, if attachment is not fully formed, the baby will not feel secure enough to explore the surrounding environment and as a result – in the long term – will suffer slow cognitive development.

## KEY THEORIES AND RESEARCH STUDIES

- Lorenz (1935): research with geese on imprinting.

- Harlow (1958): "The nature of love" studies with rhesus monkeys; contact comfort hypothesis was tested in experiment 1 and secure base hypothesis was tested in experiment 2.

- Bowlby (1958): psychological theory of attachment.

- Ainsworth *et al* (1978): research using the "strange situation paradigm"; discovery of attachment styles.

- Schaffer and Emerson (1964): an observational longitudinal study of attachment with 60 babies from Glasgow.

- Van Ijzendoorn and Kroonenberg (1988): cross-cultural meta-analysis of studies using the "strange situation paradigm".

- Shaver and Hazan (1988): a study of adult patterns of attachment in connection with infant attachment styles.

## ›› COMMON ERRORS

If you use animal research in a response, make sure you discuss the possibility of applying the findings to understanding human behaviour and development.

Harlow's research triggered important changes in childcare (in particular in orphanages), but it was also heavily criticized on the grounds of generalizability and ethics.

The first attempts to generalize these findings to humans can be found in the work of John Bowlby, who developed a theory of attachment consisting of two components: the attachment behavioural system (a biological component) and the internal working model (a cognitive component). He also suggested that there is a critical period in the formation of attachment, and if it is not formed during this period then it will never be formed. Initially he suggested the first two and a half years of life as the critical period, but he then extended this up to five years.

Bowlby's student Mary Ainsworth designed a research procedure known as the "strange situation paradigm" and used it to investigate attachment styles in human infants. This led to identifying three key attachment styles: secure attachment, insecure avoidant and insecure ambivalent. Later these attachment styles were investigated in cross-cultural contexts, and it was shown that intercultural variability of attachment styles is smaller than intracultural variability. Attachment styles probably differ more with socio-economic status than with culture.

Quite strong links were demonstrated between attachment styles in infancy and attachment styles that adults prefer in romantic relationships later in life. This shows that the effects of attachment in infancy are long-lasting and, to some extent, irreversible. This research, however, is mainly correlational and retrospective.

Play is a very complex behaviour and as such it goes through a series of stages in its development. Immature forms of play are especially interesting because they allow us to understand what components contribute to play. Development of play goes through three main stages.

- The first stage is object manipulation, which is predominant roughly at ages 1–2. The child's attention at this stage is grabbed by objects and their properties (colours, textures, tactile qualities).

- The next stage is pretend play, which is fully formed around ages 3–5. Here the object gradually stops being important and the focus is shifted to its function or the social meaning behind it.

- The next key stage is play with rules (ages 6–7). At this stage rules of social interaction become the focus of attention; play becomes very complex and involves many players. Examples include "cops and robbers" or sport games.

▲ **Figure 6.6.1** Object manipulation is the first stage of development of play

The role of peers in development was viewed differently in the theories of Piaget and Vygotsky. For Piaget, the key component of peer interaction that matters for cognitive development is constant perspective-taking. Through peer interaction, children realize that their perspectives may be different from the perspectives of others, and this uncomfortable realization causes them to explore problems more deeply. Piaget also thought that perspectives of peers are more influential than perspectives of adults because peers are more relatable. In contrast, Vygotsky believed that development is triggered when a child interacts with a more knowledgeable other – someone who is more competent in a certain situation. This could be an adult or another child; what matters is that this person is more knowledgeable.

Both these views have been empirically supported to some extent. For example, it was shown that children's moral development at ages 6–9 progresses faster when they are engaging in a discussion with peers rather than an adult. This supports Piaget's views. At the same time, it was shown that playing with a more knowledgeable other can also speed up the process of cognitive development. For example, cognitive egocentrism is overcome more easily.

As far as the influence of peers on social development is concerned, peer interaction is important for the development of perspective-taking and theory of mind. Perhaps for this reason it has been demonstrated in research that a lack of peer interaction in childhood may result in poor social adjustment in adulthood.

## 🔍 KEY RESEARCH STUDIES

- Damon and Killen (1982): developing of moral reasoning in children who have a chance to compare peer perspectives (supports Piaget).

- Nedospasova (1985): cognitive egocentrism in children who interact with a more knowledgeable other (supports Vygotsky).

- Sylva, Bruner and Genova (1976): object manipulation in the process of play and its relation to cognitive development.

- Andersen and Kekelis (1986): development of language in blind children in the process of interaction with siblings versus parents (supports Piaget).

- Suomi and Harlow (1975): long-term effects of a lack of interaction with peers in rhesus monkeys.

- Hollos and Cowan (1973): social and cognitive development in children who grew up on isolated farms in Norway.

## ≫ COMMON ERRORS

Piaget and Vygotsky had different perspectives on the role of peers and play in human development, and this can be effectively used in essays. However, do not be tempted to provide general descriptions of Piaget's and Vygotsky's theories, such as describing Piaget's stages of cognitive development (sensorimotor, pre-operational, concrete operations, formal operations). This should be avoided, and focus should be maintained in the essay on the role of peers and play.

# 6.7 CHILDHOOD TRAUMA AND RESILIENCE

This content heading is one of the three exceptions to the rule that any content connected by "and" cannot be decoupled.

In this particular case, "childhood trauma and resilience" can be decoupled in exam questions. This means that the question may refer to childhood trauma only, or to resilience only, or to both.

Trauma is an emotionally painful experience that has long-lasting effects on an individual's development and well-being. The same experience may cause trauma in one person but not in another person, depending on the individual's vulnerability and perception. Likewise, even a seemingly neutral experience may be traumatic to an individual if the person is vulnerable.

Conceptually, trauma is closely linked to deprivation. A traumatic event may be a one-time occurrence, but deprivation is continuous exposure to adverse conditions. Deprivation may be less acute, but due to its prolonged action it is no less traumatic. That is why the concepts of trauma and deprivation are often studied together.

Resilience is the ability to recover from the adverse effects of traumatic situations. In other words, it is the ability to resist trauma and deprivation and "bounce back" after a period of adversity.

The effects of deprivation on development are especially visible when deprivation occurs during a critical period. The effects of deprivation during critical periods are not easy to study due to ethical reasons. The two sources of information we have are animal studies, where animals are intentionally deprived during a period of their early life (also strongly criticized for ethical reasons), and case studies of human children who were raised in severely deprived conditions. Such studies seem to suggest that deprivation in the critical period irreversibly damages psychological development.

The most widely researched effect of trauma on human development is PTSD (post-traumatic stress disorder).

Despite the fact that the effects of trauma (such as PTSD) have been demonstrated to be deep and long-lasting, human children also have considerable potential for resilience. The resilience of children has been shown to depend to a large degree on the resilience of their parents. For example, children who are exposed to war experiences and yet react resiliently usually have more resilient parents who make themselves available to the emotional needs of their child. Another reason parents' resilience contributes to the resilience of their children is vicarious reinforcement: children observe parents' model behaviour and learn from it, especially while going through a traumatic experience.

## 🔍 KEY RESEARCH STUDIES

- Case studies of children who suffered prolonged language deprivation at an early age: the case of Genie (Curtiss *et al* 1974), the case of Anna (Davis 1947), the case of Isabelle (Mason 1942).

- Bowlby (1944): the "44 thieves" study of maternal deprivation (interviews with juvenile thieves).

- Rutter *et al* (1998): a study of developmental progress among Romanian orphans adopted before two years of age.

- Koluchová (1976): a case study of failure to form an attachment, also known as the "Czech twins" case study.

- Fieldman and Vengrober (2011): a study investigating PTSD symptoms and resilience in children living in the Gaza Strip and exposed to war trauma.

- McFarlane (1987): a study of children in families who were affected by devastating Australian bushfires in 1983.

- Betancourt *et al* (2013): a study of resilience and social readjustment in former child soldiers in Sierra Leone.

Whether or not poverty has an effect on cognitive and social development is not debatable – it does. Other research questions are of much larger significance.

- What exactly is the influencing factor? Is it low family income or one of the multiple factors associated with it (such as living in a criminal neighbourhood, a higher prevalence of mental disorders in parents, poor parenting skills and so on)?

- Do the effects of poverty on development depend on the timing of poverty episodes?

- Are the effects of poverty on development reversible?

Poverty is a complex combination of factors, and it is important to know which factor precisely is the main trigger of developmental problems. There are two main viewpoints.

- The family stress model asserts that the main factor ("pathway") of poverty is interpersonal interaction between parents and children.

- The investment model claims that the main factors are those associated with material goods, for example nutrition, educational opportunities and enriched environments.

It is not an easy task to isolate the effects of family income from other associated variables. Two main methods that can be used for this purpose are the statistical separation of effects and natural longitudinal experiments.

In a statistical separation of effects, a correlational study is conducted and sophisticated statistical techniques are used to estimate the correlation between family income and cognitive development after the effects of other confounding variables are statistically removed. Research using this technique supports the investment model more than the family stress model.

In natural longitudinal experiments, researchers investigate populations where one of the groups suddenly changes their poverty status due to an external influence. Such studies confirm that family income (the amount of money in the family) has an effect on social development of children over and above the other associated variables.

Finally, in relation to the other two questions posed above, research has typically shown the following.

- Early episodes of poverty have a more profound and lasting effect on cognitive development of children than relatively late episodes.

- Effects of poverty on social development are more reversible than effects of poverty on cognitive development; the earlier the poverty episode occurs, the less reversible its effects.

## KEY RESEARCH STUDIES

**Statistical separation of effects**

- Dickerson and Popli (2016): the "UK Millennium Cohort Study"; a longitudinal study of 19,000 children.

**Natural longitudinal experiments**

- Costello *et al* (2003): the "Great Smoky Mountains" study; a study with Native American families that moved out of poverty due to the construction of a casino and the emergence of new jobs.

- Dahl and Lochner (2010): used the timing and location of tax credits to estimate the effects of higher income on children's achievement in poor families.

- Jacob and Ludwig (2007): investigated the effects of receiving housing vouchers on children's outcomes.

- Mani *et al* (2013): examined cycles of poverty among sugarcane farmers in Tamil Nadu.

# SAMPLE QUESTIONS

Below are two example ERQs that you might see on Developmental psychology. Read the sample student answers and the accompanying comments, which will help you to understand what the students have done well and what they could do better.

## ERQ example 1

**QUESTION PRACTICE**

Discuss biological and sociocultural approaches to understanding human development as a learner. [22]

**SAMPLE STUDENT ANSWER**

The development of a growing person is a complex, multi-determined process. We know that the factors driving human development can be categorized into biological, cognitive and sociocultural ones, and for a long time we have wanted to know which group of factors is the major/primary influence. For example, the old nature-nurture debate is essentially a question of whether biological factors play a larger role in development than environmental factors.

However, the problem with this debate is that it ignores the complex nature of development, where different factors influence each other in turn and the result is always an interplay of multiple factors. For example, nature may influence nurture through niche-picking, and nurture can influence nature through epigenetics. If research finds evidence of environmental influences on development, how do we know these environmental factors were not themselves the result of a genetic influence?

A related problem is that when it comes to empirical research, it has necessarily got to be reductionist in the sense that it must assume one factor to be the leading one. Otherwise research is not possible. The reason for this is that the key method of scientific research – the experiment – is a model of influence (where one variable influences another), but it cannot model interaction (where variables interact). We have to assume a one-way influence to do science.

This may be the reason why different influential theories of human development exist, each taking one of the factors as a starting point.

For example, Piaget's theory of cognitive development assumes that the leading factor of development is biological maturation

▲ The problem implied in the question is explicitly identified and explained. It is linked to the nature-nurture debate, and the debate itself is brought into question.

▲ The two major arguments proposed in the essay (that the nature-nurture debate does not account for a dynamic interaction of factors and that experiments are necessarily reductionist) are both rooted in TOK.

of the brain. Piaget believed that cognitive development is a kind of adaptation (again, a biological concept), manifesting itself either as assimilation or accommodation, depending on whether the child's schemas adapt to his or her experiences with the environment or vice versa. Piaget suggested that cognitive development occurs in a progressive series of stages, and much of his empirical effort was directed at describing these stages and defining their age brackets. Research took the form of a typical task that children only start solving correctly once they reach a certain age. From this, Piaget inferred the existence of a cognitive ability that gradually matures and becomes available to the child at that age.

An example of a supporting research study is Piaget and Inhelder (1956) with their three mountains task. In this study, a child was shown a 3D model of three mountains with various details scattered around the model. For example, there was a tree on one side and some snow on the opposite side. The researcher and the child sat opposite each other and the researcher asked the child to describe what he or she saw and what the researcher saw (What do you see from where you sit? Now what do I see from where I sit?). Piaget and Inhelder found that most children at the age of 4 are cognitively egocentric – they do not understand that what the researcher sees from his or her perspective is different from what they see.

Cognitive egocentrism was found to be overcome by ages 7–8, when most children passed the task successfully. Piaget and Inhelder concluded that cognitive egocentrism is characteristic of the pre-operational stage of cognitive development, and that children naturally grow out of it by age 7 when they enter the concrete operational stage. This study (just like any other typical study of Piaget and his team) does not directly test the idea that it is biological maturation that drives cognitive development. But this is a plausible inference from the results. How else can we explain the fact that children fail the three mountains task at a certain age, and then start passing it once they get older? They are not formally taught how to solve the task. They must share some common factor that explains why they are getting better at approximately the same rate – perhaps biological maturation.

▲ Rather than simply describing Piaget's theory, the essay is focused on the requirements of the question.

▲ Knowledge and understanding of supporting research is shown, although more details could be necessary for full marks on criterion B.

▲ Critical thinking is demonstrated through linking results of the research to the conceptual level of analysis in the essay.

But the same study can be looked at from a different perspective. Critics of the study said that young children could fail the task not because they lack a cognitive ability, but simply because the instruction is too difficult for them to understand. Borke (1975) replicated the three mountains task with some modifications, where he made the task more interesting/relatable to the children, and the instruction itself was easier to understand. Results showed that 4-year-old children consistently passed the three mountains task, suggesting that at age 4 they are no longer influenced by cognitive egocentrism. So which is it? Is the performance of children on the three mountains task the result of age (biological maturation) or experimental instructions (environmental influence)? Building on that, Nedospasova (1985) repeated the three mountains task, but this time scaffolding the instruction for children. Children started with a role-play where they had to assume the role of one of three dolls and say how many siblings the dolls had (These dolls are three sisters; imagine that you are this doll; how many sisters do you have? How many sisters does this other doll have?). Children were prompted until they answered correctly, which is when they moved on to similar but more abstract tasks (for example, replacing dolls with circles drawn on paper). After this short "pedagogical intervention", Nedospasova found that children successfully passed the classic three mountains task (at an age when they were not supposed to be able to do so, according to Piaget). In Nedospasova's study, the focus is on sociocultural influences – the interaction between the experimenter and the child. This interaction was happening in each one of Piaget's studies, too, but it was never the focus of Piaget's attention.

We must conclude that it is impossible to directly compare biological and sociocultural influences on cognitive development in a research study. Such conclusions are a matter of inference. One and the same study (such as the three mountains task) can be conducted from the biological perspective and from the sociocultural perspective. In the first case, researchers will emphasize age and commonality between children. In the second case, researchers will emphasize the interaction between the child and the experimenter (which is a sociocultural variable).

▲ Research studies are effectively selected to support different sides of the argument and demonstrate the key controversy (all three studies used the same procedure, but obtained the results differently and hence reached different conclusions). Research is used to develop the argument.

▲ The concluding remarks clearly link results of the research back to the problem outlined in the introduction.

Curiously, both approaches will result in data supporting either the biological or the sociocultural perspective.

It is probably the case that in reality both types of influences exist in a dynamic interaction with each other. They influence each other and even transform into each other (for example, through niche-picking a child may evoke different sociocultural influences). But when we conduct research, we must isolate one variable as the independent variable and manipulate it, and this is inevitably reductionist. Experiments cannot model interaction, only influence. For that reason, we have experiments that support biological maturation, and we have experiments (using the same procedure) that support sociocultural influences.

**This response could have achieved 21/22 marks.**

**Focus on the question:** 2/2. The answer is focused both on the question and the command term. The problem implicit in the question is clearly identified and explained. Additionally, the problem is clearly categorized in TOK terms.

**Knowledge and understanding:** 5/6. Knowledge and understanding of concepts is clearly demonstrated throughout the response. Research selected to support the answer is relevant and used correctly. However, there could be more details demonstrating knowledge related specifically to the problem of cognitive development (details of relevant theories and research studies).

**Use of research to support answer:** 6/6. Research is used to support the development of the argument at all times. Research is not used for the sake of using research. The three studies that are selected all use the same procedure (the three mountains task), but emphasize different independent variables (age versus interpersonal interaction between the child and the experimenter). This is an effective choice of research because it directly supports the key arguments made in the essay.

**Critical thinking:** 6/6. Critical thinking is demonstrated through precise analysis of concepts; linking the question to key debates in psychology (nature-nurture) and TOK concepts (reductionism); and analysing the limitations of theoretical approaches and individual research studies, with clear conclusions.

**Clarity and organization:** 2/2. The essay is clear and well organized.

## ERQ example 2

QUESTION PRACTICE

Contrast two theories of cognitive development.                          [22]

SAMPLE STUDENT ANSWER

▼ Vygotsky's theory of cognitive development is relevant, but the second theory is incorrectly identified. The "environmental theory" of cognitive development does not exist, and what the candidate probably refers to is simply the general idea that cognitive development may be influenced by environmental factors.

▼ There is no "environmental theory" of cognitive development, so the candidate cannot get credit for the second theory in the essay. Additionally, the case study of Genie demonstrates how deprivation may be a factor affecting development, but it does not really support any theory of cognitive development. For this reason, the case study of Genie is not relevant to the question.

There are two theories of human development that have been studied in class, which are the Vygotsky theory and the environmental theory. The two theories of cognitive development can be compared and contrasted with three studies: Genie, Merecheva and Nichols. Cognitive development is the development of memory, thinking and academic performance. The first theory, environmental theory in cognitive development, states that the environmental factor is an important factor that influences the cognitive development of an individual. The environment of an individual's childhood may affect their cognitive development. Genie is a great example to explain this theory. The study of Genie aimed to see if the environmental factor influences cognitive development and the formation of attachment. This study used several methods to investigate. Genie was found in a locked room, and tied with a potty chair. She got beaten for making any noise. She had almost zero development of cognitive ability to speak and think, and mental retardation (not clear if it is the result of abuse or natural). After she lived with researchers, she gradually formed some attachment with them and learned vocabulary. She could speak, but not grammatically correct sentences – having some cognitive development. The environment Genie grew up in was horrible, a closed world without any attachment to the outside world, tied to a potty chair, meaning that she could not walk properly. No one talked to her before she was found. As a result, her cognitive development was minimal. This study is supported by the environmental theory. The strength of the study is ecological validity and no demand characteristics, which makes the study and theory more reliable. The limitation is no cause-and-effect relationship, there may be other factors that can affect the result.

Another theory of cognitive development is Vygotsky's theory. It states that the social factor is an important factor in cognitive development. The brain gets motivated when having social interaction and pushes cognitive development. Merecheva and Nichols are two studies that can help to explain the theory. Merecheva is an experiment that aimed to compare the test performance of two groups of students. Independent variables are one group of students were assigned to study with their own computer, and the other group studied in a group. Dependent variable is the test performance. Two groups were studied for 5 weeks with each strategy, and after 5 weeks a test was done by students. The test results showed that those who studied in a group had better performance than those who studied individually. This supports Vygotsky's theory that the brain gets motivation when students study together in a group, and push to get more cognitive development. The strengths are cause and effect, since the research method of experiment has been used, and maximum control of the variables. The limitation is no ecological validity, since it has not happened in real life. Nichols is another study that can support Vygotsky's theory. It is a similar study to Merecheva. It aimed to see the influence of social factors in cognitive development. It used the research method of experiment. Independent variables are one group with a traditional teaching method and one group that studied in small groups. Two groups were assigned to study the same materials and get a test after 9 weeks to compare the test results. The results showed that students who studied in small groups scored higher than students who studied with traditional teaching methods. This result is similar to Merecheva and also shows the reliability of Vygotsky's theory. Students who studied in groups got motivation to get more cognitive development.

Two theories of cognitive development are the environment theory and the Vygotsky theory. The similarity is that both theories indicate the factors that influence cognitive development – one is environmental factor and another is social factor. Both theories have support from studies. The difference between the two theories is that different factors have been mentioned to influence cognitive development. The environment theory focused more on the environment of an individual's childhood. However, Vygotsky's theory focused on the social effect on the learning period.

Three studies are conducted by different researchers, in different countries and with different research methods (case study

▼ The theory is not sufficiently explained, and the link between the theory and the study is superficial.

▼ Some critical thinking is demonstrated in the essay, but this is limited to evaluating studies. The evaluation points are also repetitive.

▼ Two studies here are used to support the same argument.

▼ Some conclusions are not justified by the evidence.

▼ Requirements of the command term are explicitly addressed only in this paragraph. Similarities are not required and the discussion of differences is very superficial.

▼ There is a further attempt at evaluation, but the use of terminology is not appropriate here.

and experiment), and all supported by theories. One is the environment theory and one is Vygotsky's theory. Therefore, the method, researcher, data and theory triangulation have been achieved. Therefore the two theories and three studies are reliable. In conclusion, the two theories of cognitive development are the environment theory and Vygotsky's theory, explained by three studies: Genie, Merecheva and Nichols. The environment theory states that the environment of an individual's childhood influences the level of cognitive development. And Vygotsky's theory states that brains get motivation when they have social interaction, and it pushes to get higher levels of cognitive development.

**This response could have achieved 7/22 marks.**

**Focus on the question:** 0/2. The problem/issue raised in the question is not clearly identified. The essay is mostly focused on describing the two theories separately and providing empirical support for them. With the second theory not identified correctly, contrasting two theories becomes impossible.

**Knowledge and understanding:** 2/6. The response demonstrates very limited relevant knowledge and understanding. Psychological terminology is used, but with errors. Some terms are applied properly, but some other terms are applied in incorrect contexts. And while this incorrect use of terminology does not hamper understanding, it shows a lack of knowledge.

**Use of research to support answer:** 2/6. Limited relevant psychological research is used in the response. One of the three research studies used in the essay is irrelevant to the question. The other two research studies serve to repeat points already made. Conclusions in the studies are not justified by the results.

**Critical thinking:** 2/6. There is limited critical thinking and the response is mainly descriptive. Some evaluation and discussion is present, but it is superficial. Evaluation points, when present, are not linked to the requirements of the question.

**Clarity and organization:** 1/2. The answer demonstrates some organization and clarity, but this is not sustained throughout the response. There are many repetitions, especially at the end of the essay.

# 7 HEALTH PSYCHOLOGY

In discussing topics and content headings related to Health psychology, you are allowed to look at several health-related phenomena or focus on a single one, and both approaches are equally acceptable. The chosen health problems should come from the categories:

✔ stress
✔ addiction
✔ obesity
✔ chronic pain
✔ sexual health.

For this book we have chosen to focus mainly on obesity as a health problem. This is done in order to demonstrate a variety of conceptual understandings relevant to a single phenomenon. However, you should remember that other health problems may also be chosen.

## 7.1 BIOPSYCHOSOCIAL MODEL OF HEALTH AND WELL-BEING

The biomedical model of health reduced health to biological factors (if there is a health problem, there must be a specific biological reason causing it). In contrast, the biopsychosocial (BPS) model claims that health is multi-determined by biological, cognitive and sociocultural factors. In this sense, the biomedical model is a reductionist approach and the BPS model is a holistic approach to health and well-being.

Proposed by George Engel (1977), the BPS model emphasizes the interacting nature of the three broad determinants of health. For example, it is believed that patients' subjective experiences and interpretations are important because they can cause certain biological changes as well as trigger certain societal responses to illness. Similarly, the patient's social environment may be a major contributor to both biological factors and subjective suffering. The influence of psychological factors on biological symptoms is known as psychosomatic phenomena.

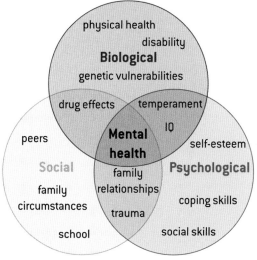

▲ Figure 7.1.1 The biopsychosocial model of health

The BPS approach emphasizes that the patient is responsible for the disease and can influence the disease through, for example, correctly interpreting the problem and selecting an appropriate lifestyle.

> Empirical evidence supporting the BPS model of health and well-being comes from two sources.

• Biological, psychological and social explanations of health problems are investigated. The more explanations that gain empirical support, the more obvious it becomes that health is multi-determined. For example, there is a considerable body of research on the influence of health beliefs (the psychological factor) on health-related behaviour.

- The effectiveness of treatment programmes designed on the principles of the BPS approach is investigated, as opposed to investigating the effectiveness of more traditional biomedical treatments.

As applied to obesity, the BPS model encourages researchers to investigate a variety of factors responsible for it. Biological factors of obesity include genetic predisposition. Cognitive factors of obesity may include a range of beliefs about eating behaviour, exercising and a healthy lifestyle. Social factors may include peer influence, availability of healthy food, culturally accepted lifestyles and so on. Additionally, it has been shown that treatment programmes based on the BPS model are more effective than their reductionist counterparts.

### 🔍 KEY RESEARCH STUDIES

- Nguyen *et al* (2017) on the effectiveness of the biopsychosocial approach to the treatment of obesity.

- Haworth *et al* (2008) on genetic determinants of obesity.

- Jokela *et al* (2012) on the relationship between dispositional factors (personality traits) and obesity.

- Rosenstock (1974) on the health belief model (HBM) of health, emphasizing cognitive variables as predictors of health behaviour.

- Curtis (2004) on some social determinants of obesity in the island states of Oceania.

### ≫ COMMON ERRORS

The focus in your exam responses should be on the holistic nature of interacting variables and not on listing multiple possible determinants of health. The idea that health is multi-determined is not limited to the statement "There are many various factors that influence health". This idea also implies the following.

- There is a complex interaction between these factors. For example, cognition may influence biology either directly (psychosomatics) or through sociocultural factors (health-related lifestyle).

- In a concrete research study it is impossible to study all the interacting variables at once, so research studies are necessarily reductionist and the BPS model is an overarching explanation rather than a concrete testable model.

- Treatments that take into consideration multiple interacting factors are more successful than treatments based on more reductionist approaches.

# 7.2 DISPOSITIONAL FACTORS AND HEALTH BELIEFS

This content heading is one of the three exceptions to the rule that any content connected by "and" cannot be decoupled.

In this particular case, "dispositional factors and health beliefs" can be decoupled in exam questions. This means that the question may refer to dispositional factors only, or to health beliefs only, or to both.

Dispositional factors and health beliefs are related to psychological explanations of health problems. Broadly speaking, psychological variables may be thought of as mediators between biological and environmental (sociocultural) determinants of health behaviour. Psychological variables determine how biological and environmental factors are perceived and interpreted. This influences health-related behaviours and lifestyles. Research into psychological determinants of health is also pertinent because these factors may be more easily changeable as compared to biological and environmental influences. For example, it is not possible to change one's genetic predisposition to obesity, and some social variables are equally not within a person's control. However, individuals may change their beliefs about having a healthy lifestyle and eating habits.

Dispositional factors (in the narrow sense of the term; that is, personality traits) contribute to health behaviour because they are stable characteristics that mediate a person's lifestyle, affecting life choices in a variety of ways. A popular model to describe personality traits is the "Big Five" model (openness to experience, conscientiousness, extraversion, agreeableness and neuroticism). One personality trait that has been pointed at in numerous research studies as being related to health behaviour is conscientiousness. Obesity is not an exception: conscientiousness has been investigated as a predictor of developing obesity over time.

Since many different beliefs may contribute to health-related behaviours, there is a need to develop an integrated model of health beliefs. A good model should be simple and at the same time should include the most essential variables that allow us to predict health-related behaviour successfully. Two most prominent attempts in this area are the health belief model (HBM) and the theory of planned behaviour (TPB). Both these models have been applied to obesity and proved reasonably effective in predicting obesity-related behaviour.

There is little doubt that cognitive variables such as health beliefs influence health behaviour. Debatable questions are as follows.

- What is the relative contribution of health beliefs to health behaviour as compared to biological and sociocultural factors?

- What exactly is the predictive power of health belief models (that is, what percentage of health behaviour can be predicted from cognitive variables alone)?

- Is this predictive power better in some areas of health behaviour and worse in other areas?

 **KEY THEORIES AND RESEARCH STUDIES**

**Models of health beliefs and their predictive validity**

- Rosenstock (1974): the health belief model (HBM).

- Deshpande, Basil and Basil (2009): an investigation of the predictive validity of the health belief model.

- Ajzen (1985): the theory of planned behaviour (TPB).

- Godin and Kok (1996), Baranowski *et al* (2003): the predictive validity and explanatory power of TPB in relation to a variety of health problems.

- Dunn *et al* (2011): using TPB to predict consumption of fast food.

**Personality factors as predictors of health problems**

- Jokela *et al* (2012): a meta-analysis on the link between personality traits and the risk of obesity.

- Sutin *et al* (2011): a longitudinal study on the personality traits most predictive of developing obesity over time.

- Kobasa and Greenwald (1979): hardiness as a personality factor protecting against the effects of stress.

- Friedman and Rosenman (1974): type A and type B personalities in connection to the risk of developing disease.

# 7.3 RISK AND PROTECTIVE FACTORS

Risk factors are factors that increase the chances of developing a disease or illness. Protective factors are factors that reduce such chances.

Risk and protective factors may come from all three categories: biological, cognitive and sociocultural. However, traditionally research in this field has focused on social variables (that is, something present in the individual's environment).

When studying risk and protective factors of health problems, it is important to be aware of the presence of confounding (mediating) variables. A mediating variable is something that strengthens or weakens the relationship between a risk or protective factor and health-related behaviour. Its influence may be so strong that the link between a risk or protective factor and a health-related behaviour actually disappears once you take into account the mediating variable.

An example of this is the influence of wealth on life expectancy. When looked at in isolation, being wealthier may be predictive of living a longer life, but this relationship disappears once you take into account using medical services. Using good medical services is the actual cause of longer life expectancy, and being wealthier just happens to correlate with using good medical services.

Since such variables exist, one needs to make a distinction between two types of research in this area:

- research correlating health behaviour with each potential risk and protective factor separately
- research investigating multiple risk and protective factors simultaneously and their interaction with each other.

The second approach allows researchers to have more unbiased estimates of the importance of risk and protective factors, but it is also much more complex and requires larger sample sizes, as well as the use of more sophisticated statistical techniques.

Research in obesity has identified a large number of both risk and protective factors. Among the relatively more obvious risk factors are: parental obesity, body dissatisfaction and low socio-economic status. Among the relatively more obvious protective factors are: regular physical activity, self-efficacy and a high intake of fruit and vegetables. However, research investigating multiple risk and protective factors simultaneously has also identified less obvious, "non-traditional" risk factors. For example, sleep duration was shown to be predictive of obesity.

## >> COMMON ERRORS

Remember that discussing risk and protective factors of a health problem is not the same as discussing sociocultural explanations of this problem. You should make sure to maintain the focus on risk and protective factors.

- Unlike sociocultural explanations, risk and protective factors may not be primary causes of a health problem; they merely influence the chance of its occurrence.

- There is the problem of confounding (mediating) variables in risk and protective factor research. It is pertinent because given the existence of a large number of risk and protective factors of a health problem, it is necessary to define their importance relative to each other.

## 🔍 KEY RESEARCH STUDIES

- Padez *et al* (2005): a study on family variables as risk and protective factors of obesity.

- Haines *et al* (2006): a longitudinal study on risk and protective factors of obesity in adolescence – the "Project EAT (Eating Among Teens)" study.

- Chaput (2009): a study of multiple interacting risk and protective factors of obesity (the "Quebec Family Study").

Commonly mentioned biological explanations of obesity are: genetic factors, hormonal factors (leptin and insulin) and patterns of brain activation.

Biological processes that have been linked to obesity point to the major role played by leptin: a hormone that signals fat to the brain. Leptin is also linked to a specific gene (the ob gene). This suggests a genetic predisposition to obesity; an expectation that has been confirmed in a number of research studies based on the idea of genetic similarity (for example, twin studies).

Investigation of the neurological basis of behaviours related to addiction has also revealed mechanisms that may explain such behaviours. One example is the activation of dopaminergic pathways (the brain reward system). Another example is the pattern of brain activation in response to food-related stimuli. Differences in such patterns between obese and non-obese individuals suggest that the "obese brain" reacts to food differently, although it is unclear if it is this reaction that causes the health problem or vice versa.

Cognitive explanations of obesity have included a wide range of cognitive variables, such as inhibitory control, subjective perception of one's own weight, perception of health risks, attitudes, perceived threat of the illness, perceived effectiveness of a health behaviour and so on. To handle this variety, researchers have suggested integrated models of health beliefs. Essentially, a health belief model is a system of cognitive variables that are deemed necessary and sufficient to predict a wide range of health-related behaviours. Among the most popular models of health beliefs are Rosenstock's (1974) health belief model (HBM) and Ajzen's (1985) theory of planned behaviour (TPB).

The explanatory power of these models has been investigated (and compared) in a variety of fields. Overall results suggest that a successful model of health beliefs can explain about one third of the observed variation in health-related behaviours. This suggests an important role of cognitive variables in health.

Social explanations of obesity have focused on such factors as a sedentary lifestyle and the consumption of added sugars. Sedentary lifestyles may be the result of better economic development and Westernization. Since food with added sugars tends to be cheaper, consumption of added sugars also links directly to an individual's socio-economic status. Apart from these two key social determinants of obesity, there is a large variety of additional social factors that either contribute to obesity or prevent it (thus becoming either risk or protective factors of obesity).

▲ **Figure 7.4.1** The consumption of added sugars is one social factor contributing to obesity

## KEY RESEARCH STUDIES

- Haworth *et al* (2008): a twin study on genetic inheritance of obesity.

- DelParigi *et al* (2005): a PET study on patterns of brain activation in response to food stimuli.

- Research on health beliefs and other cognitive variables: Craeynest *et al* (2008), Lewis *et al* (2010), Rosenstock (1974), Deshpande, Basil and Basil (2009), Ajzen (1985), Godin and Kok (1996), Baranowski *et al* (2003), Dunn *et al* (2011).

- Drewnowski (2004) on the relation between the cost of food and its energy density.

- Curtis (2004) on the obesity epidemic among island populations of Oceania.

See also research studies for the content headings "Dispositional factors and health beliefs" (page 125) and "Risk and protective factors" (page 126).

## >> COMMON ERRORS

Remember not to misinterpret "health problems" as mental health issues. This is not correct. The list of health problems acceptable for the IB Psychology course is given in the Subject Guide: stress, addiction, obesity, chronic pain and sexual health.

# 7.5 PREVALENCE RATES OF HEALTH PROBLEMS

Epidemiology is the study of the spread of diseases in populations. Several metrics are used to describe the spread, the most basic metric being morbidity – the percentage of a population that is affected by a disease. Morbidity includes incidence and prevalence. Prevalence is the percentage of a population that is experiencing a given health problem. Incidence is the percentage of previously healthy individuals that develop a health problem in a given period of time (for example, 1-year incidence). Incidence shows the rate at which a health problem is developing.

Epidemiological research depends considerably on the problem of thresholds: deciding on the exact criteria for classifying a health problem as present versus absent. For example, for obesity this takes the form of deciding on the cut-off BMI score. Individuals immediately after this cut-off point are classified as obese while those immediately before it are classified as non-obese.

This links to the issue of the validity of health problem indices. Is the index an adequate reflection of the health problem? For example, doubts have been raised that BMI is a good index for obesity. One argument is that there is no clear relationship between BMI and mortality.

Once we have selected an indicator of a health problem that we have reasons to believe is valid, and once we have selected and justified a cut-off score on this indicator, we face the task of reliably measuring prevalence and incidence of the health problem in a given population. This task is not without challenges either.

- We need to select a reliable source of data.

- We need to take into account potential biases. For example, a major problem is reporting bias. This may distort epidemiological data.

- We need to measure carefully epidemiological data in sub-groups. For example, prevalence and incidence of health problems might be very different in groups of males and females, as well as groups differing in culture, age, educational level and so on.

## 🔍 KEY RESEARCH STUDIES

- Hruby and Hu (2015), Nguyen and El-Serag (2010): prevalence of obesity.

- Pan *et al* (2011): incidence of obesity.

In line with the biopsychosocial model of health, it is reasonable to suggest that a successful health promotion programme will target multiple factors potentially influencing health behaviour. The idea that health promotion needs to target various layers of environmental determinants of health is known as the ecological approach to health promotion. The ecological approach addresses determinants of health on individual, interpersonal, organizational, community and policy levels.

- On an individual level, health promotion takes the form of changing a person's health beliefs and developing more constructive attitudes towards health and health-related behaviours. Practically this may be achieved in individual counselling sessions, however, this is of course dependent on whether or not people take initiative and seek counselling.

- On an interpersonal level, health promotion takes the form of social networking campaigns where interaction with other people encourages healthy lifestyles.

- On an organizational level, health promotion includes holistic campaigns affecting the daily functioning of an organization, such as installing exercise facilities at a workplace to promote physical activity and prevent obesity.

- On a community level, an example would be a mass media campaign promoting a healthy lifestyle or specific health-related behaviours (for example, daily exercise or getting a mammography done).

- Finally, on the level of national policy, health promotion may take the form of specific legislative acts, such as legislation for food labelling or taxation to make unhealthy food products less profitable to companies.

Below are some examples of health promotion programmes.

- The "Challenge!" health promotion model (Black *et al* 2010) is an example of a prevention initiative on the interpersonal level. It was a mentorship model of health promotion and obesity prevention among African-American adolescents, based on social cognitive theory. Participants were each paired with a mentor who accompanied them on trips to grocery stores and had regular meetings with them to discuss their attitudes and health beliefs. Research showed that the programme was effective in preventing weight gain and changing some unhealthy eating habits.

- An example of an organizational-level intervention is the World Health Organization's "Health Promoting Schools" (HPS) framework. Evaluation of the effectiveness of this programme produced mixed results. For example, acceptability of the programme was high but family involvement proved to be the weakest component.

- An example of a social marketing campaign to counteract obesity (on a community level) is the campaign "Canada on the Move". Step counters were disseminated in grocery stores in Canada. The campaign proved to be effective for the increase of daily physical activity (walking).

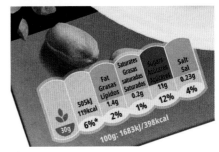

▲ **Figure 7.6.1** "Traffic light" food labelling was introduced in the UK to promote healthier choices

## KEY RESEARCH STUDIES

- Black *et al* (2010) on the effectiveness of the "Challenge!" health promotion programme.

- Langford *et al* (2015): evaluation of the "Health Promoting Schools" framework.

- Craig, Tudor-Locke and Bauman (2006) on the effectiveness of the "Canada on the Move" programme.

- Malterud and Tonstad (2009) on the common challenges in implementing anti-obesity prevention programmmes.

## >> COMMON ERRORS

Students sometimes address this content heading in the exam in a superficial manner by discussing healthy lifestyles. This is not correct. The focus must be on specific health promotion programmes.

# SAMPLE QUESTIONS

Below are two example ERQs that you might see on Health psychology. Read the sample student answers and the accompanying comments, which will help you to understand what the students have done well and what they could do better.

## ERQ example 1

**QUESTION PRACTICE**

Discuss ethical considerations relevant in the study of health problems.      [22]

**SAMPLE STUDENT ANSWER**

▼ The problem/issue raised in the question is identified but not sufficiently explained.

Ethical considerations in psychological research can be broadly divided into the following categories: ethical considerations when conducting the research, ethical considerations when reporting the findings and ethical considerations when applying the findings. They are all important in the study of health problems because they regulate how researchers go about obtaining data and then using it.

The study of health problems includes research into the determinants of health problems as well as research into their prevalence in a population. In this response I will focus on obesity as an example of a health problem.

In conducting a research study it is important to observe the following ethical considerations: protection from harm, confidentiality, informed consent, debriefing, opportunity to withdraw from participation and the use of deception.

▶ This section demonstrates clear knowledge of the range of ethical considerations involved in conducting a study as well as reporting and applying its results. However, it is not linked directly to the question (health problem). This makes the section marginally relevant.

In reporting the results of the study it is important to consider potential harmful effects for the participants from knowing this information. Results may be anticipated and incidental. It is ethical to foresee the kinds of results that can potentially be obtained in the study (both anticipated and incidental) and explain the strategy for dealing with such results in the informed consent form. For example, participants may be asked to agree explicitly that incidental findings not related to the original research question will not be shared with them. But even in this case, if incidental results are discovered that may be of vital importance to the individual (for example, a brain scan revealed a brain tumour), researchers may make the decision to share the result with the participant.

In applying the results of a study it is important to consider their credibility and generalizability. Making sweeping generalizations on the basis of a single research study to inform public policy is unethical because in this case people's lives are affected based on questionable evidence.

One research study that investigated biological determinants of obesity was Haworth et al (2008). This was a twin study where more than 5,500 same-sex pairs of twins were given questionnaires asking them about their height and weight. Based on that information their BMI index was calculated. Based on that, they were categorized as normal weight, overweight or obese. BMI correlations were further compared in pairs of monozygotic versus dizygotic twins. Researchers found that genetic inheritance could be used to explain up to 70% of the observed variation in BMI. This led them to conclude that BMI and obesity are genetically determined to a large extent.

The typical ethical considerations for conducting a study are applicable to this example. In a study like this, participants should be given informed consent, briefed and debriefed, and their data should be stored in an anonymized format. However, apart from the typical ethical protocol for any research study, no special requirements exist. Simply providing information on their height and weight does not hurt participants in any way, neither physically nor mentally. There are also no unique ethical considerations in reporting the individual results to participants. It is not likely that any potentially harmful information will be revealed incidentally. However, applying the results of the study does raise ethical concerns.

Essentially the conclusion of the study is that BMI and obesity are inherited (up to 70%). If such results are taken at face value and presented as an undeniable scientific fact, policy makers may misinterpret them to mean that health promotion programmes are ineffective and that there is nothing an individual can do to control his or her obesity. Such conclusions are harmful because they undermine the attempts to control obesity in the population by targeting environmental factors or cognitive factors (through changing people's health beliefs). For this reason, when results of this study are published in a peer-reviewed journal, ethical considerations dictate that

▼ The candidate jumps straight to the description of a research study. Clear knowledge is demonstrated, but the argument/conceptual understanding demonstrated by the study is not explained.

▲ This is a comprehensive analysis of ethical considerations in the context of the given research study. Critical thinking is demonstrated by discussing which ethical considerations are most relevant in this context and why.

▼ The discussion is limited to one individual research study, not to the field in general as requested by the question.

▲ A second example of research is given, and clear knowledge of research details is demonstrated.

▲ Once again, there is a comprehensive analysis of ethical considerations in the context of a particular research study. Critical thinking is shown through the application of generic ethical guidelines to specific research.

important limitations must be recognized and the degree of generalizability must be honestly described. For example, it must be recognized that what applied to the population of MZ and DZ twins does not necessarily apply to a wider population. Lewis et al (2010) investigated the influence of health beliefs on obesity. Participants in the study were around 150 Australian adults with moderate and severe obesity. Semi-structured telephone interviews were conducted. The interviews were transcribed and content analysis was conducted using the transcripts. In the process of content analysis, researchers identified emerging themes and compared these themes between groups of moderately and severely obese individuals. Important differences were identified in the participants' responses. For example, moderately obese participants believed that their weight is caused by environmental factors, while severely obese participants had a tendency to blame themselves. For moderately obese participants the main motivation to lose weight was social pressure, while for severely obese participants the main motivation was the medical risks that they recognized. Researchers concluded that there are differences in how moderately and severely obese individuals appraise the situation, and that these differences should be taken into account in health promotion programmes.

This study used quite a sensitive topic for the telephone interview. Questions on people's beliefs about the reasons and consequences of their obesity, the amount of control they have over it, and their healthy and unhealthy behaviours might be uncomfortable for participants and harm their self-esteem. For this reason it is important to have a detailed informed consent form that outlines the nature of the questions asked. Researchers should also make sure that participants finish the interview in a stable state of mind, on a positive note. Extra attention should be paid to allowing participants to withdraw any time during the interview, as well as to withdraw the results from the study database. Confidentiality is also an important issue in the context of this study. It should be clearly explained to participants how exactly their individual data will be used, and data should be stored in a way that makes it impossible to trace the responses back to individual participants.

At the same time, incidental findings are not an issue in the context of this particular study because it is unlikely that information previously unknown to the participant will be discovered in the course of the interview.

Overall, as we have seen, the study of health problems has a number of important ethical considerations to be taken into account. Which of the ethical considerations are most relevant depends on the context of a particular research study. However, the most common ones are linked to reminding participants about the right to withdraw (due to the sensitive nature of the investigation), reporting findings to individual participants (especially when incidental findings are discovered in the process of research, such as a brain tumour that the participant did not know about), and applying the results to designing health prevention programmes (care should be taken not to make sweeping generalizations based on research with limited samples).

▼ The focus is on the research study rather than a broader conceptual understanding about research into health problems in general.

▲ In the conclusion an attempt is made to connect the discussed examples back to the question and formulate broad conceptual understandings about ethics in the study of health problems in general.

**This response could have achieved 15/22 marks.**

**Focus on the question:** 1/2. The answer identifies the problem raised in the question, but does not sufficiently explain it (why exactly ethical considerations are important in the study of health problems).

**Knowledge and understanding:** 5/6. The response demonstrates relevant, detailed knowledge and understanding. Psychological terminology is used accurately and appropriately. Clarity of knowledge is especially evident in the details of individual research studies, as well as knowledge of ethical guidelines in psychological research in general.

**Use of research to support answer:** 4/6. Relevant psychological research is chosen to support the answer. However, the two research studies used in the answer are simply used as examples from the study of health problems. These studies are not used in the answer to illustrate a broader conceptual understanding related to the question. In this sense, the research selected partially develops the argument. On the plus side, the two research examples illustrate slightly different ethical considerations, giving the response more breadth.

**Critical thinking:** 3/6. The response contains critical thinking, but lacks development. Mostly critical thinking is limited to the application of generic ethical guidelines to a specific research study. Discussion and evaluation of the problem raised in the question (ethics in the study of health problems in general) is attempted but not well developed.

**Clarity and organization:** 2/2. The answer demonstrates clarity and organization that is sufficiently sustained throughout the response, although the conclusion is somewhat underdeveloped.

## ERQ example 2

Discuss two or more factors related to the development
of one health problem. [22]

SAMPLE STUDENT ANSWER

▼ The problem raised in the question is identified, but not thoroughly explained. The candidate just defines addiction and states that it is influenced by both biological and sociocultural factors.

Substance abuse can be defined as the maintained use of an unhealthy substance despite knowing the negative consequences. Addiction is a horrible disorder that negatively affects the health of an individual. This essay will discuss addiction to nicotine (or smoking) and discuss the factors related to the development of this addiction. The addictive nature of nicotine along with sociocultural factors such as parental smoking and peer pressure will be discussed in the essay. Biological factors relate to the development of nicotine addiction due to the nature of the source of addiction.

▲ Biological factors are both explained on a conceptual level and supported with an appropriate research study.

Nicotine is a psychoactive drug that promotes the secretion of neurotransmitters and changes neural pathways. Nicotine leads to the secretion of noradrenalide, serotonin and acetylcholine. Noradrenaline leads to a temporary increase in heart rate and blood pressure, serotonin alters mood, and acetylcholine is associated with improved memory. Dopamine, the feel-good hormone, is also released, giving the smoker a feeling of pleasure. DiFranza et al (2006) investigated the biologically addictive nature of nicotine using a sample of Massachusetts teens with a mean age of 12. The participants filled out questionnaires on their own smoking history, their environment, their attitudes to smoking and their parents' views or habits on smoking. A group of 11 teens were also interviewed. The researchers found that around 60% of the teens recalled a relaxation effect after their

▲ Sufficiently good knowledge of the study's details is shown.

first time smoking. Of this 60%, 90% felt they were addicted and 60% felt they had lost control. In the group that did not experience an initial relaxation effect, considerably fewer teens felt addicted.

▲ Diverse critical thinking points are raised regarding the study (generalizability, methodology, ethical considerations).

This study demonstrates the addictive nature of nicotine, as the participants in the sample experienced a relaxation effect and many felt addicted. The sample may be less generalizable as it consisted of teenage boys from Massachusetts. It may apply to other US teens but could vary by gender and culture. The study has some ethical concerns due to the nature of teens smoking. It is not mentioned that the researchers offered the teens help with smoking cessation or even encouraged them to stop, though this could have potentially affected the data. The methodology consisted of self-reporting, which may be biased, and the teens may have been eager to seem more rebellious by lying about smoking in the past. Interviews were used for a small portion of the sample (as the sample was too big for everyone to be interviewed), and this made the study more effective. Overall, the study aids in demonstrating the addictive nature of nicotine, as it creates a relaxed feeling that could encourage consistent smoking.

Sociocultural factors such as parental smoking and peer pressure could also affect the development of addictive behaviour. Bauman (1980) studied US teens and their smoking history based on whether or not their own parents smoked. If their parents didn't smoke, 80% of the teens had never tried themselves, but 50% had tried if their parents had smoked. This study demonstrates how parental smoking can create a model for children who will then be more likely to smoke. Based on Bandura's social learning theory, it makes sense that the children of parents who smoke are more likely to try it as they see models doing it.

Having friends who smoke could also increase the likelihood of smoking. According to the UN (2004), peer pressure is one of the biggest reasons for teen smoking. Unger et al (2001) studied teen smoking in a self-selected sample of Californian teens. The sample was very large, consisting of around 20,000 teens. Questionnaires were filled out by the sample asking whether their friends smoked and whether they themselves had ever tried it. The study found that European-American teens with friends who smoked were more likely to try smoking than African-American, Asian-American or Hispanic teens with friends who smoked. This demonstrates peer pressure and the role of culture on smoking.

The Unger et al study demonstrates how peer pressure, or simply having friends who smoke, can increase the likelihood of smoking. The European-American teens were more likely to

▲ Evaluation of the study is clearly linked back to the question.

▲ Clear knowledge of sociocultural factors is shown and effectively supported by research. Details of research studies are few but sufficient for the purposes of making the argument.

▼ Evaluation is focused a bit too much on the problem of generalizability (other aspects could be given equal attention).

▲ Some effective critical thinking points are made. Evaluation of research studies is diverse and links back to the conceptual arguments (the problem raised in the question).

▲ Balanced conclusions are made.

▲ The main arguments of the essay are effectively summarized in the conclusion, contributing to the clear focus and organization of the essay.

smoke due to the individualistic cultural dimension, where teens often rebel to set themselves apart from their parents. The teens of different races were explained to be of a more collectivistic culture where family and honesty are important. Therefore race or culture can affect the likelihood of smoking. The study is strong as it is cross-cultural and includes boys and girls, but it is only in California so the results may vary in different countries. Like DiFranza's study, an ethical concern of this study could be the lack of promoting or encouraging smoking cessation in place of getting results on teen smoking. The methodology could be limited as self-reporting was required, which is not always reliable as some individuals may have lied and this could have tampered with the results. But the study is still strong and reliable due to the large sample size, the cross-cultural aspect and the consideration of cultural background. The study may be generalizable to other teenagers, but this may vary by state or by country. The study is focused on teen smoking so it must not be generalizable to different age groups. Overall the study offers insight into how having friends who smoke can increase the likelihood of smoking, but also how culture can affect the likelihood as well.

Smoking is a highly addictive behaviour. Both biological and sociocultural factors play a role in the development of the addiction. In terms of biological factors, nicotine is a psychoactive drug, and as DiFrenza demonstrated it has a relaxation effect that can lead to addiction. Bauman demonstrated how parental smoking can increase the likelihood of addiction, while Unger et al demonstrated the effect of peer pressure on teen smoking, and how cultural differences can also affect the likelihood of smoking. Overall, it is evident that both biological and sociocultural factors play a role in the development of addictive behaviour such as nicotine addiction, even in people as young as 12.

This response could have achieved 18/22 marks.

**Focus on the question:** 1/2. The problem/issue raised in the question is identified but not sufficiently explained.

**Knowledge and understanding:** 5/6. The response demonstrates relevant, sufficiently detailed knowledge and understanding that is clearly linked to the requirements of the question. Psychological terminology is used appropriately.

**Use of research to support answer:** 5/6. Relevant psychological research is used to support the response, pieces of evidence are relevant to the arguments they support, and research conclusions are linked to the question on a conceptual level.

**Critical thinking:** 5/6. The response demonstrates well-developed critical thinking with some diverse evaluation points (although the focus throughout the response is mostly on the generalizability of results).

**Clarity and organization:** 2/2. The answer demonstrates clarity and organization throughout.

## 8.1    FORMATION OF PERSONAL RELATIONSHIP

The formation of romantic relationships is a complex process influenced by an array of biological, cognitive and sociocultural factors all interacting with each other.

On the biological level, there have been many attempts to explain the feeling of physical attraction.

For example, evolutionary theories have looked at attraction as an indicator of a higher likelihood of producing healthy offspring. All evolutionary explanations in psychology are essentially models, and to test a model certain predictions are formulated that are then tested against observational data. With the evolutionary explanation of attraction, such predictions include the following (among others).

▲ **Figure 8.1.1** Attraction is influenced by biological, cognitive and sociocultural factors

- Females will be more attracted to males who can provide better economic care to the offspring.

- Males will be more attracted to younger females with a healthy body.

- Features of facial symmetry will be important predictors of attraction because they correlate with health.

- In less developed countries, females will be more attracted to traits such as loyalty.

Other dimensions of biological explanations are genetic (the association between physical attraction and markers of genetic compatibility such as the major histocompatibility complex), and neurochemical (the association between physical attraction and hormones such as oxytocin, neurotransmitters such as dopamine, and pheromones).

On the cognitive level, explanations for the formation of romantic relationships have focused on cognitive schemas and interpretations that mediate our reactions to a potential partner. The similarity-attraction hypothesis claims that attraction to others depends on how similar we think they are to ourselves. The related matching hypothesis suggests we are attracted to people whose level of attractiveness is (according to our judgment) similar to that of our own.

It should be noted that most research on cognitive determinants of attraction focuses on one factor (or a small number of factors) at a time, which makes it difficult to assess the relative contributions of biological and cognitive factors in developing an attraction. Thus a question that remains open is: are cognitive factors primary determinants in their own right, or are they simply mediators for biological determinants?

Similar to cognitive explanations, multiple determining (or perhaps mediating) factors have been identified in the sociocultural approach to behaviour. Examples include (but are not limited to) familiarity, proximity and social proof.

- The idea of familiarity suggests that merely being exposed to each other more frequently (for example, attending the same class) has an effect on attraction.

- The idea of proximity implies that there is a correlation between feelings of attraction and living in close proximity to each other.

- The idea of social proof is that we tend to be more attracted to a person if we see that other people are attracted to that person as well.

## KEY RESEARCH STUDIES

- Buss (1989): a cross-cultural study of mate preferences.

- Wedekind *et al* (1995): the "dirty T-shirt" study of the major histocompatibility complex.

- Byrne (1961): an experiment to support similarity-attraction hypothesis.

- Walster *et al* (1966), Berscheid *et al* (1971): experiments testing the matching hypothesis.

- Festinger, Schachter and Back (1950): a study supporting the correlation between physical proximity and friendship.

- Zayonc (1968) on the mere exposure effect.

- Moreland and Beach (1992) on the effects of familiarity on attraction.

- Jones *et al* (2007): a study showing that cues of social proof may contribute to feelings of attraction.

# 8.2   ROLE OF COMMUNICATION IN PERSONAL RELATIONSHIPS

Communication plays a role in all stages of the development of personal relationships. We will focus here on the role of communication in maintaining an established relationship.

Many theories and models have been proposed to explain the role of communication in relationships. Some of the most prominent ones are: social penetration theory, approaches based on the concept of attributional styles, and approaches based on the concept of patterns of accommodation.

Social penetration theory views a developing relationship as a gradual movement through "layers" of communication, from superficial interaction to self-disclosure. Research in support of this theory suggests that self-disclosure increases mutual liking, the longevity of relationships and the self-reported depth of interpersonal interaction.

Attribution is the process of assigning causes to one's own behaviour or other people's behaviour. With a negative attributional style, the negative behaviour of a partner is typically attributed (by the other partner) to dispositional factors, whereas positive behaviour is typically attributed to situational factors. The opposite is true for the positive attributional style. Supporting research in this area has shown that problems in maintaining relationships (for example, families in relational distress) frequently demonstrate negative attributional styles. It may be difficult, however, to establish a direction of causality here: is it the attributional style that influences relationship problems, or is it the other way around?

The idea of patterns of accommodation refers to the strategies used by partners to resolve emerging conflicts or disagreements. These strategies might differ in terms of their constructiveness. Results of supporting studies demonstrate that couples who voice their disagreements and solve conflicts actively and constructively tend to be more satisfied with their relationship, and the relationship itself tends to be more stable.

## 🔍 KEY THEORIES AND RESEARCH STUDIES

- Altman and Taylor (1973): social penetration theory.

- Sheldon (2009) on self-disclosure on Facebook.

- Heider (1958): the theory of attribution.

- Stratton (2003) on attributional styles in distressed families.

- Rusbult and Zembrodt (1983) on four strategies of conflict resolution in relationships.

- Gottman and Krokoff (1989): longitudinal observation of couples using conflict resolution.

There is an overlap between this content heading and "role of communication in personal relationships", which is not at all surprising because communication (or a lack of it) is responsible for how relationships change. However, there has been a more specific research interest in the process of a break-up, with research questions such as: what causes a break-up, how does it start, what phases does it go through, and is it reversible?

Several prominent models have been proposed to describe and explain the process of relationship dissolution. One such model is Gottman's "Four horsemen of relationship apocalypse". This model is based on longitudinal research that aimed to identify the characteristics of communication that are most predictive of break-up. Other examples include Rollie and Duck's (2006) five-stage model of relationship breakdown (the intrapsychic stage, the dyadic stage, the social stage, grave dressing and resurrection), Knapp's relationship termination model and the fatal attraction hypothesis.

Empirical support for such models is difficult for several reasons.

- Most data is based on self-report or observation; self-report is not too reliable and the credibility of observational data depends largely on how artificial the research conditions are. In addition, participants are likely to change their behaviour when they know they are being observed.

- Self-reports are often retrospective (asking participants to describe the history of their relationships), which raises the problem of biases associated with reconstructive memory.

- The nature of the research question is such that longitudinal research is required. Such research is difficult to conduct for practical reasons (for example, sample attrition).

- There are cultural differences in relationship dissolution. For example, many collectivist cultures have arranged marriages.

- There is the possibility of biased samples, as most of the participants in research are either university students participating for course credit or couples seeking relationship counselling.

- Research is often focused on heterosexual relationships, making generalizability of the results limited.

As a result of this, there is no single research study that can support a model of relationship breakdown in its entirety. Such models are based on a large number of research studies, each investigating a limited aspect.

### KEY THEORIES AND RESEARCH STUDIES

- Research at the Gottman Institute ("The Love Lab").

- Models of relationship breakdown: Rollie and Duck (2006), Lee (1984).

- Knapp, Vangelisti and Caughlin (2014): Knapp's model of relationship development and termination.

- Felmlee (1995): the fatal attraction hypothesis.

- LeFebvre, Blackburn and Brody (2014): an application of Rollie and Duck's (2006) model to Facebook behaviour during relationship dissolution.

- Flora and Segrin (2003) on the association between self-reported relationship well-being and relational history.

# 8.4    COOPERATION AND COMPETITION

Competition is behaviour that benefits a person or group at the expense of the interests of another person or group. In contrast, cooperation is behaviour that benefits another person or group. Cooperative behaviour may or may not pursue goals of self-interest; it is the outcome for another party that matters.

Both competition and cooperation can manifest on an interpersonal level and on an intergroup level. In the history of psychological research, these levels of competition and cooperation have been approached differently, with distinct sets of theories and research studies for both.

| | Interpersonal level | Intergroup level |
|---|---|---|
| **Competition** | Evolutionary explanation (survival) | Realistic group conflict theory |
| **Cooperation** | Kin selection theory, reciprocal altruism theory, empathy-altruism model | Social identity theory |

▲ Table 8.4.1   Theories linked to competition and cooperation

## Interpersonal level

Competitive behaviour has often been explained from the evolutionary standpoint: individuals compete with each other because resources are limited and they want to maximize their chance for survival. With limited resources, disadvantaging another individual may be evolutionarily beneficial.

However, cooperative behaviour presents a dilemma from the evolutionary point of view. Why do individuals cooperate with each other even when resources are limited? This seems counterintuitive. Solutions to this dilemma include the following.

- Kin selection theory (Hamilton 1964). This theory suggests that the reason for cooperative behaviour is the desire to maximize the survival potential of your genes.

- Reciprocal altruism theory (Trivers 1971). This theory explains that the reason you are being cooperative with another individual is that you expect this behaviour to be reciprocated in the future.

- Empathy-altruism model (Batson 1981). This suggests that humans, unlike animals, are capable of genuine altruistic behaviour stemming from an empathic concern for the well-being of others.

## Intergroup level

Several prominent theories have been suggested to provide an explanation of cooperation and competition on the intergroup level. One of them is the realistic group conflict theory (Campbell 1965). This theory suggests that the cause of intergroup competition is scarce resources and incompatible goals regarding those resources (when one group gains, another loses). As a step forward, the theory also suggests that it is possible to overcome competition and induce cooperation by substituting incompatible goals with superordinate goals (when both groups win if they cooperate). In any case, the theory places the causal factors of cooperation and competition in the environment.

By contrast, social identity theory (Tajfel and Turner, 1979) emphasizes internal determinants of cooperative/competitive behaviour – the way an individual identifies with his or her group. The theory suggests that when individuals identify with a social group, their self-esteem becomes dependent on the positive distinctiveness between their group and other social groups. As a result of this, there is a desire to maximize positive distinctiveness through ingroup favouritism and outgroup discrimination.

Cooperation and competition are behavioural decisions made in the context of some external parameters (such as the scarcity of resources) and the anticipated actions of the other party. Such situations are effectively described by game theory: the field of research that applies mathematical methods to explain the most rational behaviour of an "agent" in a system of interacting agents. When this is applied to actual human behaviour in similar situations, we are dealing with behavioural game theory. Behavioural game theory has produced some insightful results about how and when people cooperate or compete with each other.

## KEY THEORIES AND RESEARCH STUDIES

**Theories of competition and cooperation**

- Hamilton (1964): kin selection theory.
- Trivers (1971): reciprocal altruism theory.
- Batson *et al* (1981): empathy-altruism model.
- Campbell (1965): realistic group conflict theory.
- Tajfel and Turner (1979): social identity theory.

**Empirical support for the theories**

- Sherif *et al* (1961): "Robber's Cave" studies (to support realistic group conflict theory).
- Tajfel *et al* (1971): minimal group studies (to support social identity theory).

- Batson's studies to support the empathy-altruism model – Batson *et al* (1981): the "Elaine" study;
Toi, Batson (1982): the "Carol" study.

- Research with human participants to support kin selection, such as Madsen *et al* (2007).

- Burton-Chellew, Ross-Gillespie and West (2010): a study using behavioural game theory to explain that cooperation between individuals may be the result of competition between groups.

## >> COMMON ERRORS

The content heading "cooperation and competition" is conceptually close to content headings such as "origins of conflict and conflict resolution" and "prosocial behaviour", but there are still unique emphases in all these content headings that need to be preserved for your responses to stay focused on the questions.

Competition is a broader concept than conflict, and in a similar manner cooperation is broader than

prosocial behaviour. Although examples of conflict and prosocial behaviour may be used to illustrate certain points, you need to be careful not to reduce competition to conflict and cooperation to prosocial behaviour. Keep the focus on demonstrating the general principles underlying competition and cooperation. Also remember about the two levels of analysis involved in this research (the interpersonal level and the intergroup level).

# 8.5 PREJUDICE AND DISCRIMINATION

In the triad of concepts that are linked to this content heading – stereotypes, prejudice and discrimination – stereotypes describe cognitions, prejudice describes attitudes, and discrimination relates to behaviour. Stereotypes (generalized perceptions based on a person's group membership) form the basis for the other two. Prejudice is a negative attitude towards an individual or a group of people (again, based on their group membership). When prejudice translates into behaviour, it becomes discrimination.

There is an important distinction between explicit prejudice (openly expressed and consciously accepted negative attitudes) and implicit prejudice (when people do not accept or do not realize that they are in fact prejudiced against a certain group). Today, research into implicit prejudice is becoming more popular because people tend to demonstrate less explicit prejudice due to social desirability. It does not mean, however, that people are becoming less prejudiced on the implicit level. Implicit Association Tests (IATs) are used to measure such prejudice.

Implicit prejudice may influence decision-making and behaviour in subtle ways (without the individual being consciously aware of this influence). At the same time, implicit prejudice may itself be influenced by factors such as being exposed to counter-stereotypical examples.

There is a complex relationship between intergroup prejudice and group size. Contradictory predictions have been made regarding what will happen to prejudice as the size of the outgroup grows. Realistic group conflict theory predicts that as the size of the outgroup increases, so will the perceived threat, which means that prejudice and discrimination towards the outgroup should increase. On the other hand, the contact hypothesis predicts that a larger outgroup size means more personal contact with its members and, as a result, less prejudice. Research in this area has in fact revealed a curvilinear relationship between prejudice and the size of the outgroup: one increases as the other increases, but only to a certain point, after which the relationship becomes inverse.

## >> COMMON ERRORS

Although it may be claimed that prejudice arises from stereotypes, remember that prejudice and stereotypes are still not the same thing. Stereotypes are cognitions while prejudice is an attitude. Cognitions and attitudes are measured in different ways. Hence, although you can explain the link between stereotypes and prejudice on a conceptual level, when it comes to using supporting research to explain prejudice, you need to select research studies that measure attitudes, not cognitions.

Similarly, although conceptual similarities exist between "discrimination" and "competition", the concepts are not identical. A research study demonstrating competition does not necessarily demonstrate discrimination. Competitive behaviour may be a consequence of ingroup favouritism rather than outgroup discrimination. To stay focused on the question, it would be better to select supporting research that shows outgroup discrimination explicitly.

## 🔍 KEY RESEARCH STUDIES

- Greenwald, McGhee and Schwartz (1998): introduced Implicit Association Tests as a method.

- Levinson, Cai and Young (2010) on the influence of implicit prejudice on discriminatory decision-making in a legal context.

- Columb and Plant (2011) on the Obama effect (malleability of implicit prejudice in the presence of counter-stereotypical examples).

- Savelkoul *et al* (2011) on the curvilinear relationship between intergroup prejudice and the size of the outgroup.

# 8.6 ORIGINS OF CONFLICT AND CONFLICT RESOLUTION

As concepts, "competition" and "conflict" are related. Competition is any interpersonal (or intergroup) behaviour that benefits the interests of the actor at the cost of the other party involved. In other words, what makes behaviour competitive is the anticipated outcome: the "I win, you lose" situation. But not every competitive behaviour is a conflict, such as healthy economic competition in a free market society. Competition becomes conflict when it becomes explicit and when disadvantaging the other party becomes a goal in itself.

One of the pertinent research questions in this area is the question of conflict origins. Multiple theories exist regarding the primary causal factors of conflict, including the following.

- Realistic group conflict theory (Sherif *et al* 1961): focuses on the role of competition over scarce resources.

- Social identity theory (Tajfel, Turner 1979): focuses on the role of social categorization.

- The instrumental model of group conflict (Esses *et al* 2001): focuses on the combination of resource stress and the perceived salience of a potentially competitive outgroup.

All theories are supported by empirical evidence to some extent, but they differ in their ability to explain various instances of conflict.

Another pertinent research question is that of conflict resolution. Again, several approaches have been suggested, the most prominent of these being the contact hypothesis. This suggests that conflict will reduce when interpersonal contact between members of rival groups increases. However, in order for this to happen, intergroup contact has to meet a number of conditions (Allport 1954):

- In the contact situation, the two groups should be equal.

- Groups should depend on each other in this situation.

- They should have common goals.

- The contact should be supported by authorities or social norms.

Studies have shown that intergroup contact is indeed an effective measure against prejudice and conflict. A number of additional findings show, for example, that contact with one outgroup is also associated with reduced prejudice towards other outgroups.

It is often the case that one of the conflicting groups is dominant and the other one is non-dominant. In such situations, the effects of contact on conflict reduction are asymmetric: members of the dominant group respond more positively to perspective-taking (listening to and hearing the other group), while members of the non-dominant group respond more positively to perspective-giving (expressing themselves and allowing themselves to be heard).

## KEY THEORIES AND RESEARCH STUDIES

- Theories of conflict origins: Sherif *et al* (1961), Tajfel and Turner (1979), Esses *et al* (2001).

- Staub (1999) on aggravating factors of conflict.

- Allport (1954): the contact hypothesis in its original form.

- Pettigrew and Tropp (2006): a meta-analysis of the contact hypothesis.

- Bruneau and Saxe (2012) on the differential role of perspective-giving and perspective-taking in the resolution of conflict.

## >> COMMON ERRORS

Remember that although the concepts "conflict", "competition", "discrimination" and "prejudice" are similar and overlapping, they are not the same. This means that not every research study (or theory) illustrating one of the concepts would be suitable to support another.

## 8.7 BYSTANDERISM

▲ **Figure 8.7.1** Bystanderism increases when there are more onlookers

Bystanderism (or the bystander effect) is the phenomenon where an individual witnesses an emergency situation yet does not help the victim due to the presence of other observers (onlookers). It has been demonstrated that a greater number of other observers is associated with the decreased likelihood of helping the victim. This seems like a paradox, so a psychological theory was required to explain it.

The theory of unresponsive behaviour was proposed by Latané and Darley (1970). This theory suggests that there are five cognitive steps involved in the decision to intervene (or not intervene):

1. noticing the event

2. interpreting the event as an emergency

3. assuming personal responsibility

4. choosing the way to help

5. implementing the decision.

If there is a disruption of any of these steps, help will not be rendered. Investigation of the psychological factors that increase the likelihood of bystanderism has been focused mostly on steps 2 and 3 in this model (interpreting the event as an emergency and assuming personal responsibility). This research has led to the discovery of several key phenomena explaining bystanderism.

- Pluralistic ignorance. In their interpretation of ambiguous situations, people tend to rely on the reactions of others. If others do not react to a situation as an emergency, chances are that the individual will not interpret it as one either.

- Evaluation apprehension. This refers to an individual's fear of being judged when acting publicly. Such anticipated judgment may make individuals reluctant to take responsibility.

- Diffusion of responsibility. This refers to the perception that the other onlookers present in the same situation share a part of the responsibility for intervention, so the more onlookers the less likely it is that any individual will feel personally responsible.

These psychological phenomena are key mechanisms of bystanderism.

### ›› COMMON ERRORS

Bystanderism is a specific phenomenon observed in human behaviour. It has a certain history of research associated with it. Although it may link conceptually to other content headings, such as "prosocial behaviour", "social identity theory" and "social cognitive theory", using research from those content headings to address questions on bystanderism would not be appropriate.

### 🔍 KEY THEORIES AND RESEARCH STUDIES

- Latané and Darley (1970): the theory of unresponsive behaviour.

- Latané and Darley (1968): the "smoke-filled room study" (demonstrated pluralistic ignorance).

- Darley and Latané (1968): the "intercom study" (demonstrated diffusion of responsibility).

- Piliavin, Rodin and Piliavin (1969): the "New York subway study".

Prosocial behaviour is any behaviour that benefits others. It is this outcome for other people that defines a behaviour as prosocial, regardless of the motives. Such behaviours where the motivation is egoistic but the outcome is beneficial to others can be explained by the theory of evolution. These behaviours are also easily modelled in behavioural game theory: in a typical game, all individuals pursue self-interest, but the outcome for other players might also be enhanced depending on the structure of the pay-offs.

However, when prosocial behaviour occurs at some cost to the helper (a special case of prosocial behaviour known as altruism), this becomes more difficult to explain. Why do individuals sacrifice their own interests to help others?

To answer this question, some theories have tried to find hidden egoistic motives behind seemingly altruistic acts, while other theories have claimed that humans, unlike animals, are capable of truly selfless altruism.

Some prominent theories in this field are summarized here.

- Kin selection theory (Hamilton 1964). The egoistic motive behind altruistic acts, according to this theory, is the desire to maximize the survival potential of one's genes. This explains, for example, why relatives receive helping behaviour more often than non-relatives. Studies have demonstrated to some extent the applicability of this theory to both humans and animals.

- Reciprocal altruism theory (Trivers 1971). The egoistic motive this theory suggests is the anticipation that altruistic behaviour will be returned in the future. Research has shown that altruism is more likely when the perceived likelihood of such reciprocation is higher.

- Empathy-altruism model (Batson *et al* 1981). This model suggests that truly selfless behaviour is a reality in human beings, and it is driven by empathic concern for others. Supporting research has shown, for example, that personal identification with the victim increases feelings of empathic concern and, as a result, increases the likelihood of altruistic behaviour.

Selecting the "best" explanation is a task that is challenging and perhaps impossible. It comes down to identifying the deepest hidden motivation behind people's actions; something that is only possible through self-report measures. Given the limitations of such data, we need to accept the limitations of any conclusions based on it.

## KEY THEORIES AND RESEARCH STUDIES

- Theories of altruism: Hamilton (1964), Trivers (1971), Batson (1981).

- Madsen *et al* (2007): support for kin selection theory with human participants.

- Batson *et al* (1981): the Elaine study; support for the empathy-altruism model.

# 8.9   PROMOTING PROSOCIAL BEHAVIOUR

Various strategies for promoting prosocial behaviour have been suggested and investigated. These may be broadly grouped into two categories:

- strategies targeting incentives for prosocial behaviour
- strategies targeting psychological variables responsible for prosocial behaviour.

▲ **Figure 8.9.1**   Prosocial behaviour can be encouraged through school curricula

Strategies in the first group increase the cost of non-helping and reduce the cost of helping. An example is the "Good Samaritan" laws accepted in some countries (for example, Australia, Canada, Ireland and Germany). Different versions of this law reduce the cost of helping by not holding helpers legally responsible if their help results in unintentional harm. They also increase the cost of non-helping by legally punishing bystanders who do not help even though this does not put them in any danger, and so on. The effectiveness of Good Samaritan laws has been demonstrated in a variety of contexts, for example in increasing the incidence of reporting drug overdoses.

Strategies in the second group aim to teach people skills associated with prosocial behaviour or generally train people to be more socially responsible. Such strategies are commonly incorporated into educational programmes. Examples include a mindfulness-based kindness curriculum for children and compassion training through meditation sessions for adults. The effectiveness of such strategies has been demonstrated in a variety of studies, with effects that are both short-term and long-term.

## 🔍 KEY RESEARCH STUDIES

- Nguyen and Parker (2018) on the effectiveness of Good Samaritan laws.

- Flook *et al* (2015): an investigation of the effects of a mindfulness-based kindness curriculum for pre-school children on prosocial attitudes and behaviours.

- Hutcherson, Seppala and Gross (2008): showed that brief meditation sessions for adults could be effective for increasing positivity towards strangers.

- Leiberg, Klimecki and Singer (2011) on the effects of short-term compassion training on prosocial behaviour (as measured in a specially designed computer-based simulation).

# SAMPLE QUESTIONS

Below are two example ERQs that you might see on Psychology of human relationships. Read the sample student answers and the accompanying comments, which will help you to understand what the students have done well and what they could do better.

## ERQ example 1

Discuss two or more approaches to research used in the study of group dynamics. [22]

Group dynamics is the study of the ways in which groups come into contact with each other, and how this contact evolves. The study of group dynamics embraces phenomena like cooperation, competition and conflict. It also looks at related issues of prejudice and discrimination. While cooperation, competition and conflict are more bidirectional, prejudice and discrimination are more unidirectional (one group mistreats another).

The study of group dynamics is not easy because there are multiple factors involved in how intergroup interaction will progress. To take all of these factors into account, a lot of variables need to be measured. Also when it comes to groups, it is much harder to control confounding variables. For example, a laboratory experiment with separate individuals is obviously much simpler than a laboratory experiment with two groups. Many methods may be used to study group dynamics, and this essay will discuss several of them.

Sherif et al (1961) conducted the famous "Robber's Cave" study to investigate how competition over resources may be responsible for intergroup competition and conflict. On the basis of that research, a theory was proposed that became known as the realistic group conflict theory. This theory states that conflict between groups is the result of scarce resources over which groups compete. If you increase the availability of resources, conflict will be resolved.

In the study itself, researchers posed as camp leaders in a summer camp. The study involved 24 12-year-old boys. The boys attended a summer camp and did not know that they

▲ The scope of research into "group dynamics" is correctly identified.

▼ There is an attempt to explain the problem implicit in the question, but there is not enough focus on approaches to research. The question is restated but not further explained.

▼ The Sherif *et al* study is described in a very detailed way, but the research method used in the study is not identified. This part of the essay is descriptive and does not link directly to the requirements of the question.

149

were part of a psychological study. The study included three stages. In the first stage (the stage of group formation), boys were randomly split into two groups and the groups were given lodgings at opposite sides of the camp so they did not know about the existence of the other group. The groups took the names of the Rattlers and the Eagles. The behaviour of boys was observed and it was noted, for example, that they quickly established certain group traditions, rituals, internal norms and habits.

During the second stage (inducing conflict), the researchers introduced the groups to each other and organized a series of highly competitive activities between the two teams. Activities were designed in such a way that there were clear winners (who got an attractive prize) and losers (who did not get anything, not even a consolation prize), so both groups were motivated to win at the expense of each other. Observations at this stage of the study showed that the teams started demonstrating outgroup discrimination: they called members of the other group names, and on one occasion even burned their flag and raided their cabins.

In the third stage, however, researchers wanted to see if they could reduce the conflict they had created. For this they designed another set of activities where the goals of the two groups were no longer incompatible. In fact, they introduced activities with superordinate goals, meaning that the two groups had to work together to be successful. Observations showed that the introduction of such activities led to the reduction of outgroup discrimination and less conflict. After the end of the programme, many boys even volunteered to share a bus with members of the other group on their way home. This study demonstrated how competition over resources (such as attractive prizes) may create outgroup discrimination and conflict. The study was strong in its ecological validity since it was conducted in the naturalistic setting of a summer camp for boys. The fact that participants did not know they were being studied and did not give their informed consent certainly presents an ethical issue. However, it is also true that without this degree of deception, the boys' behaviour would not have been natural. External variables were carefully controlled where possible, increasing the validity of results. Detailed observations

▼ Some evaluation of the research study is attempted, but it is limited because a particular research study is being evaluated, not an approach to research in the study of group dynamics (as the question requires).

were carried out at each of the three stages of the research study, providing rich data. At the same time, a lot of things could have gone wrong. For example, we cannot be absolutely sure that at the first stage boys really did not suspect that there was another team on the camp site.

Another example of research in the area of group dynamics is Levinson et al (2010). These researchers investigated implicit racial prejudice and how it affects legal decision-making in the court. Implicit prejudice is different from explicit prejudice in that it manifests in behaviour, but people do not admit they have it. Since implicit prejudice cannot be captured by questionnaires and other self-report measures, measurement of implicit prejudice is done via a special class of tests known as IATs (Implicit Association Tests). These tests are built on the idea that it takes less time for the brain to process information that is in line with a stereotype and more time to process information that is counter-stereotypical. So for a person who is racially prejudiced against black people, for example, reaction times for the category "black/not guilty" will be longer than reaction times for the category "black/guilty". By presenting participants with a series of stimuli and asking them to categorize the stimuli into such categories, researchers calculate the average reaction times and infer implicit prejudice if there is a difference in averages for the different categories.

Levinson et al designed an implicit association test and a robbery evidence evaluation task. In the robbery evidence task, participants were given a story of a robbery as well as a series of pictures of evidence from the crime scene. For each piece of evidence they had to rate the extent to which they thought it was indicative of guilt. Results of this study showed that participants who scored higher on the implicit racial prejudice IAT were also more likely to think that evidence was indicative of the perpetrator's guilt, but only when the supposed perpetrator was black. In other words, implicit prejudice translated into biased decisions in the court against black people.

Levinson's experiment was highly controlled to ensure that confounding variables did not distort findings. Implicit Association Tests are a reliable measure of implicit prejudice that is not dependent on participants' attempts to provide

▼ Another research study is described and explained. The study is relevant to group dynamics, but again the research method is not identified.

▼ This is marginally relevant to the question because the focus is on an individual research study, not on a research method used to investigate group dynamics.

> ▶ There is some relevant evaluation of the research study, but it is not linked directly to the overarching topic of "approaches to research".

socially desirable responses. The evidence evaluation task is a good approximation of real-life legal decision-making, where investigators (or judges) review evidence that is often ambiguous and need to decide if that evidence is enough for a guilty verdict. Levinson's study is also socially significant as today people rarely admit to racial prejudice, but that does not mean that such prejudice does not manifest in behaviour. However, it might be claimed that the evidence evaluation task lacks ecological validity. Real-life decision-making in a court is much more complex. Also, participants in this study knew they were taking part in a psychological experiment, so their behaviour may have been unnatural due to demand characteristics.

Overall, different approaches to research may be used in the study of group dynamics. Studies such as Sherif et al (1961) helped us establish theories of intergroup conflict. Research such as Levinson's (2010) looked at implicit prejudice and its role in outgroup discrimination. Experiments are especially valuable because they allow us to make cause-effect inferences, so we can establish reasons for the occurrence of conflict or discrimination.

> ▼ Essentially the essay is built upon two concrete examples of research studies. While these are relevant, just describing and evaluating these examples is not enough to do justice to the generic nature of the question.

**This response could have achieved 10/22 marks.**

**Focus on the question:** 1/2. The problem/issue raised in the question is identified but not explained.

**Knowledge and understanding:** 2/6. The response demonstrates very limited knowledge and understanding relevant to the question (it focuses on specific examples rather than approaches to research in general). Relevant terminology is not used; for example, the research method for the two examples is not identified.

**Use of research to support answer:** 3/6. Relevant psychological research is used in support of the response and partly explained, but research is sometimes only vaguely linked to the question. The research selected could be used to develop the argument more effectively.

**Critical thinking:** 3/6. The response contains critical thinking but lacks development. Most critical thinking points are limited to evaluation of individual research examples.

**Clarity and organization:** 1/2. The answer demonstrates some organization and clarity, but this is not sustained throughout the response.

# ERQ example 2

QUESTION PRACTICE

Evaluate one theory explaining prosocial behaviour in humans.    [22]

SAMPLE STUDENT ANSWER

One theory explaining altruism in humans is kin selection theory. Altruism is a type of prosocial behaviour with no reward and sometimes at a cost to oneself. There are several definitions of altruism, and researchers have not agreed on one definition. Kin selection theory is a biological explanation of altruism, or more specifically it is an evolutionary explanation. The theory proposes that the degree of altruism depends on the number of genes shared with the person. The more genes shared, the more one person will help the other. Since it is an evolutionary explanation, it proposes that our genes drive us in a way to maximize our survival, and that our genes are passed down to the next generation either by personal reproduction or through the reproduction of others that carry our genes. The theory is also based on the idea that helping behaviour has survived through evolution because those who have helped had a greater chance to survive.

One strength of this theory is that it is supported by several animal studies. But one problem is that it is not known to what extent the results can be generalized to human behaviour, because it is known that human behaviour is influenced by cultural factors.

However, there is experimental research on humans that shows that the degree of altruism is influenced by the number of genes shared. One study is Madsen et al (2007). The aim was to investigate how kinship influences altruism. Thirteen female and eleven male students from London were used, and also two Zulu populations. The independent variable was the number of genes shared with the beneficiary, and the dependent variable was helping, operationalized as the amount of time a painful position was held. Participants were asked to do a standard isometric ski-training exercise, which is like sitting on an imaginary chair with your back against a wall. This became increasingly painful with time. The time held would be transferred into material wealth, which was money to the students from London and food to the male participants from

▲ The introduction to the essay defines the main terms and identifies the theory in focus. The problem inherent in the question is not explained in the introduction, but explained later on.

▲ The essay is focused on the question. Animal studies are acknowledged, but not described as they are not directly relevant.

▲ A relevant research study is effectively explained in connection to the question. Elements of research methodology are correctly applied.

▲ The study is linked explicitly to the conceptual understanding relevant to the question.

the Zulu population. The money or food would be sent to the person nominated, and if this was the participant then the money or food would be given to him or her directly.

This study supports kin selection theory because it shows that the degree of altruism, which was operationalized as the time the participant held an increasingly painful position, is influenced by the number of genes shared. The more genes shared, the longer the position was held.

One strength of this study that supports kin selection theory is that it took culture into consideration. Both students from London (which is considered an individualistic culture) and males from the Zulu population were used. This makes it possible to generalize the results. However, only a small sample of 24 students was used from London, which makes the results difficult to generalize to the rest of the population. And the researchers only used men from the Zulu population, which makes the results difficult to generalize to females in the Zulu population.

▶ This is a relevant but limited evaluation in terms of generalizability.

Another strength of the study that supports kin selection theory is that it found gender differences. Females made less of a distinction between close and less close relatives.

The researchers also found that the Zulu participants made less of a distinction between their close and less close relatives. However, this can be considered a limitation. The researchers investigated how kinship influences altruism in a collectivistic culture using the theory and method they developed in an individualistic culture. This is called an ethnocentric approach. However, they did give the Zulu population something that they value, which is food instead of money.

▲ Further evaluation of the study is made, with several more appropriate critical thinking points.

Madsen et al (2007) was the first experimental study to support kin selection theory. Previous research tended to be self-reporting, or only imposed a hypothetical time cost on the participants. But Madsen et al (2007) showed that the number of genes shared do influence the degree of altruism. Therefore one can conclude that kinship influences altruism. On the other hand, experimental research is considered artificial and lacks ecological validity. People might not behave in the same way in real-life situations. However, Sime (1983) analysed how people escape from a burning building. The results were that those who are unrelated

▲ A general evaluation of the theory of altruism is made – this is an effective link back to the question. Counter-evidence is considered.

tend to separate, but those who are related tend to stay together. This is a real-life situation.

One limitation of kin selection theory is that it is difficult to operationalize altruism, but the way it was operationalized in Madsen's experiment was ingenious.

One limitation of kin selection theory is that it is a post-hoc explanation, because it is an evolutionary explanation. Researchers develop theories and test them on humans today and draw a conclusion on how people have evolved. Kin selection theory draws the conclusion that helping behaviour has survived through evolution because those who helped had a greater chance to survive. Madsen et al tested this hypothesis or theory in 2007, and supports what kin selection suggests about how people have evolved. Another problem with evolutionary explanations is that they cannot be falsified.

Another limitation of kin selection theory is that it has a reductionist approach. It only takes a biological explanation of altruism into consideration. There are other explanations too, such as the negative state relief model (which is a cognitive explanation of altruism), which is also supported by research such as McMillan and Austin (1971). Theories explaining complex behaviours such as altruism should have an interactionist approach and take biological, cognitive and also sociocultural factors into consideration. On the other hand, it is difficult to investigate the role of several factors in one study.

Another problem with kin selection theory is that it does not explain why we help complete strangers. If the motive for helping is to make sure that your genes are passed down to the next generation, then why do we adopt children or help strangers?

In conclusion, the strength of kin selection theory is that it is supported by several animal research studies, experimental research on humans such as Madsen et al (2007), and also real-life situations analysed by Sime in 1983. Limitations concerning kin selection theory are that experimental research that supports it lacks ecological validity and is artificial, it is based on post-hoc explanations and cannot be falsified, and it does not explain why people help strangers. Another limitation is that it has a reductionist approach and takes only biological factors into consideration.

▲ Although this lacks clarity, an effective link is made to evolutionary explanations in psychology. This allows the candidate to touch on a range of evaluation points uncovering essential limitations of the theory of altruism.

▶ Several more limitations (and counter-arguments) are mentioned, although the structure of the response becomes somewhat broken at this point.

**This response could have achieved 16/22 marks.**

**Focus on the question:** 2/2. The essay is focused on the question and meets the requirements of the command term. The problem/issue raised in the question is explained.

**Knowledge and understanding:** 4/6. The response demonstrates relevant knowledge of concepts and research evidence relevant to the question, but lacks detail. Terminology is applied properly and used in appropriate contexts.

**Use of research to support answer:** 4/6. Relevant psychological research is used. The response is mostly based on one key research study, but other research is also used to support the points made. The use of research is effective in terms of using the findings to illustrate key arguments/conceptual understandings.

**Critical thinking:** 5/6. The response contains extensive evidence of critical thinking. Evaluation of relevant areas is consistently well developed and a diverse range of arguments is made regarding the strengths and limitations of kin selection theory.

**Clarity and organization:** 1/2. The answer demonstrates some organization and clarity, but this is not sustained throughout the response. Closer to the end of the essay the structure is somewhat broken.

# PAPER 3 (HL ONLY)

## 9.1    PAPER 3 STRUCTURE AND TIPS

Higher level (HL) students will be formally assessed on research methods and ethics in paper 3. The paper will include a stimulus material based on a research study (qualitative, quantitative or a mix of the two). You will be asked the following questions based on this stimulus material.

### Question 1

Question 1 has three compulsory parts.

a.  **Identify** the research method used and **outline** two characteristics of the method [3 marks].

b.  **Describe** the sampling method used in the study [3 marks].

c.  **Suggest** one alternative or one additional research method that could be used to investigate the aim of the original study, giving one reason for your choice [3 marks].

### Question 2

The second question will be one of the following.

*   **Describe** the ethical considerations that were applied in the study and **explain** if further ethical considerations could be applied [6 marks].

*   **Describe** the ethical considerations in reporting the results and **explain** additional ethical considerations that could be taken into account when applying the findings of the study [6 marks].

### Question 3

The third question will be one of the following.

*   **Discuss** the possibility of generalizing/transferring[1] the findings of the study [9 marks].

*   **Discuss** how a researcher could ensure that the results of the study are credible [9 marks].

*   **Discuss** how the researcher in the study could avoid bias [9 marks].

The total number of marks for this paper is 24.

## Question 1 (a): Identify the research method

Since the study in the stimulus material may be quantitative, qualitative or even a mix of the two, an important first step is to identify the research method by relating it clearly to one of the broad

---

1 Only the relevant term ("generalizing" or "transferring") will be used in exams, depending on whether the question relates to a quantitative or qualitative study.

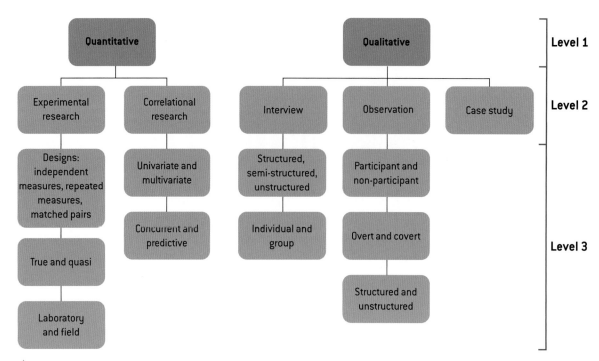

▲ Figure 9.1.1 Hierarchy of research methods

categories. Try to identify the method as precisely as possible, and be aware of the difference between a research method and a technique used to measure variables.

In your identification of the method, start with the most general (defining) characteristics. For example, is it quantitative or qualitative? Then make your way down the hierarchy, identifying the specific sub-type. Figure 9.1.1 provides an example of the hierarchy of types and sub-types that you may want to use.

When you identify the research method, it is recommended to identify it at "level 2" first (see Figure 9.1.1); then determine as many additional sub-types as possible from the given description. For example: "This research used the qualitative method of observation. More specifically, it was a non-participant, structured, overt naturalistic observation."

When it comes to "level 3" sub-types, remember that they are not necessarily mutually exclusive. For example, it is possible to have a true laboratory experiment with an independent measures design. Other examples are: a field quasi-experiment with a repeated measures design; a structured, non-participant, covert laboratory observation; a semi-structured individual interview; and a multivariate, longitudinal correlational study.

The options given in the hierarchy in Figure 9.1.1 do not exhaust all the possibilities. You should decide on the most suitable identification based on the specific study given in the stimulus material, especially when the study is mixed (qualitative in some aspects and quantitative in others).

The difference between a research method and a technique used to measure variables is that a research method provides a direct test of the hypothesis (in a quantitative study) or a direct response to the research question (in a qualitative study), whereas the measurement of variables in itself does not test the hypothesis/does not answer the research question.

For example, suppose the hypothesis of the study is that anxiety (A) influences biases in thinking and decision-making (B). This hypothesis is a statement of a cause-effect relationship between A and B. So the **method** used to test this hypothesis has to be an experiment (experiments are the only method that allows cause-effect inferences). Variable A will be manipulated by the researcher and variable B measured. **Techniques** used to measure this variable may be diverse: observation (you could make a checklist of biased decisions and observe people in their everyday environments), questionnaires, brain scanning technology (if you know brain areas are associated with certain cognitive biases, you may expect activity in these brain areas to increase with the increase in anxiety levels), a specially designed computer-based task, an interview and so on.

## Question 1 (a): Outline two characteristics of the method

Once you have identified the method, you are asked to outline its two characteristics. There are various ways to approach this, but it is important that the characteristics you choose to outline are **essential** to the method. They should be **defining** characteristics (that is, something that makes this method different from other methods). The defining characteristics will probably be different depending on the method – whether it is experimental, correlational or qualitative research.

The tips given below are merely suggestions. In no way is there any "prescribed correct answer" to these questions, and you are encouraged to make your own decisions on the basis of the specific stimulus material you have been provided. However, some starting points for a typical situation are worth considering.

In general, the recommendation is for one of the characteristics to be something that makes the method different from other methods at level 2 (see Figure 9.1.1). The other characteristic could be something that makes a particular sub-type of the method different from other sub-types of the same method at level 3. Examples are given below.

In **experimental research**, one of the characteristics may be what defines the study as an experiment: the fact that the independent variable is manipulated, the dependent variable is measured, the confounding variables are controlled, and all this gives us the possibility to make cause-effect inferences. This makes experimental research different from other research methods at level 2 (see Figure 9.1.1). Another characteristic of the method could be one that helps you to distinguish between sub-types at level 3. For example, you could characterize the experimental design (independent measures, repeated measured, matched pairs or mixed).

In a similar way, for **correlational research** one of the characteristics that you outline may refer to level 2 of the hierarchy and the other to level 3. Namely, one characteristic may be that variables are measured but not manipulated by the researcher, hence cause-effect inferences cannot be made. Another characteristic may refer to the way the variables are measured; the correlational method of research is defined by the way data is processed, not by the method of gathering data. So in a particular correlational study, variables may be measured through the use of various techniques, such as questionnaires or brain scanning technology.

For **qualitative methods**, one of the characteristics may be what separates one qualitative method from all the others. For example, if you identified the research method as a semi-structured interview, you might talk about how interviews are different from other qualitative methods (such as observations and case studies). The unique feature of interviews is that they rely on the natural narrative produced by participants, which is then analysed. Another characteristic may be one that distinguishes semi-structured interviews from other types of interview: the fact that there is an interview guide with a set of topics to be discussed with the interviewee, but flexibility exists in what questions will be asked and in what order.

## Question 1 (b): Describe the sampling method used in the study

This is a fairly straightforward question. Remember that sampling methods are different for qualitative and quantitative research. For example, random sampling may be used in quantitative research, but not qualitative. The opposite applies to purposive sampling.

Since this is a "describe" question, you need to give details. It is not enough simply to identify the sampling method. Describe how the researchers carried out the actual sampling process (for example, for random sampling, how they ensured that every member of the target population had an equal chance of being included in the sample).

According to the assessment criteria, one mark will be given for correctly naming the sampling method, and up to two marks for accurately describing at least two characteristics of the method.

## Question 1 (c): Suggest one alternative or one additional research method that could be used to investigate the aim of the original study, giving one reason for your choice

In order to answer this question effectively, you need to consider three things.

1. What was the researchers' original intention, hypothesis or research question?

2. How does the method that was used by the researchers limit the nature of the conclusions they can make, in terms of the original hypothesis or research question?

3. What would be the best alternative method to overcome such limitations?

Focusing on these three questions will help you to avoid making superficial suggestions. For example, it is always possible to claim that a case study lacks sample-to-population generalizability, so an alternative would be an experiment with a large random sample. But this is a superficial claim because it does not take into account the original research question. Since researchers chose to conduct a case study, they were clearly not interested in this aspect of generalizability. Instead they were interested in an in-depth investigation of a unique individual or group.

For example, suppose that researchers investigated the relationship between anxiety and test performance. For this they conducted a correlational study with an opportunity sample of undergraduate students: students were given a questionnaire measuring their anxiety (as a personality trait) and they were required to take an ability test. Scores on the test were then correlated with anxiety scores. The obvious limitation of this study is the inability to make cause-effect inferences due to its correlational nature. We could perhaps specify the hypothesis to the form "A influences B", make anxiety the independent variable and manipulate it – for example, by telling one half of the participants that results of the test will be used in calculating their achievement grade (although that, of course, raises several ethical issues).

When suggesting an alternative (or additional) research method, it is advisable to select alternatives from level 2 of the hierarchy (Figure 9.1.1). For example, if the stimulus describes a semi-structured interview, avoid suggesting a structured interview as an alternative method. Arguably, both structured and semi-structured interviews are examples of one single method – the interview. Instead, select your alternatives from the methods on level 2: experiment, correlational study, observation, interview and case study.

## Question 2 (a): Describe the ethical considerations that were applied in the study and explain if further ethical considerations could be applied

Here are some guidelines that you can follow when answering this question.

- Keep in mind a list of the most common ethical considerations that are relevant for research with humans, and a separate list for animals. For example, some students use the mnemonic "Can Do, Can't Do With Participants" for human research: Confidentiality, Deception, informed Consent, Debriefing, the right to Withdraw, Protection from harm.

- Based on the given study, decide which ethical guidelines would be most relevant.

- Carefully read the stimulus material for signs of the application of ethical considerations. Describe how they were applied.

- If some of the guidelines you considered relevant were not mentioned in the stimulus, explain how they could have been applied.

- Make a clear distinction between ethics in conducting a study and ethics in reporting or applying its results. Question 2 (a) deals with ethics in conducting a study, while ethics in reporting and applying results is the focus of question 2 (b). These are two separate questions.

## Question 2 (b): Describe the ethical considerations in reporting the results and explain additional ethical considerations that could be taken into account when applying the findings of the study

Ethical considerations in **reporting the results** of a study revolve around two aspects: reporting results back to individual participants and reporting results to a wider community (through publication).

Guidelines regarding the reporting of individual results to participants may include (but are not limited to) the following points.

- Undertaking a full debriefing where the true aim of the study is revealed to participants. During the debriefing it should be explained to participants how their data will be stored, handled and reported.

- Developing a plan for handling and communicating incidental findings. For example, if researchers saw a brain tumour in the brain of one of the participants, should this information be revealed? It is good ethical practice to anticipate the possibility of incidental findings and discuss it in the consent form, where the participant agrees to receive (or not receive) such information.

- Conducting a cost-benefit analysis for reporting unanticipated incidental findings.

- Giving participants an opportunity to withdraw their data after debriefing.

- Offering counselling if the participant is in distress as a result of the study.

Guidelines regarding the publication of results may include (but are not limited to the following points.

- Maintaining confidentiality (it must not be possible to establish a participant's identity from the publication of results).

- Watching out for data fabrication (avoiding it and reporting it to the scientific community).

- Sharing research data for verification.

- Considering social implications of reporting scientific results, such as enhancing the stereotyping or discrimination of certain social groups.

Ethical considerations in **applying the findings** of a study refer to using the published results to design intervention programmes, to inform campaigns or to make any other decisions that have social implications. For example, a researcher conducted interviews with high school students at a particular school and found that many of them report cheating or at least planning to cheat prior to major tests and exams. The school management read the report and decided to install surveillance cameras in the exam hall. Other schools followed this example. Was this decision to install cameras ethical? That should be the focus of the answer in "applying the findings of a study".

Ethical considerations in applying the findings of a study may include (but are not limited to) these recommendations.

- Considering credibility, generalizability and replicability of published research before applying the findings in high-stakes projects driving social change. Interventions will be biased if findings are misinterpreted. For this reason, any practical project applying scientific results must be especially meticulous about analysing the limits of their applicability. In our example, could it be that results are limited to one particular school?

- Considering the risk of stigmatizing certain social groups. In our example, installing cameras may send students the wrong message that they are not trusted.

- Considering the risk of discrimination or reinforcing the marginalization of various social groups. In this case, installing cameras may interfere with considerations of personal privacy.

- Watching out for other considerations involving any sort of physical or mental harm or discomfort caused by actions taken based on the published research.

## Question 3 (a): Discuss the possibility of generalizing/transferring the findings of the study

It is important to remember that the concept of "generalizability" manifests itself differently in quantitative and qualitative research, and that terminology is different.

Another important aspect that you need to keep in mind is that generalizing the results of a study from a sample to a wider population is only one of the aspects of generalizability. There are three types of generalizability (Firestone 1993):

1. sample-to-population generalizability (from participants who took part in the study to larger groups of people)

2. case-to-case generalizability (from the setting of the research study to other similar settings)

3. theoretical generalizability (from the findings of the research study to the underlying theory).

In qualitative research, using these three terms for the types of generalizability is acceptable.

In quantitative (experimental) research, these three types of generalizability are referred to as types of validity.

1. Population validity is the same idea as sample-to-population generalizability in qualitative research.

2. Ecological validity is the extent to which findings can be generalized from experimental settings to real-life situations. In this sense it resembles case-to-case generalizability in qualitative research.

3. Construct validity is the extent to which results of the study can be generalized from operationalizations to theoretical constructs (which resembles theoretical generalization in qualitative research).

Qualitative research methodology approaches generalizability of results differently from quantitative research: more emphasis is on theoretical and case-to-case generalizability (known as transferability) and less on sample-to-population generalizability. This is due to the non-probabilistic nature of samples in qualitative research.

Thus to answer this question it would be advisable to start by explaining the three types of generalizability. Then explain how they should be referred to in the context of the given study (quantitative or qualitative), and outline which types of generalizability should be the focus of discussion. For example, sample-to-population generalizability is not the most important in qualitative research, so to focus your response on it when the study is qualitative would not be appropriate. Having given your explanation, you can discuss the limits of generalizability of the study, with reference to the details provided in the stimulus material.

## Questions 3 (b) and 3 (c): Discuss how a researcher could ensure that the results of the study are credible/Discuss how the researcher in the study could avoid bias

There is a lot of overlap between these two questions in paper 3. Credibility and bias are two sides of the same phenomenon: the less bias, the higher credibility. Ensuring that there is little bias automatically implies ensuring that the study is credible.

In **experimental studies**, credibility is referred to as internal validity. An experiment is internally valid when the independent variable (IV) has been manipulated, the dependent variable (DV) has been measured, and potential confounding variables have been controlled (either eliminated or kept constant). If there are reasons to suspect that some confounding variables influenced the DV and this influence was not the same at all levels of the IV, credibility decreases because you cannot unambiguously attribute the change in the DV to the changing IV. In other words, if something interferes in the relationship between the IV and the DV, the internal validity (credibility) of the experiment gets compromised.

Confounding variables that most commonly interfere in the relationship between the IV and the DV are known as threats to internal validity (Campbell 1965), and they are the most common sources of bias in experimental research. Threats to internal validity include: the Hawthorne effect, demand characteristics, experimental mortality, the testing effect, experimenter bias, regression to the mean, maturation, instrumentation, selection and the history effect. But remember that there are other sources of bias, so in your analysis of the study you should not feel limited by these nine commonly occurring threats.

To increase credibility, researchers should control potential biases through random allocation into groups or conditions, controlling confounding variables by keeping them constant in all conditions, replicating research and supporting it with additional evidence from other sources.

In **correlational studies**, credibility is the extent to which the results of the study reflect the reality that is being investigated, as opposed to artificial findings created by bias in the research itself (facts as opposed to artifacts). The difference, however, is that there is no IV that is being manipulated by the researcher, so sources of bias are different. Bias in correlational research can occur on two levels: on the level of variable measurement and on the level of interpretation of the findings.

- On the level of variable measurement, sources of bias depend on the techniques that were used to measure the variables. For example, if some variables were measured using brain scanning technology, all the biases inherent in this measurement (such as limitations of the temporal and spatial resolution of the scanner, "noise" from fidgeting and background brain activity) will also reduce credibility of the correlational study.

- On the level of interpretation of the findings, the common sources of bias are curvilinear relationships, the third variable problem and spurious correlations.

To increase credibility, researchers should take into account potential third variables (and measure them to assess their contribution to the results), study scatter plots to spot curvilinear relationships, and avoid formulating hypotheses after the dataset has been obtained.

In **qualitative research**, the term "validity" is not used. The idea of credibility (the extent to which research findings reflect the reality that is being investigated) is expressed using two terms: "credibility" itself and "trustworthiness". These terms may be used interchangeably. Ways to increase credibility and potential sources of bias in qualitative research may depend on the specific method being used. For example, there are sources of bias specific to the interview.

Common sources of bias associated with qualitative research include, but are not limited to: acquiescence, social desirability, dominant respondent bias, sensitivity bias (these four are biases caused by the participants), confirmation bias, leading questions bias, question order bias, sampling bias and biased reporting (these are biases caused by the researcher).

To increase credibility (trustworthiness) in qualitative research, researchers can use triangulation, reflexivity and credibility checks. They should also make sure that good rapport with the participant is established and that "rich" descriptions are used when reporting the findings.

To answer this question it is therefore crucial to keep in mind the type of study described in the stimulus material (quantitative, qualitative or mixed) and use appropriate types of bias. Identify the biases that are most relevant in the context of the study. Avoid simply discussing all known biases in general terms. For example, if the stimulus material described an experiment and experimental mortality was a real problem in it, focus on experimental mortality rather than discussing all typical biases one by one. Marks will be awarded for relevant arguments that demonstrate not only general understanding of bias and credibility in quantitative and qualitative research, but also the ability to apply this understanding to the context of a specific research study.

## 9.2 SAMPLE PAPER 3 AND RESPONSES

### Sample paper 3

The stimulus material below is based on a study of gender differences in online empathy.

A research study was conducted with the aim of investigating gender differences in online empathy among high school students in an international school in Switzerland. It is projected
5 that the proportion of online interpersonal interactions among high school students will increase exponentially in the near future. This means that interpersonal interactions of students will happen online more and more frequently
10 than face to face. Concerns have been raised regarding how this is likely to impact students' empathy. Do online interactions lead to deeper empathy because students are exposed to more personal stories more easily, or do they weaken
15 empathy because online interactions do not feel real? And what are the gender differences in patterns of online communication and online empathy? In any case, increasing online interpersonal communication will become a
20 reality, and it is necessary to understand how empathy will develop in this context.

A female researcher in Switzerland was interested in the patterns of interpersonal communication of high school students on social media and
25 internet forums. The study was carried out in an international school in Switzerland, where the researcher herself also happened to be a teacher and classroom tutor. The sample for this research was recruited during breaks, inviting
30 students who were available at that time and willing to participate. They were allowed to be late for the following lesson. Overall, 50 students participated (34 female and 16 male). All the participants were high school students enrolled in
35 years 1 and 2 of the IB Diploma Programme.

Data was collected using unstructured interviews. Participants signed informed consent forms and were debriefed after the interview. Both before and after the interview, it was stressed by the researcher that their anonymity and confidentiality would be guaranteed. In addition to the interviews, to understand the nature of gender differences in online empathy deeper, the researcher also conducted a focus group with eight female students. Students for the focus group were recruited via convenience sampling (they were free due to the absence of their teacher on that day). In the focus group, participants were asked to discuss their experiences in empathy-related online communication. Information revealed by participants of the focus group (their stories and selected quotes) were used extensively in the final research report.

Results demonstrated that male and female students have distinctly different empathy-related behaviours in online communication. Gender differences in perceived barriers to displays of empathy were also analysed. For example, results showed that male students have a more impersonal approach to online communication, and react with disapproval to public displays of empathy, which prevents female students from showing signs of empathy as much as they would like to. It was difficult for female students to be empathetic online when such empathy was being stigmatized by male students. Discussing the practical implications of these results, the researcher suggested that training sessions need to be conducted for male students to help them improve their online communication behaviour and create fewer obstacles for female students in expressing their empathy.

Answer **all** of the following three questions, referring to the stimulus material in your answers. Marks will be awarded for demonstration of knowledge and understanding of research methodology.

1. **(a)** Identify the research method used and outline **two** characteristics of the method. [3]

   **(b)** Describe the sampling method used in the study. [3]

   **(c)** Suggest **one** alternative or **one** additional research method that could be used to investigate the aim of the original study, giving **one** reason for your choice. [3]

2. Describe the ethical considerations in reporting the results and explain additional ethical considerations that could be taken into account when applying the findings of the study. [6]

3. Discuss the possibility of generalizing the findings of the study. [9]

## Sample response 1

SAMPLE STUDENT ANSWER

**1 (a)** Identify the research method used and outline **two** characteristics of the method. [3]

The main method used in the study is the unstructured interview. It is a type of interview, a qualitative research method. Additionally, as a follow-up to the main procedure, the researcher also used a focus group, which is also a special case of the interview. It is not specified whether the focus group was structured or unstructured. In any case, the unstructured interview is the main method here.

One characteristic of interviews is that (unlike other methods) they rely on verbal self-reports, which allows researchers to get an insight into subjective experiences that are otherwise unobservable. For example, for this study no other method would perhaps be able to demonstrate that female participants were intimidated by males in their online behaviour.

Another characteristic of the method is that (unlike structured and semi-structured interviews), unstructured interviews do not

▲ The method is correctly identified (additionally, the main and the supplementary methods are identified).

▲ Two characteristics are outlined. The characteristics are clearly stated.

have a prescribed set of questions or even an expected flow for the conversation. This allows for the method to be highly narrative and reflect the participants' experience in the most natural way.

**1 (b)** Describe the sampling method used in the study. [3]

> ▲ The sampling method is correctly identified.

This study used convenience sampling. The recruitment of participants was not driven by considerations of representativeness; it was only important for the researcher that the participants are suitable for investigating the aim of the study. In this particular case, this had to be high school students. Since the researcher herself was a teacher and classroom tutor in an international school, taking students from that very school

> ▲ Descriptive details are provided about the process of sampling.

was the most cost-effective option. Volunteer participants were recruited during breaks. They were also allowed to be late for the following lesson (some participants may have used this as a motivation to participate).

**1 (c)** Suggest **one** alternative or **one** additional research method that could be used to investigate the aim of the original study, giving **one** reason for your choice. [3]

> ▲ The candidate clearly states that this is a suggestion for an additional (not alternative) method. The method is linked to the original aim of the study.

A quasi-experiment may be suggested as an additional method of research in this context. Originally the aim of the research was to investigate "patterns of interpersonal communication of high school students on social media and internet forums" (lines 17–19). The aim was left very open and no specific hypotheses were made. Representativeness was not the goal in selecting a sample, hence gender distribution in the sample happened to be uneven. However, the key finding that emerged in the study was gender-related. One may wonder if this could be an artifact of a larger number of female participants in the study. Therefore, the next step in conducting this research would be to confirm the findings more rigorously/quantitatively.

> ▲ A clear reason is given for the choice of method.

For these reasons, the results of this qualitative study could be used to construct a questionnaire asking participants to rate various aspects of their empathy-related online experiences, and administer this questionnaire to a more representative group of male and female students. This will present the opportunity to corroborate and triangulate the findings of the unstructured interviews.

**2** Describe the ethical considerations in reporting the results and explain additional ethical considerations that could be taken into account when applying the findings of the study.　　　[6]

The topic of this research may be quite sensitive in nature, especially given that a finding emerged that suggested the presence of a hidden online conflict between male and female participants.

> ▲ The candidate explains what the key ethical issue is in the context of the study.

One consideration that is important in reporting is debriefing. Participants in this study were fully debriefed, and it was stressed that their anonymity and confidentiality were guaranteed. In the debriefing it is important to let participants know how results will be used and how data will be stored.

> ▶ This is correct, but could be explained a little more.

Confidentiality and anonymity are another consideration in reporting. When results are published, it must be ensured that particular statements or quotations cannot be traced back to individual participants. It may be difficult in this particular study, for example, because only eight female students participated in the focus group, and quotes from that discussion were extensively used in the report. From the quotes it may be possible to identify individuals.

> ▲ This is a relevant ethical consideration, linked to the context of the study.

The third consideration in reporting is dealing with incidental findings. It may have become known to the researcher that there were some instances of unethical behaviour online. The question is then what the researcher should do with such findings (should they be reported to the principal?). These considerations should be thought through and decided in advance, and participants should know from their consent form what the researcher is going to do with such incidental findings.

> ▲ This is a relevant ethical consideration, linked to the context of the study.

In terms of applying the findings of the study, the researcher "suggested that training sessions need to be conducted for male students to help them improve their online communication behaviour and create fewer obstacles for female students in expressing their empathy" (lines 52–56). Considerations here include the following.

> ▲ Ethical considerations in applying the findings of the study are clearly separated and relevant.

- Data may be insufficient to make a conclusion that male participants need training. Male participants may be offended by this suggestion, and to be fair they were under-represented in this research. Additional research is necessary and such recommendations cannot be warranted.

▶ Three ethical considerations are outlined, but there is some overlap between them.

- Online empathy is a new phenomenon, and any regulative measures in this sphere may be counter-productive. This research can certainly be used to gain insight into the process, but it can hardly be the basis for designing intervention programmes.
- One should remember about the possible consequences of bringing the results of the study to the attention of authorities. For example, school management may misinterpret the results as meaning that male students are offensive in their online behaviour, which again could lead to counter-productive administrative measures.

**3.** Discuss the possibility of generalizing the findings of the study.    [9]

▲ The candidate demonstrates understanding that quantitative and qualitative research studies approach the issue of generalizability differently.

Qualitative studies are characterized by three types of generalizability: sample-to-population, case-to-case and theoretical generalizability (Firestone 1993). Since this is a qualitative study, these three types apply here.

Sample-to-population generalizability is the extent to which results may be generalized from the participants in the study to a wider population. However, sampling in qualitative research is non-probabilistic in nature and generalizing to a population is not the goal. For example, in this particular study the goal was to investigate patterns of interpersonal communication of high school students. While it could be claimed that sample-to-population generalizability of this study is severely limited because of the uneven gender distribution, it must also be noted that gender differences were not the original focus of the study. They emerged in the process of investigation.

▲ Knowledge of non-probabilistic sampling in qualitative research is demonstrated.

Case-to-case generalizability is the extent to which findings could be applicable to other settings, for example, students in another school. Case-to-case generalizability depends to a large extent on how detailed the report is, and how rich the data that was collected. For example, when a teacher from another school reads the report, he or she will need to decide if results are applicable to that school. This will depend on how the results are reported, for example, how detailed the descriptions of participant responses are and how well contextual details were integrated in the analysis. But in general it is probably true that case-to-case generalizability of the unstructured interviews is high. There is no reason to expect that

▲ There is a balanced judgment of case-to-case generalizability.

▼ The candidate could further explain what conditions have to be met for the results to be generalized from this school to another similar school.

in that particular school empathy-related online experiences of teenagers are somehow different from those of other teenagers. Theoretical generalizability is the extent to which the study's findings may be generalized to a broader theory. It is probably true that the findings may be interpreted in the framework of a more general theory of gender differences (for example, some theories claim that male teenagers are less emotional). Such theories also corroborate the findings, which leads me to say that the theoretical generalizability of this study is sufficient.

> ▶ This is correct, but could be expressed a little more clearly.

**This response could have achieved 22/24 marks.**

**Question 1 (a):** 3/3. The method is identified correctly and two characteristics of the method are clearly outlined.

**Question 1 (b):** 3/3. The sampling method is correctly identified and described with a sufficient level of detail.

**Question 1 (c):** 3/3. A relevant additional method has been suggested and linked to the original aim of the study. A clear reason is given for the choice of method. It is also clearly explained why the method in this context works as an additional one, not an alternative.

**Question 2:** 5/6. Ethical considerations in the answer are clearly separated into two groups (reporting results and applying findings). Three ethical considerations are given for both groups, but some of them overlap (especially in applying the findings). They could be separated a little more clearly.

**Question 3:** 8/9. In general, the candidate demonstrated good understanding of qualitative terminology and effectively used all terms in appropriate contexts. However, some examples could be explained a little further, and for some arguments supporting details from the study could be provided.

## Sample response 2

SAMPLE STUDENT ANSWER

**1 (a)** Identify the research method used and outline **two** characteristics of the method. [3]

The research project used unstructured interviews. Unstructured interviews are more informal interviews, they usually do not use an interview schedule and contain open-ended questions that can be asked in any order. Being quite informal, questions can be made up and added or removed during the time the interview is being conducted, therefore it is a relatively flexible research method as the questions can be adapted and changed, according to the answers given. The use of open-ended questions yields qualitative data as it allows respondents to talk in depth and allows them to give their own opinions.

> ▼ If "not using a schedule" and "containing open-ended questions" are the two characteristics, they are not clearly separated.

**1 (b)** Describe the sampling method used in the study.     [3]

> ▶ Sampling method is correctly identified, but its non-probability nature could be further unpacked.

The sampling method used was convenience sampling. Convenience sampling is a non-probability method of sampling through collecting samples from people who are available at the time the study is being carried out. Samples are usually collected from the most convenient location around where the study is being conducted. The researcher conducted the interviews at the same school she worked at. Convenience sampling is a quick and easy method of sampling, therefore it is often used for research in schools and universities, as it was in this one.

**1 (c)** Suggest **one** alternative or **one** additional research method that could be used to investigate the aim of the original study, giving **one** reason for your choice.     [3]

> ▼ Only one reason for the choice of method is required. Additionally, what the candidate describes is not a survey but a quasi-experiment because the focus is on gender differences.

An alternative research method that could be used is a survey. A survey would allow for the researchers to ask specific questions in relation to gender differences in online communication for high school students in Switzerland, such as specific questions regarding their online communication habits, time spent online and so on. Also, using a survey could allow for a larger sample size as it would be easier to obtain results, especially if used with random sampling. This would further increase the generalizability of the results.

> ▼ In terms of ethical considerations involved in **reporting** results of a study, consent forms are important because they may contain information on how results will be reported. Consent to participate in the study itself may be categorized as an ethical consideration in **conducting** a study. It is not clear from the candidate's response which of the two aspects is meant here.

**2** Describe the ethical considerations in reporting the results and explain additional ethical considerations that could be taken into account when applying the findings of the study.     [6]

The participants were given consent forms to sign and were fully debriefed after the interviews were completed. They were also guaranteed full anonymity and confidentiality of their results after the interviews were conducted, which ensures that the identities behind the results were fully protected after the interviews were conducted. Confidentiality and anonymity must have been ensured as the unstructured interviews were carried out individually between the researcher and the participant. This is important as some people may feel insecure about their answers and uncomfortable having this information known by others. However, their information

> ▼ The candidate should focus on confidentiality in reporting results rather than promising confidentiality to participants.

may not have stayed completely confidential as a focus group met after the interviews, therefore information discussed during the focus group could be spread by participants. The researchers could have potentially asked the participants of the focus group to sign forms ensuring that what was discussed would not be shared.

Furthermore, participants should have been told afterwards that they could contact the researchers if they had any questions or wanted to know where their data was going to be used. Participants should also have been informed before the study about their right to withdraw, so they could withdraw their own participation as well as any data collected from the experiment at any given time.

> ▼ Two other considerations relevant to reporting results are mentioned here, but only very briefly.

**3.** Discuss the possibility of generalizing the findings of the study. [9]

The sampling method used was convenience sampling (where participants are selected based on convenience and selection criteria). Convenience sampling is a type of non-probability sampling. It follows a different logic from random sampling. The sample was limited to students at a high school in Switzerland and therefore was not representative of the communication styles used in different countries. The sample was relatively small with only 50 participants, therefore it is not considered to be statistically representative of the greater population. Furthermore there was a greater amount of females (34) in comparison to males (only 16), and the uneven number of males to females shows that it is not representative of different genders. Also, as the data received was qualitative, the amount of participants was significantly less, therefore it is not as generalizable. To make it more generalizable, a different sampling method such as random sampling could have been used, as well as a less specific research method, to allow for more participants to be included.

> ▲ There is some recognition of qualitative research being different from quantitative research in terms of generalization.

> ▼ The rest of the response uses the quantitative logic of representative sampling.

**This response could have achieved 10/24 marks.**

**Question 1 (a):** 2/3. The method is stated, but it could be more fully specified. One characteristic is outlined. The second characteristic is not clearly outlined or separated from the first one.

**Question 1 (b):** 2/3. The sampling method is correctly identified and some descriptive details are given. References are made to the stimulus material. However, the non-probability nature of convenience sampling could be further demonstrated.

**Question 1 (c):** 1/3. A survey as described by the candidate would be an additional method rather than an alternative. Exploring gender differences was not the aim of the original study. Gender differences emerged in the process of undertaking interviews. Therefore, the survey could be used to follow-up on these results. However, it can also be argued that the method the candidate described in the response is not a survey, but a quasi-experiment. If a survey is used to collect data and then investigate gender differences, the method is a quasi-experiment and the survey is a technique to measure a variable. In addition, it is not clear what the main reason is for choosing this method (the question requires only one reason).

**Question 2:** 2/6. Confidentiality in reporting results may be considered one ethical consideration that is fully described (1 mark awarded). Two other ethical considerations relevant to reporting (letting participants know how their data is going to be used and allowing participants to withdraw data after debriefing) are mentioned, but only very briefly (1 mark awarded rather than 2). The response does not explain any ethical considerations in applying the findings of the study (no marks awarded).

**Question 3:** 3/9. The candidate started with a recognition of the fact that qualitative research uses non-probability sampling and hence sample-to-population generalizability is usually not the aim. However, the rest of the answer is focused on explaining why sample-to-population generalizability of the study is limited, which contradicts the first part of the answer. Students should not judge generalizability of qualitative research on the basis of standards of quantitative research. Additionally, the candidate could have discussed other types of generalizability (case-to-case generalizability and theoretical generalizability).

# 10 INTERNAL ASSESSMENT

The internal assessment (IA) task is very different from writing essays. It requires you to conduct and analyse a study, it is done in a team, and it is not performed under timed exam conditions. But it is also quite "algorithmic". This means that you maximize your chances of getting a high mark if you strictly follow some existing algorithms and conventions.

In this section of this book we will do the following.

✔ Unpack assessment criteria for the IA.

✔ Provide a checklist that can be used prior to submitting the final version of your IA. Follow this checklist to make sure you have included all required elements and observed all the standards.

✔ Suggest a "study menu" from which to pick a study for your IA. This will not be an exhaustive list and you are free to choose anything beyond it, but it will give examples of research studies that could be linked clearly to a background theory or model.

Note that the focus of this book is on assessment, so we are not speaking about how the IA project should be conducted. We are looking only at the final report and discussing what makes some reports better than others.

## 10.1  UNPACKING IA ASSESSMENT CRITERIA

### Criterion I: Introduction (6 marks)

There are several things to note here.

The **aim** of the investigation is a very important element of the IA report, and you should formulate it carefully and precisely. (This is the aim of your own investigation, not the aim of the study you are replicating, although in many cases these two aims will be similar.) One way to state the aim is "To investigate the influence of A on B in a sample of C". This template is relevant because your study will be experimental (it is a requirement for the IA), hence there will be an independent variable (A) influencing the dependent variable (B). It may be a good idea to specify the sample because it will be different from the original study, so replicating the research on a new sample to check the generalizability of the conclusions may be considered one of the reasons why you are conducting this investigation.

To explain the **relevance** of the aim means to explain its relation to the original study that you are replicating and to explain why your investigation is worth carrying out. In terms of relation to the original study, you can speak about how your investigation will contribute to the theory or model upon which it is based. For example, you might have modified the original experiment a little and your investigation will test the applicability of the model in these new modified conditions. Or you simply have reasons to believe that applicability of the model may be limited in modern times, so this needs to be tested. In terms of practical relevance, you can speak about how results of the investigation might be used in real life.

The **theory or model** upon which your investigation is based is another important element of the IA report that is responsible for a lot of marks. Every experimental study published in a peer-reviewed journal provides an empirical test for some background theory or model. It is true that sometimes this theory or model is not explicitly identified

**The highest markband for this criterion requires the following:**

| 5–6 | The aim of the investigation is stated and its relevance is explained. |
|---|---|
| | The theory or model upon which the student's investigation is based is described and the link to the student's investigation is explained. |
| | The independent and dependent variables are stated and operationalized in the null or research hypothesis. |

or explained in the original publication. The trick is either to replicate a study where such links are already explicitly made in the published paper, or to "extract" information on the background theory or model from related publications. Below in the IA "study menu" we will provide some examples of published experiments with clear links to their respective background theories/models.

Although technically the assessment criteria do not require a separate statement of variables (they can be included in the research and null hypotheses), it is still advisable to define the independent and dependent variables and provide their operationalizations, and then formulate the null hypothesis and the research hypothesis using these operationalized variables.

## Criterion II: Exploration (4 marks)

**The highest markband for this criterion requires the following:**

| 3–4 | The research design is explained. |
| --- | --- |
| | The sampling technique is explained. |
| | The choice of participants is explained. |
| | Controlled variables are explained. |
| | The choice of materials is explained. |

Two things are especially important for this assessment criterion.

- Include all necessary elements in the report. There are five elements: design, sampling technique, choice of participants, controlled variables and choice of materials. Technically you are not required to separate these by individual headings, but it is advisable to do so.

- All five elements need to be explained (as opposed to simply described). This means that you should explain why you have chosen this particular element (design, sampling technique and so on) and exactly how it works. Some examples below will clarify this.

Note that a description of the experimental procedure is not explicitly mentioned in the criteria, but it is still advisable to include it. It will not be assessed because the procedure may be identical for all members of the group, but it is still an essential element of any experimental report and without it the rest of the report will make little sense.

## Criterion III: Analysis (6 marks)

**The highest markband for this criterion requires the following:**

| 5–6 | Descriptive and inferential statistics are appropriately and accurately applied. |
| --- | --- |
| | The graph is correctly presented and addresses the hypothesis. |
| | The statistical findings are interpreted with regard to the data and linked to the hypothesis. |

To appropriately and accurately apply **descriptive and inferential statistics** means to choose the appropriate statistical tests (and explain why they have been chosen), to carry out calculations correctly, and to report the results accurately and in accordance with all conventions. The choice of statistical tests may depend on factors such as the level of measurement (nominal, ordinal, interval, ratio), the presence of outliers in raw data and the experimental design (repeated measures or independent measures). In reporting inferential results, it is important to choose between a two-tailed and one-tailed test, to choose an appropriate level of statistical significance, and to make a correct conclusion (for example, reject the null hypothesis if the result of an inferential test is statistically significant).

The **graph addresses the hypothesis** when the elements of the graph are directly related to the key comparison that is being tested. For example, in an independent measures design, if the hypothesis requires a comparison between two groups of participants, the graph will include two bars denoting the measures of central tendency for the two groups, and two error bars denoting the measure of dispersion. The graph should not contain any unnecessary data (for example, it is not appropriate to include individual results). The graph is correctly presented when it follows the requirements of a standard publication style (for example, APA). Some of the common rules include the requirement that the graph does not contain any unnecessary elements hindering understanding, that the $y$-axis starts with a 0 and that there is a clear legend explaining the meaning of all elements in the graph.

To **link statistical findings to the hypothesis** means to interpret the findings correctly in terms of your original hypothetical prediction. For example, if results of the inferential test are not significant, you should accept the null hypothesis and reject the research hypothesis. It is important to make a correct conclusion.

Note that some elements of the report are not explicitly mentioned in the criteria, but it is still advisable to include them (namely, a table of results with descriptive statistics).

## Criterion IV: Evaluation (6 marks)

Once again, this assessment criterion looks at the link between your investigation and the background theory or model. This means that if the theory or model is not accurately and explicitly identified in the introduction, you are likely to lose marks for your evaluation too. It is important to ensure that **results are discussed in relation to the theory or model**, not just the replicated study. To say that your results coincide with those of the original study and therefore corroborate the theory is a little too superficial. You have modified the original study in some aspect (at the very least, you used a new sample coming from a different place and time) – what does this mean in terms of supporting or refuting the theory?

For **strengths and limitations**, it is advisable to give strengths and limitations related to the three elements of design, sample and procedure. Strengths and limitations should be relevant to the investigation, therefore they should not be generic. For example, stating that a limitation of the sample is that the sample size was too small is not really relevant – it is not specific to your investigation, and this limitation can be said to apply to any study.

Finally, **modifications** should follow on from the limitations you identified, and there should be relevant suggestions for how the limitations could be overcome.

**The highest markband for this criterion requires the following.**

| 5–6 | The findings of the student's investigation are discussed with reference to the background theory or model. |
| --- | --- |
| | Strengths and limitations of the design, sample and procedure are stated and explained and relevant to the investigation. |
| | Modifications are explicitly linked to the limitations of the student's investigation and fully justified. |

# 10.2  THE IA CHECKLIST

This checklist is designed to assist you in making sure that your final IA report includes all the required elements. You can also use it in the process of writing as a guide to what needs to be mentioned and in which section.

| Item | Check? |
|---|:---:|
| **Title page** | |
| Write a title of the IA report. It can be in the following form: *"An experiment to investigate the influence of … on … : a replication of Smith and Smith (1979)"* | ❏ |
| Include the word count. | ❏ |
| Include your own alphanumeric candidate code and candidate codes of your teammates (alphanumeric candidate codes are in the format xyz123). | ❏ |
| Include your exam session (for example, May 2021). | ❏ |
| **Introduction** | |
| Describe the theory or model upon which your investigation is based. This should be the theory or model that was tested in the original study that you are replicating. | ❏ |
| Include a description of the original study you are replicating (this part is not assessed and is not part of the markband, but it is necessary for the logic of the report; be brief and only report the details that are essential in the context of your own investigation). | ❏ |
| Briefly explain the modifications you have made to the original study and justify them. | ❏ |
| State the aim of your investigation. The aim should be written in theoretical terms (constructs, not operationalizations). | ❏ |
| Explain the relevance of your aim for the background theory or model and for any potential practical applications. | ❏ |
| Explain how your own investigation is linked to the background theory or model, for example how your investigation will contribute to testing or clarifying the theory or model. | ❏ |
| Name your variables (independent and dependent), first as a construct and then its operationalization (for example, "the IV is post-event information, operationalized as emotional intensity of the verb in the leading question"). | ❏ |
| State your research hypothesis using operationalized variables. | ❏ |
| Specify whether the hypothesis is one-tailed or two-tailed. | ❏ |
| State your null hypothesis (this should be a statement opposite to the research hypothesis). | ❏ |
| **Exploration** | |
| Break this section down into six sub-headings: design, sampling technique, participants, controlled variables, choice of materials, procedure (the last one is not assessed because it may be identical to your teammates' but it must be included for the clarity and continuity of the report). | ❏ |
| Identify your experimental design and state which design was used. | ❏ |
| Explain the choice of this experimental design (for example, refer to avoiding order effects, participant guessing, participant variability). Why was this design preferred to other possible designs? | ❏ |
| Acknowledge the limitations of your experimental design. | ❏ |
| State the sampling technique that was used in your investigation. | ❏ |
| Explain how sampling was performed. | ❏ |
| Explain the choice of the sampling technique – why was it preferred to other options? | ❏ |
| Describe the relevant characteristics of participants in your study, especially the parameters that are relevant in the context of your investigation – for example, driving experience in a replication of Loftus and Palmer (1974). | ❏ |
| Explain how the characteristics of your sample affect the generalizability of results in your investigation. | ❏ |
| State your target population (individuals to which the results of your investigation can be generalized). | ❏ |
| List the variables you controlled (by eliminating them or keeping them constant in all conditions), and state how you controlled them. | ❏ |
| Explain why it was important to control these variables. | ❏ |
| List all materials you used for the study (for example, PowerPoint slides with a memory stimulus, a stopwatch, a standardized questionnaire, a standard instruction). | ❏ |

▲ Table 10.2.1  The IA checklist                                                      *(Continued)*

| Item | Check? |
|---|:---:|
| **Exploration** | |
| For the most relevant ones, explain why these materials were chosen (for example, PowerPoint slides were chosen because it is easy to change the slides automatically after a certain amount of time). | ❏ |
| Include a step-by step description of the experimental procedure. Make sure that it is brief but includes all details necessary for an independent researcher to replicate your investigation exactly. | ❏ |
| Include references to relevant appendices in the procedure. For example: "Participants were invited into the classroom and given a consent form (Appendix 1)". | ❏ |
| Make sure to include (in the procedure section) an indication of how ethical guidelines were followed in the investigation. For example, participants were given a consent form, debriefed and given an opportunity to withdraw from participation/withdraw their results. | ❏ |
| **Analysis** | |
| Include two sub-headings: one for descriptive statistics and one for inferential statistics. | ❏ |
| State the measure of central tendency that was used in your investigation. Explain the choice of this measure of central tendency (for example, you can refer to the level of measurement, outliers, normality of distribution). | ❏ |
| State the measure of dispersion that was used in your investigation. Explain the choice of this measure of dispersion. | ❏ |
| State descriptive results in the text ("The mean number of words recalled in the first condition was … "). | ❏ |
| Include a table for the results of descriptive statistics. | ❏ |
| Include a clear, self-sufficient title for the table. Avoid non-specific terms for this (such as "experimental group", "control group", "group 1", "group 2"). | ❏ |
| Include a graph for the same results. | ❏ |
| Include a clear, self-sufficient title for the graph. | ❏ |
| Align the graph with your hypothesis. For example, if the hypothesis is about the comparison of two groups, the graph must show aggregated data (one measure of central tendency and one measure of dispersion) for the two groups. Most commonly, your graph will be a bar graph with error bars. | ❏ |
| Include a clear legend for the graph, explaining what each element of the graph stands for. | ❏ |
| Start the $y$-axis with 0 to avoid misrepresenting small differences. | ❏ |
| Include an appendix showing the calculations of descriptive statistics. Make sure to demonstrate the working and not only the end result. (If you used software to calculate results, screenshots are necessary that show how the calculations were performed. For example, in a screenshot from a spreadsheet you should show the formula that was written into a cell calculating the measure of central tendency.) | ❏ |
| State the inferential statistical test that has been used. | ❏ |
| Explain the choice of inferential statistics (you can make references to the level of measurement, experimental design, presence of outliers/normality of distribution). | ❏ |
| Report results of the inferential test in a standardized format (for example, following the APA conventions). | ❏ |
| Make sure to mention the value of the inferential test (for example, the U value for the Mann-Whitney test), the level of statistical significance and the type of test of significance that was used (one-tailed or two-tailed). | ❏ |
| Include an appendix showing calculations of inferential statistics. Make sure to demonstrate the working and not only the final result. (For example, if online software was used to calculate results, include screenshots clearly demonstrating which options were selected and which parts of the output were used in the reporting of results.) | ❏ |
| Formulate the conclusion in terms of accepting or rejecting the null hypothesis. (For example, "The result was statistically significant, therefore the null hypothesis was rejected and the research hypothesis accepted".) | ❏ |
| Formulate the conclusion in the language of the hypothesis that was accepted. | ❏ |
| **Evaluation** | |
| Link the findings of your investigation to the background theory or model. For example, explain the significance of your findings for the theory. | ❏ |
| Name and explain at least one strength for each of the following elements: design, sampling, procedure. | ❏ |
| Name and explain at least one limitation for each of the following elements: design, sampling, procedure. | ❏ |
| Make sure that the strengths and limitations are specific to your investigation and not generic points that can be applied to any study. | ❏ |
| Make sure that the limitations of procedure were unavoidable (otherwise they are considered poor planning on your part rather than a limitation of the procedure). | ❏ |
| Explain modifications that can be made to the study in future research to overcome the limitations that you identified earlier. Make sure that the suggested modifications are linked to the limitations. | ❏ |

*(Continued)*

| Item | Check? |
|---|---|
| **References and in-text citations** ||
| Make sure that you are consistently using one of the accepted publication formats in your references and in-text citations. (APA is advisable for Psychology. The items below will assume that you are using APA.) | ❏ |
| Make sure that all ideas in your report are properly cited and referenced. | ❏ |
| Make sure that there is a one-to-one correspondence between in-text citations and references: for every in-text citation there must be a reference at the end, and for every reference there must be an in-text citation. | ❏ |
| Make sure that you are citing relevant, credible sources (avoid popular educational websites and prioritize publications in academic, peer-reviewed journals). | ❏ |
| Make sure that all references have all required elements (such as author initials, year of publication, the name of the journal, the number of the journal issue, page numbers). | ❏ |
| For online sources, make sure you have included a URL or DOI and date of retrieval. | ❏ |
| Make sure journal names are not abbreviated in your bibliography entries (for example, *Journal of Personality and Social Psychology* is not abbreviated as *J Pers Soc Psychol*). | ❏ |
| If you use a direct quote in quotation marks, include the page number in the in-text citation (for example, Loftus and Palmer, 1974, p.586). | ❏ |
| If in doubt, consult the latest edition of the relevant citation manual. You should be able to find it online. | ❏ |
| Do not blindly trust automated citation tools. If you use them, cross-check manually that references are correct and contain all required elements. | ❏ |
| **Appendices** ||
| Include all necessary appendices, such as the consent form, briefing instructions, debriefing instructions, stimulus materials, raw data, and calculations of descriptive and inferential statistics. | ❏ |
| Clearly label each appendix with a number and a title. | ❏ |
| For the consent form, include a pro-forma (not filled out). | ❏ |
| In the raw data, delete the names of participants. | ❏ |
| **General formatting** ||
| Anonymize the IA report by making sure your name, the names of your teammates or the name of your school do not appear anywhere in the report. If names do appear in the report, you can replace them with "XXXXXX". | ❏ |
| If your email address or other contact details appear on the consent form or the debriefing form, anonymize these too. | ❏ |
| Make sure that your report is within the word count of 1,800–2,200 words (not included in the word count are: tables and graphs, references, appendices and in-text citations). | ❏ |
| Include a clear table of contents. | ❏ |

This "study menu" is meant to give you some examples of research studies that have been popular in the past for replication in a Psychology IA project, together with a brief description of the background thoery or model for each study. The purpose is to demonstrate what counts as the background theory or model.

By no means is this list exhaustive. Nor is it a suggestion that these studies are somehow "better" for Psychology IA than any other studies you might want to use for your investigation.

Note that full texts of all publications cited here at the time of writing this book were accessible online for free.

| Description | Theory/model | Notes |
| --- | --- | --- |
| **Study: Loftus and Palmer (1974)** | | |
| Participants were shown clips of a car crash and asked to estimate the speed of a car. A verb was changed in the leading question. | The theory of reconstructive memory: post-event information can get integrated with the original memory of the event, altering this memory. In the study, post-event information is operationalized as the emotional intensity of the verb used in the leading question (such as "contacted", "smashed into") and memory of the original event is operationalized as an estimation of the speed of the car in the video. | The theory is described on the last page of the original Loftus and Palmer (1974) publication: Loftus, EF and Palmer, JC 1974. "Reconstruction of Automobile Destruction: an Example of the Interaction between Language and Memory." *Journal of Verbal Learning and Verbal Behaviour.* Vol 13, pp 585–589.<br><br>See the "Discussion" section in this publication. |
| **Study: Strack and Mussweiler (1997)** | | |
| A study of anchoring bias. Participants were first asked a question with an unreasonably low or unreasonably high anchor ("Did Mahatma Gandhi die before or after the age of 9 years old?"; "Did Mahatma Gandhi die before or after the age of 140 years old?"). Then participants were asked the key question requiring them to make a decision ("How old was Mahatma Gandhi when he died?"). | Anchoring bias is based on the selective accessibility model. This model explains that when participants are given the comparative task (such as "Did Mahatma Gandhi die before or after the age of 140 years old?"), they test the possibility that the target (Gandhi) possesses the anchor value (140) by constructing a mental image that is as consistent with this value as possible. Subsequently this mental image becomes highly accessible and therefore impacts further judgments. | Selective accessibility model is explained in detail (and related to the results of the study) on the last page of Strack and Mussweiler's paper: Strack, F and Mussweiler, T. 1997. "Explaining the Enigmatic Anchoring Effect: Mechanisms of Selective Accessibility." *Journal of Personality and Social Psychology.* Vol 73, number 3, pp 437–446.<br><br>For a more detailed discussion, see also: Mussweiler, T and Strack, F. 2001. "Considering the Impossible: Explaining the Effects of Implausible Anchors." *Social Cognition.* Vol 19, number 2, pp 145–160. |
| **Study: Glanzer and Cunitz (1966)** | | |
| A study on the influence of recall delay on serial position effect. In one of the experiments (experiment 2), researchers presented participants with a list of words and varied the amount of time between the end of the list and when the words had to be recalled. The researchers found that a delay between the end of the list and recall affects the recall of the last words on the list (recency), but not the recall of the first words (primacy). | The research study supports the multi-store memory model (MSMM), and in particular the thesis that short-term memory and long-term memory are two separate memory stores. Introducing a delay between the end of the list and recall prevents the non-rehearsed words from the end of the list from being transferred from short-term memory into the long-term memory store. As a result, recall of these words is affected. At the same time, the fact that the first words on the list are not affected is also consistent with MSMM because, theoretically, these words were rehearsed and therefore entered a separate memory store (long-term memory) that is not affected by the delay. | Glanzer, M, and Cunitz, AR. 1966. "Two Storage Mechanisms in Free Recall." *Journal of Verbal Learning and Verbal Behaviour.* Vol 5, number 4, pp 351–360.<br><br>This paper reports on two separate experiments. They are both acceptable for the IA (with some simplifications), but experiment 2 is more straightforward. |

▲ Table 10.3.1  The IA study menu: example studies and background theories or models

(*Continued*)

| Description | Theory/model | Notes |
|---|---|---|
| **Study: Tversky and Kahneman (1981)** | | |
| A study on the framing effect. Participants were presented with a hypothetical scenario involving an outbreak of a disease that can potentially kill 600 people, and the necessity for the government to pick one of two proposed strategies. The pairs of strategies presented to the two groups of participants were logically identical, but differed in how they were framed: in terms of gains ("200 people will be saved") or in terms of losses ("400 people will die"). | This and other similar research conducted by Tversky and Kahneman observed reversal of choice in risky decision problems depending on how the problem is framed. They claim that such dependence of decisions on framing presents a challenge for the traditional normative theory of decision-making under risk – the expected utility theory. As an alternative to this theory that incorporates their new experimental data, they suggest the prospect theory of decision-making. Prospect theory is the background theory or model that may be used for this study. It is also reasonable to discuss the expected utility theory in this context.<br><br>Prospect theory suggests that decision-making under risk consists of two phases: an initial phase in which outcomes are framed and a reference point set, and the final phase in which outcomes are evaluated. The theory also suggests that outcomes are expressed as positive or negative deviations from the reference point originally established (and where the reference point will be placed depends on how the problem is framed). | Tversky, A and Kahneman, D. 1981. "The Framing of Decisions and the Psychology of Choice." *Science.* Vol 211, number 4481, pp453–458.<br><br>Tvesky and Kahneman describe prospect theory in an accessible way in their 1981 publication (although the theory itself was developed a little earlier).<br><br>Their explanation is also accompanied by a graphical representation that is worth reviewing. |
| **Study: Craik and Tulving (1975)** | | |
| A study on the influence of depth of processing on the retention of words in memory. Ten separate experiments are described in the original paper, but experiment 2 is chosen as an example here. In this experiment participants were first shown a list of 60 words, and before each of the words asked one of three questions (Is the word written in uppercase? Does the word rhyme with … ? Does the word fit in the sentence " … "?). Following this, rate of recall was compared for the three groups of words preceded by different questions. | The theoretical model for this study, as well as all 10 experiments reported in the paper, is the levels of processing (LOP) framework for human memory proposed by Craik and Lockhart (1972).<br><br>The levels of processing model suggests that the duration of a memory trace depends on the depth of processing at the stage of encoding. There are three levels of processing described in the model: structural, phonetic and semantic. Structural and phonetic processing are examples of "shallow" processing, while semantic processing is "deep". According to the theoretical prediction, deep processing will result in better memory (a longer-lasting memory trace). | The theory is described in detail in the following publication (see pp 675–677 especially):<br><br>Craik, FIM and Lockhart, RS. 1972. "Levels of Processing: A Framework for Memory Research." *Journal of Verbal Learning and Verbal Behaviour.* Vol 11, pp 671–684.<br><br>The study itself:<br><br>Craik, FIM and Tulving, E. 1975. "Depth of Processing and the Retention of Words in Episodic Memory." *Journal of Experimental Psychology.* Vol 104, number 3, pp 268–294. |
| **Study: Iyengar and Lepper (2000)** | | |
| Groups of participants were offered a selection of chocolates. One group had a selection of 6 choices whereas the other group had a selection of 24 choices. The study predicted that when there is too much choice, participants will be less likely to make any choice at all and less likely to be satisfied with the choice they made. (In a variation of this study, chocolates were replaced by a choice of optional class essay assignments.) | The model behind this study is the choice overload hypothesis. The model states that there are different motivational consequences of limited (psychologically manageable) and extensive (psychologically excessive) choices. It further asserts that the provision of excessive choices may be seen as desirable at first, but proves to be unexpectedly demotivating in the end. This is explained in the following way: being presented with an extensive choice results in a greater enjoyment of the choice-making process (because of the opportunities provided), but also in an increased feeling of responsibility for the choice. This feeling of responsibility is later translated into a greater dissatisfaction with the choice that was made. | Iyengar, SS and Lepper, MR. 2000. "When Choice is Demotivating: Can One Desire be Too Much of a Good Thing?" *Journal of Personality and Social Psychology.* Vol 79, number 6, pp 995–1006.<br><br>The choice overload hypothesis is described in the original publication: see both the introductory section (pp 995–996) and "general discussion" (pp 1003–1004). |

Below you will find a sample internal assessment report from a student who replicated Strack and Mussweiler's (1997) study on the effects of anchoring on decision-making. This report was selected for several reasons. First, it is well written and follows the checklist of necessary elements quite accurately. Second, it is quite detailed and provides a good example of writing about various aspects where students often lack confidence (such as explaining the choice of inferential statistics, describing participant characteristics). Third, Strack and Mussweiler's research is a popular choice for student IAs. There are examiner comments throughout the report itself as well as holistic comments at the end. Marks are provided for all criteria and the allocation of marks is explained. To make sure that the example is complete, all appendices are also included.

## Title page

*Psychology Internal Assessment*

Enigmatic Anchoring Effect: A replication of Strack and Mussweiler (1997)

*An experiment to investigate the effect of anchoring bias on decision-making*

▲ Clear title based on the aim of the investigation.

Session: XXXXX

Candidate code: XXXXX

Candidate codes of team members: XXXXX

Psychology HL

Word count: 2199

## Contents

▲ The table of contents is helpful. All appendices clearly labelled and easy to follow.

## Introduction

Humans are subject to systematic errors in thinking known as cognitive biases, which result from heuristics: rules of thumb that individuals rely on to simplify decision-making (Todd 2001). Employed when one uses system 1 thinking (Stanovich & West 2000), heuristics facilitate fast decision-making by reducing cognitive load, but introduce errors when real-world situations deviate from one's assumptions.

One cognitive bias is anchoring bias: "disproportionate influence on decision-makers to make judgments that are biased toward an initially presented value" (Furnham & Boo, 2011, p. 35). Explaining this paradigm, Mussweiler and Strack (1999) proposed the selective accessibility model. According to this model, when provided with an anchor, individuals adopt a positive test strategy, in which they test the possibility that the anchor is the true value. In doing so, they selectively increase the accessibility of anchor-congruent knowledge, leading individuals to rely on this when generating their absolute estimates. This manifests itself in an assimilation of the absolute estimate towards the anchor.

Strack and Mussweiler (1997) examined the influence of anchoring on decision-making by giving a general-knowledge question to 69 university students. Each question had two components: a comparative judgment followed by an absolute judgment. Participants were randomly allocated to one of two groups and were given an implausible high or low anchor. One question asked Gandhi's age at death. Those in the high anchor group were asked whether Gandhi died before or after the age of 140, whereas the low anchor group were given the age of 9. Afterwards, participants were asked to estimate Gandhi's actual age of death. Results showed that participants' judgments were biased towards the number provided in the first question (anchor). With the high anchor, age estimates averaged 66.7, compared to 50.1 with the low anchor. Explaining this in terms of the selective accessibility model, participants given age 140 as the anchor, for example, generated their comparative judgment by testing the possibility that Gandhi's age at death is 140. In this process, they selectively recalled anchor-consistent knowledge, for example that Gandhi had many accomplishments, which implies that he was long-lived. Activating such knowledge increases its accessibility, prompting participants to base their absolute judgment upon this anchor-congruent evidence.

The following research is a partial replication of Strack and Mussweiler's study, aiming to investigate the influence of an implausible anchor on decision-making, specifically an age of death estimation. Instead of Gandhi, participants will estimate Abraham Lincoln's age at death, since Lincoln is better-known in this population. In addition to making a link to the selective accessibility model, the findings of this study will also demonstrate human limits to rationality, supporting the dual process model, specifically system 1 thinking – that individuals test the possibility that the anchor is true because "system 1 understands sentences by trying to make them true" (Kahneman, 2012, p. 122). Furthermore, it can help individuals to become more aware of strategic anchors in everyday life (such as in marketing or salary negotiations) and, perhaps, to make better decisions.

**H₁ – research hypothesis:** the mean values for the absolute judgment of Abraham Lincoln's age of death (years) of participants given

### Side annotations

▲ In-text citations follow the APA style consistently. For example, when a direct quote is used, the candidate also provides a page number where the quote can be found in the original paper.

▲ The background model is identified and explained.

▲ The original study is described briefly, and only details relevant to the candidate's own investigation are used. The original study is once again linked to the background model, explaining the model even further.

▲ The aim is stated.

▲ The modification is explained.

▲ The practical relevance of the aim is explained.

▲ The research and null hypotheses are clearly stated, the type of hypothesis is identified (one-tailed).

an implausible high anchor (140 years of age) will be higher than participants given an implausible low anchor (9 years of age).

A one-tailed hypothesis was chosen as there is previous research that supports this claim (Strack & Mussweiler 1997).

**H₀ – null hypothesis:** there will be no significant difference in the mean values for the absolute judgment of Abraham Lincoln's age of death (years) between participants given an implausible high anchor (140 years of age) and participants given an implausible low anchor (9 years of age).

## Exploration

### Design

To replicate the original study's design, an independent measures design was used, with participants randomly allocated to either an implausible high or implausible low anchor condition. As participants in both conditions answered questions regarding Lincoln's age at death, a repeated measures design was not feasible: participants' absolute estimate in their second condition will likely remain the same as their estimate in their first condition regardless of the anchor.

> ▲ The choice of design is explained.

### Sampling technique

As researchers had limited available time for testing due to scheduling conflicts, participants were limited to only those who were available during those times. Therefore, opportunity sampling was used, where available students belonging to the target population were approached and invited to participate. As anchoring bias is a universal phenomenon, the lack of representativeness that may occur from opportunity sampling will not reduce the generalizability of this study's findings.

> ▲ The sampling technique (opportunity sampling) is explained with reference to an argument rarely mentioned but relevant in this context (the universality of the cognitive phenomenon under study).

### Participants

The sample contained 10 male and 10 female non-psychology IB students taking English A: language and literature. They were either 16 or 17 years old and of different ethnicities including Chinese. Having studied Strack and Mussweiler's experiment, psychology students were not recruited to prevent demand characteristics. As the study used English instructions and questions, fluency in English was required, hence only students taking English A: language and literature were chosen. As participants' ages and educational backgrounds can influence their numerical estimation, the target population is Year 12 students from XXXXX School.

> ▲ Participant characteristics are stated and the choice of participants is explained.

> ▲ Based on characteristics of the sample, the target population is explicitly limited to a group to which results would be generalizable.

### Procedure

> ▲ The procedure is easy to follow and fully replicable. Clear links are given to appendices where the reader can find relevant forms and materials.

1. Using a random group generator (Appendix 1), participants were randomly allocated to the implausible high or implausible low anchor condition, ensuring that there was an equal number of participants per condition.

2. Individually, the participant entered a classroom with two researchers present, one providing instructions (researcher A) and the other recording the findings in silence (researcher B). Participants were asked to sit at desks prepared with a pen and an informed consent form.

3. Informed consent (Appendix 2) was obtained.

4. Standardized instructions (Appendix 3) were read out by researcher A.

5. Participants were presented with a computer screen that displayed the comparative judgment question (Appendix 4). Participants communicated their answers verbally with "before" or "after", which was recorded digitally by researcher B.

6. Researcher A pressed the space bar to display the next question – the absolute judgment question (Appendix 5). Participants' verbal answers were recorded digitally by researcher B.

7. A debriefing statement (Appendix 6) was read out by researcher A, and participants were reminded of their freedom to withdraw.

## Variables

▲ Operationalization of the independent and dependent variables is stated.

**Independent:** Lincoln's age at death provided in the comparative judgment question (in years, 9 or 140).

**Dependent:** participants' absolute estimate of Lincoln's age at death (in years).

### Controlled

▲ Controlled variables are explained. It is precisely identified what it is that the researchers are trying to control and why.

- Object of question: questions regarding Lincoln's age at death were asked in both conditions to control content effects.

- Phrasing of questions: the lexicon and syntactic structure of the questions were controlled so that participants' interpretations of the question (which can influence their final estimates) were consistent.

- Delivery of questions: questions were always presented using a PowerPoint slide. If a researcher had been used to deliver the questions, the person's tone may have varied, which could influence how information is conveyed and consequently influence the participant's answer.

## Materials

▲ The choice of materials is explained.

- **Standardized instructions** (Appendix 3) were read to each participant before starting the experiment. Informing participants of the experiment procedure in an identical way (in terms of content, style and delivery) minimized confounding variables and experimenter bias.

- A **debriefing statement** (Appendix 6) was read by researcher A at the conclusion of the study to complete participants' understanding of the experiment.

- A **random group generator** (Appendix 1) was used to allocate participants randomly to the two experimental conditions. All participants having an equal probability of being assigned to any condition minimized participant variables.

- Two **PowerPoint presentations** were prepared – one for each condition – each with two slides: the comparative judgment question (Appendix 4) on the first slide and the absolute judgment question (Appendix 5) on the second.

## Ethical considerations

- **Informed consent:** prior to participation, all participants were informed of the nature of the experiment, what they would be required to do, how their data would be used and their right to withdraw and confidentiality preservation. Parental consent was not required because all participants were at least 16 years old. All participation was voluntary.

- **Confidentiality:** participants and their data were kept unknown to third parties by restricting access to collected data.

- **Deception:** participants were not informed that the study would look at the influence of anchoring bias on decision-making.

- **Debriefing:** at the conclusion, participants were told the study's true aims, expected results and how their data would be used and stored. Deception and justification for this were revealed, and participants were reminded of their right to withdraw with an opportunity to ask questions.

- **Withdrawal from participation:** participants' freedom to withdraw at any point of the study was made clear explicitly through the informed consent and the debriefing statement.

> ▲ Ethical considerations are explained thoroughly. Although technically this section is not assessed, a breach of ethical considerations may result in no grade being awarded for the subject. For this reason, a section on how ethical considerations were addressed is essential for the IA report (although this could be combined with the "Procedure" section).

## Analysis

### Descriptive statistics

As the ratio-level variable (age) was collected, the mean was obtained as the measure of central tendency, and standard deviation as the measure of dispersion. These facilitated precise comparisons to Strack and Mussweiler's findings since they used the same measures to summarize their data, and also allowed all individual values in the raw data to be represented (this was acceptable because there were no severe outliers).

**Table 1:** *Means and standard deviations of participants' absolute estimate of Abraham Lincoln's age at death when given an implausible high anchor versus an implausible low anchor*

| Implausible anchor | Mean (years of age) | Standard deviation |
|:---:|:---:|:---:|
| High | 69.7 | 18.7 |
| Low | 50.5 | 15.8 |

> ▲ Table and graph titles are self-sufficient; the reader can fully understand both the graph and the table without having to read the report to make sense of the information.

Table 1 reveals that the mean estimate of participants who received an implausible high anchor was 69.7, compared to 50.5 for an implausible low anchor. The average estimate of the implausible high anchor group is higher than that of the implausible low anchor group, indicating that the anchors yielded strong assimilation effects on absolute estimates. The standard deviation of those in the implausible high anchor group was 18.7, and 15.8 for the implausible low anchor group.

**Graph 1:** *Differences in the means of participants' absolute estimate of Abraham Lincoln's age at death when given an implausible high anchor versus an implausible low anchor (note that error bars denote ±1 standard deviation)*

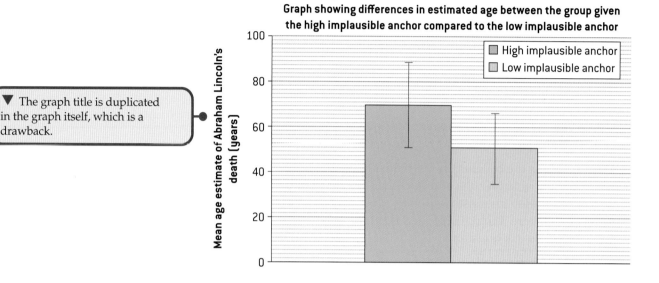

The graph title is duplicated in the graph itself, which is a drawback.

## Inferential statistics

Since normality of distribution cannot be assumed due to the small sample size, a non-parametric test was employed. As the study used an independent measures design and ratio-level data can be reduced to ordinal, the Mann-Whitney U test was applied (see Appendix 10) to look for a difference between conditions, obtaining U = 21. When compared to $p < 0.05$ at one-tailed hypothesis, this is smaller than the critical value 27, hence the data is significant at $p < 0.05$. Therefore, U = 21, $p < 0.05$, one-tailed. With less than 5% probability that results are due to chance and 95% confidence, the null hypothesis is rejected and research hypothesis is accepted: participants given an implausible high anchor indeed gave a higher mean value for the absolute judgment of Abraham Lincoln's age of death compared to participants given an implausible low anchor.

Inferential results are clearly reported using the accepted notation.

## Evaluation

The study successfully demonstrated the influence of anchoring bias on decision-making during age estimation. Given the same question regarding Lincoln's age at death, the estimates of participants given an implausible high anchor averaged 69.7, 19.2 higher than that of the implausible low anchor group (50.5). The Mann-Whitney U test revealed that this difference is significant when $p < 0.05$, supporting the study's research hypothesis and the findings of Strack and Mussweiler in that participants' absolute judgments were assimilated towards the implausible anchor.

For Strack and Mussweiler, this is due to selective accessibility of anchor-consistent information. Given their anchors, participants engaged in hypothesis testing, assessing whether their anchor value is Lincoln's actual age of death. Although this hypothesis was likely rejected due to the anchor value's implausibility, anchor-consistent evidence was nevertheless more easily retrievable, leading participants to rely on this biased evidence to make their subsequent absolute judgment. This is reflected in the absolute judgment that is assimilated towards the anchor value.

Strack and Mussweiler's study showed that the implausible low anchor had a greater impact on participants' absolute judgment than the implausible high anchor, reflecting the belief that 140 is impossible, rather than implausible. In this study, the implausible high anchor was more influential. This may be due to participant variability. Although a strength of an independent measures design is the elimination of content effects with participants in both conditions being asked Lincoln's age at death, different participants were used in each condition. Despite random allocation, participants who are more susceptible to anchoring bias due to lower cognitive abilities (Bergman, Ellingsen, Johannesson & Svensson, 2010) or introverted personalities (Eroglu & Croxton, 2010), for example, may have coincidentally been placed in the implausible higher anchor condition. A modification would be pre-testing participants with practice trials to ensure both groups have similar susceptibility to anchoring bias or increasing the sample size.

The opportunity sample gathered 10 boys and 10 girls. A strength of this is that the equal representation of gender allowed the study to support that anchoring bias is a universal phenomenon regardless of gender. However, this sample wasn't representative of the gender mix in the target population, since there are a higher proportion of girls in Year 12 at XXXXX School. To improve population validity, a modification would be studying the exact distribution of gender in the year group and recruiting participants accordingly.

Although Strack and Mussweiler presented participants with 22 pairs of comparative and absolute questions, participants in this study were asked only one pair of questions. A strength of this procedure is the prevention of fatigue effects: with more questions, participants would successively become more prone to anchoring bias with sustained cognitive demands and decision fatigue. That being said, some participants knew more about Lincoln's death. The final estimates of these participants resulted in anomalies since they relied on their knowledge rather than the anchor to make their decision. For example, knowing that Lincoln was assassinated, they gave a low estimate despite being given an implausible high anchor. To prevent the influence of participants' knowledge, a modification would be asking each condition two questions pertaining to different contents. For example, half of the group's participants might be asked about Lincoln's death and the other half about John F. Kennedy's death.

In conclusion, with the null hypothesis rejected using 0.05 level of significance, an implausible anchor did influence participants' estimates of Abraham Lincoln's age at death. This is consistent with the selective accessibility model (Mussweiler & Strack, 1999) and the dual process model (Stanovich & West, 2000).

▶ An attempt is made to link the results back to the background model (but the candidate has done a better job at analysing the original study rather than his or her own investigation).

▲ The design, sample and procedure are equally represented when discussing strengths and limitations. Suggested modifications are meaningful and clearly linked to the limitations identified earlier.

▲ Once again the link is being made to the background theories or models: the more specific selective accessibility model and the more general dual process model.

▲ References follow the APA format.

## References

Bergman, O., Ellingsen, T., Johannesson, M., & Svensson, C. (2010). Anchoring and cognitive ability. *Economics Letters, 107*(1), 66–68. https://doi.org/10.1016/j.econlet.2009.12.028

Eroglu, C., & Croxton, K. (2010). Biases in judgmental adjustments of statistical forecasts: The role of individual differences. *International Journal of Forecasting, 26*(1), 116–133. https://doi.org/10.1016/j.ijforecast.2009.02.005

Furnham, A., & Boo, H. (2011). A literature review of the anchoring effect. *The Journal of Socio-Economics, 40*(1), 35–42. https://doi.org/10.1016/j.socec.2010.10.008

Kahneman, D. (2012). *Thinking, Fast and Slow*. Penguin Books.

Mussweiler, T., & Strack, F. (1999). Hypothesis-consistent testing and semantic priming in the anchoring paradigm: A selective accessibility model. *Journal of Experimental Social Psychology, 35*(2), 136–164. https://doi.org/10.1006/jesp.1998.1364

Stanovich, K., & West, R. (2000). Individual differences in reasoning: Implications for the rationality debate? *Behavioural and Brain Sciences, 23*(5), 645–665. https://doi.org/10.1017/s0140525x00003435

Strack, F., & Mussweiler, T. (1997). Explaining the enigmatic anchoring effect: Mechanisms of selective accessibility. *Journal of Personality And Social Psychology, 73*(3), 437–446. https://doi.org/10.1037/0022-3514.73.3.437

Todd, P. (2001). Heuristics for decision and choice. *International Encyclopedia of The Social & Behavioural Sciences*, 6676–6679. https://doi.org/10.1016/b0-08-043076-7/00629-x

## Appendices

### Appendix 1: Random group generator

▲ A link is given to a website, enhancing the replicability of the investigation.

Link to website: https://www.randomlists.com/team-generator

**Random team generator**

| Group 1 | | | | | |
| --- | --- | --- | --- | --- | --- |
| 1 Participant 6 | 2 Participant 20 | 3 Participant 13 | 4 Participant 2 | 5 Participant 1 | 6 Participant 19 |
| 7 Participant 11 | 8 Participant 8 | 9 Participant 12 | 10 Participant 16 | | |

| Group 2 | | | | | |
| --- | --- | --- | --- | --- | --- |
| 1 Participant 17 | 2 Participant 5 | 3 Participant 4 | 4 Participant 15 | 5 Participant 3 | 6 Participant 9 |
| 7 Participant 18 | 8 Participant 10 | 9 Participant 7 | 10 Participant 14 | | |

## Appendix 2: Consent form

Dear participant,

We will be conducting an experiment into decision-making for our Psychology IA. This will involve taking part in a general-knowledge questionnaire. You will not be subjected to any physical or psychological harm, and all data will be kept anonymous and confidential. You may withdraw yourself and your information from this experiment at any time in case you change your mind, and all results of the experiment can be received upon request. Don't hesitate to ask questions if you have any.

I, _____, understand the nature of this experiment and I agree to participate voluntarily. I give the researchers permission to use my data as part of their experimental study. I understand that I should not reveal any information about the study afterwards.

Age: _____

Signature: _____      Date: _____

> ▲ A pro-forma consent form is given.

## Appendix 3: Standardized instructions

Welcome and thank you for agreeing to participate in this psychology experiment into decision-making. You will be presented with a computer screen with a question on it. You must not touch the computer and please answer the question verbally. After you have answered this question, I will swipe to the next slide with the second question on it. Please answer this question verbally as well. We will be recording your answers digitally on another computer. Are there any questions?

> ▲ These are the standardized instructions to be read out to each participant. This is an important element of the appendices that is often overlooked by students.

## Appendix 4: Comparative judgment questions

**Implausible low anchor:**

Did Abraham Lincoln die before or after the age of 9?

**Implausible high anchor:**

Did Abraham Lincoln die before or after the age of 140?

> ▲ Screenshots are given from the presentation that was used in the study to ask participants the key questions.

## Appendix 5: Absolute judgment question

How old was Abraham Lincoln when he died?

▲ The debriefing is clear and informative. Minor deception is revealed. Participants are given the opportunity to withdraw their results from the study. Participants are allowed to ask questions.

## Appendix 6: Debriefing statement

This experiment investigated the influence of anchoring bias on decision-making. We did not inform you of this at the beginning of the study to prevent the possibility of you changing your behaviour. There were two conditions in this experiment: an implausible high anchor or an implausible low anchor. Previous research has demonstrated that participants given the low anchor consistently guessed lower values for a person's age of death, while those with the high anchor consistently guessed higher values. The results obtained here seem to confirm that. The data we have collected today will be used for the analysis of results in our IA, and will be stored in a document with restricted access to maintain your confidentiality. Once again, we would like to remind you that you have the right to withdraw your data. Please inform us if you would like to do so and we will delete your data from all records accordingly. If you are interested you can know the full results of the experiment. Please let us know so that we can send you the information via email. Do you have any questions? Thank you very much for your participation.

▲ Raw data is anonymized.

## Appendix 7: Raw data

| Participant | Gender | Implausible anchor | Comparative judgment | Absolute judgment |
|---|---|---|---|---|
| 1 | Male | High | Before | 50 |
| 2 | Male | High | Before | 80 |
| 3 | Male | Low | After | 60 |
| 4 | Male | Low | After | 70 |
| 5 | Male | Low | After | 60 |
| 6 | Male | High | Before | 45 |
| 7 | Male | Low | After | 50 |
| 8 | Male | High | Before | 84 |
| 9 | Male | Low | After | 45 |
| 10 | Male | Low | After | 42 |
| 11 | Female | High | Before | 90 |
| 12 | Female | High | Before | 65 |
| 13 | Female | High | Before | 74 |
| 14 | Female | Low | After | 20 |
| 15 | Female | Low | After | 73 |
| 16 | Female | High | Before | 90 |
| 17 | Female | Low | After | 45 |
| 18 | Female | Low | After | 40 |
| 19 | Female | High | Before | 40 |
| 20 | Female | High | Before | 79 |

## Appendix 8: Calculation

▲ Calculations are clearly shown with screenshots.

A calculator was used to obtain the mean and standard deviations of participants' absolute estimate of Abraham Lincoln's age at death when given implausible anchors.

Link to calculator: https://www.calculatorsoup.com/calculators/statistics/statistics.php

**Implausible high anchor:**

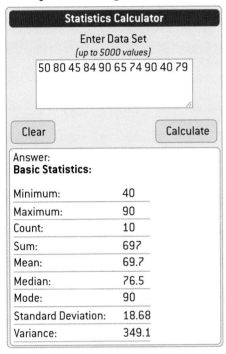

**Implausible low anchor:**

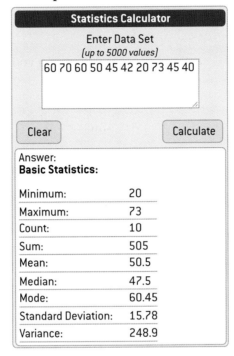

## Appendix 9: Summarized data table

| Implausible anchor | Comparative judgment | Mean absolute judgment | Standard deviation |
|---|---|---|---|
| High | Before | 69.7 | 18.7 |
| Low | After | 50.5 | 15.8 |

193

## Appendix 10: Inferential statistics

A calculator was used to apply the Mann-Whitney U test.

Link to calculator: https://www.socscistatistics.com/tests/mannwhitney/default2.aspx

▲ Calculations clearly shown with screenshots. It is shown which particular values were used as the final output. All decisions are also demonstrated (for example, the decision to use a one-tailed test of statistical significance).

| Sample 1 | Sample 2 | S1 Values | S1 Ranks | S2 Values | S2 Ranks |
|---|---|---|---|---|---|
| 50 | 60 | 40 | 2.5 | 20 | 1 |
| 80 | 70 | 45 | 6 | 40 | 2.5 |
| 45 | 60 | 50 | 8.5 | 42 | 4 |
| 84 | 50 | 65 | 12 | 45 | 6 |
| 90 | 45 | 74 | 15 | 45 | 6 |
| 65 | 42 | 79 | 16 | 50 | 8.5 |
| 74 | 20 | 80 | 17 | 60 | 10.5 |
| 90 | 73 | 84 | 18 | 60 | 10.5 |
| 40 | 45 | 90 | 19.5 | 70 | 13 |
| 79 | 40 | 90 | 19.5 | 73 | 14 |

Significance Level:

◯ 0.01

◉ 0.05

One- or two-tailed hypothesis?:

◉ One-tailed

◯ Two-tailed

**Result Details**

*Sample 1*
Sum of ranks: 134
Mean of ranks: 13.4
Expected sum of ranks: 105
Expected mean of ranks: 10.5
$U$-value: 21
Expected $U$-value: 50

*Sample 2*
Sum of ranks: 76
Mean of ranks: 7.6
Expected sum of ranks: 105
Expected mean of ranks: 10.5
$U$-value: 79
Expected $U$-value: 50

*Sample 1 & 2 Combined*
Sum of ranks: 210
Mean of ranks: 10.5
Standard Deviation: 13.2288

*Result 1 - U-value*

The $U$-value is 21. The critical value of $U$ at $p > .05$ is 27.
Therefore, the result is significant at $p > .05$.

## Examiner report

**This IA report could have achieved 19/22 marks.**

### Introduction: 5/6

Anchoring bias is correctly related to the relevant theoretical model – the selective accessibility model proposed by Strack and Mussweiler (1999). The model is clearly described. Additionally, the broader theoretical roots of the selective accessibility model (system 1 and system 2 thinking – the dual process model) are also outlined. However, there could be more clarity regarding which one of the two models (the dual process model or the selective accessibility model) is the main theoretical framework for the candidate's investigation.

The aim of the candidate's investigation is clearly stated. The aim is related to the background theory or model (selective accessibility model), although this link could be explained more explicitly. The candidate also explained the practical relevance of the aim of the investigation.

The independent and dependent variables are clearly operationalized (this is explicitly shown further on in the "Exploration" section). The variables are also operationalized in the research and null hypotheses.

### Exploration: 4/4

Research design is explained with reference to an attempt to avoid order effects (which made alternative research designs impossible or not desirable).

The sampling technique is clearly stated and explained with reference to practical considerations, as well as the universality of the phenomenon under question (opportunity sampling is acceptable because there is no reason to expect that the object of investigation – the simple cognitive phenomenon of anchoring bias – will differ from sample to sample).

The characteristics of participants in the sample are clearly described, and the choice of participants is explained with reference to the aim of the investigation (for example, the fact that psychology students were not recruited was explained by the desire to avoid demand characteristics and guessing the aim of the study).

Controlled variables are clearly stated and explained. All controlled variables were aimed at standardizing the experimental procedure so as to keep constant the factors that could potentially influence the dependent variable (such as the tone of the question when asked verbally).

The choice of materials is effectively explained. The candidate provided a justification for why each material was used in the study. Additionally, materials are clearly labelled and included in the appendices.

### Analysis: 5/6

Descriptive and inferential statistics are appropriately and accurately applied. The choice of descriptive statistics is justified by the level of measurement of the data, the absence of outliers and the fact that the original study used the same measures (to enhance comparability). Descriptive statistics are applied accurately, calculations are fully demonstrated in an appendix, and results are reported in the text as well as a table and a graph.

The graph is presented correctly and with a consideration of all conventions; there is a clear, self-sufficient title and a clear legend. The graph directly addresses the hypothesis of the investigation.

The choice of inferential statistics is correct and is fully explained with reference to the level of measurement, experimental design and expectations regarding normality of distribution. The test is accurately applied and interpreted in terms of the research hypothesis. Calculations are fully demonstrated in an appendix.

### Evaluation: 5/6

The findings of the candidate's investigation are discussed with reference to the background model. The candidate discussed how Strack and Mussweiler's findings related to the selective accessibility model, and made an attempt to link findings of his or her own investigation to the model. However, the link between the student's investigation and the background model could be investigated a little more. (For example, how does the fact that results were replicated even when the question was modified from Gandhi to Lincoln contribute to the selective accessibility model?)

Strengths and limitations of the design, sample and procedure are stated and explained. All three elements (design, sample and procedure) are represented in this explanation. Strengths and limitations outlined by the candidate are relevant to the specific context of the investigation. Meaningful modifications are suggested for future studies, and all modifications are linked to the respective limitations of the design, sample and procedure.

# 11 PRACTICE EXAM PAPERS

By this point, you will have refreshed your understanding of content headings and made sure that you are aware of the key exam requirements. You will also have picked up some techniques to refine your exam skills and probably worked out your own individual approach to revision. In this section, you are given a full exam-style paper to practise. This is an HL exam paper, but it is mostly applicable to SL students too. Remember that SL students do not take paper 3, choose one question only in paper 2, and cannot be asked HL extension questions in paper 1. This means that question 3 in paper 1 part B cannot be asked at the standard level. It is advisable that you practise the paper in timed conditions, handwriting your answers. This is to approximate the real-life exam situation as much as possible. After you have written your answers, you can check them using the markscheme that is available at www.oxfordsecondary.com/ib-prepared-support.

## Paper 1 (HL)

### Section A

Answer **all** questions in this section. Marks will be awarded for focused answers demonstrating accurate knowledge and understanding of research.

**Biological approach to understanding behaviour**

1. Explain how **one** neurotransmitter may influence **one** human behaviour. [9]

**Cognitive approach to understanding behaviour**

2. With reference to a study investigating **one** cognitive process, outline the research method used in the study. [9]

**Sociocultural approach to understanding behaviour**

3. Describe **one** research study related to acculturation. [9]

### Section B

Answer **one** question in this section. Marks will be awarded for demonstration of knowledge and understanding (which requires the use of relevant psychological research), evidence of critical thinking (for example, application, analysis, synthesis, evaluation) and organization of answers.

4. Discuss how **one or more** genes may influence behaviour. [22]

5. Evaluate **one or more** models of thinking and/or decision-making. [22]

6. Discuss the effect of the interaction of global and local influences on behaviour. [22]

# Paper 2 (HL)

Answer two questions, each from a different option. Each question is worth 22 marks.

Marks will be awarded for demonstration of knowledge and understanding (which requires the use of relevant psychological research), evidence of critical thinking (for example, application, analysis, synthesis, evaluation) and organization of answers.

## Abnormal psychology

1. Evaluate one or more research methods used to investigate factors influencing diagnosis.

2. Contrast two explanations for one mental disorder.

3. To what extent can the effectiveness of treatment of mental disorders be assessed?

## Developmental psychology

4. To what extent do peers and/or play affect cognitive and/or social development?

5. Discuss biological, cognitive and/or sociocultural influences on the development of identity.

6. Evaluate psychological research into cognitive development.

## Health psychology

7. Discuss the biopsychosocial model of health and well-being.

8. Discuss ethical considerations relevant in the study of health problems.

9. To what extent are health promotion programmes effective?

## Psychology of human relationships

10. Discuss the role of communication in personal relationships.

11. Discuss origins of conflict and/or conflict resolution.

12. Discuss the use of one or more research methods in the study of social responsibility.

# Paper 3 (HL)

Read the passage carefully and then answer all the questions.

The stimulus material below is based on a study on the influence of compassion training on prosocial behaviour.

---

5 Researchers were interested whether it is possible to promote prosocial behaviour towards strangers by means of short-term compassion training. Previously it had been shown that compassion training has positive effects on mood and health and influences participants' behaviour in the laboratory, but it remained unclear whether these effects endure outside of a laboratory setting in real-life interactions with strangers.

45 To measure prosocial behaviour towards strangers, researchers developed a new procedure called the Zurich Prosocial Game

(ZPG). It is a computer game in which the participant's task is to navigate an avatar through a maze to a treasure within a limited time. There are multiple rounds. Each treasure,
5 if reached during the round, is worth $0.50. At the same time, participants can see another avatar, controlled (as they are led to think) by another research participant in another location in Europe. In fact, the other player is a computer
10 script. As the players are moving through their mazes, red or blue gates fall in front of their characters, blocking them off from the treasure. The character has a certain number of red and blue keys that open the corresponding doors.
15 But players can also use their key to open the co-player's door if his or her character is stuck. Whether or not players give keys to their co-player (when there is a chance they will need the keys themselves) was used as a measure of
20 prosocial behaviour.

Participants in the study were 69 healthy female volunteers aged 18–34 years. Only females were included in the sample because they have higher empathy scores. All participants were recruited
25 via advertisements. The advertisements never mentioned the word "compassion". Participants were then divided into two groups: the compassion training group and the memory training group. Allocation into groups depended
30 on which slot was available at the time the participant could come. Allocation resulted in equal groups (35 and 34 participants).

Participants in the compassion group attended a one-day training based on meditation
35

techniques. Guided by an experienced meditation teacher, participants visualized various people and sent them positive thoughts, such as "May you be happy" or "May you be 45 safe". This was aimed at fostering an attitude of benevolence towards oneself and others. Participants in the memory training group underwent a one-day training in using a mnemonic technique.
50

Both groups played ZPG twice, 2–5 days before and 2–5 days after the training. Results showed that there was no change in the amount of helping in the memory training group. On the other hand, the amount of helping 55 in the compassion training group increased significantly.

Researchers concluded that short-term compassion training can promote prosocial behaviour towards strangers in real-life 60 situations, and that these effects endure beyond the training context. Researchers acknowledged that additional research needs to be carried out to clarify the effectiveness of the technique. For example, they note that compassion-focused 65 imagery may be distressing to some people, according to some clinical research. However, they recognize that "compassion training could have great societal impact when implemented in institutions of daily life" (p. 6).
70

Based on: Leiberg, S, Klimecki, O, and Singer, T. 2011. "Short-term compassion training increases prosocial behaviour in a newly developed prosocial game." PLoS ONE. Volume 6, number 3. https://doi. org/10.1371/journal.pone.0017798. 75

Answer all of the following questions, referring to the stimulus material in your answers. Marks will be awarded for demonstration of knowledge and understanding of research methodology.

1.  (a) Identify the research method used in the study and outline **two** characteristics of the method. [3]

    (b) Describe the sampling method used in the study. [3]

    (c) Suggest **one** alternative or **one** additional research method that could be used to investigate the aim of the original study, giving **one** reason for your choice. [3]

2.  Describe the ethical considerations that were applied in the study and explain whether further ethical considerations could be applied. [6]

3.  Discuss how the researcher in the study could avoid bias. [9]

# INDEX